'Give Them a Volley and Charge!'
The Battle of Inkermann, 1854

'Give Them A Volley and Charge!'

The Battle of Inkermann, 1854

PATRICK MERCER

SPELLMOUNT
Staplehurst

British Library Cataloguing in Publication Data:
A catalogue record for this book is available
from the British Library

Copyright © Patrick Mercer 1998

ISBN 1–86227–025–2

First published in the UK in 1998 by
Spellmount Limited
The Old Rectory
Staplehurst
Kent TN12 0AZ

1 3 5 7 9 8 6 4 2

The right of Patrick Mercer to be identified
as the author of this work has been asserted by him
in accordance with the Copyright, Designs
and Patents Act 1988

Typeset by Palimpsest Book Production Limited,
Polmont, Stirlingshire
Printed in Great Britain by
TJ International Ltd, Padstow, Cornwall

Contents

List of Maps

List of Plates

barrier. Note the line of the Post Road at the base of East Jut. *(Author)*

9. St Clement's Ravine today seen from the Russians' perspective. The Sandbag Battery lies within the scrub slightly to the right of the peak of the Kitspur. *(Author)*

10. The fight for the Sandbag Battery. The Footguards recapture the Battery once again, driving the Russian infantry from the tactically worthless but highly prized landmark. *(Author)*

11. Sgt Walker of the 55th (Westmorland) Regt counter-attacks the Iakoutsk Regt as the centre of the British position on Home Ridge is threatened. *(Author)*

12. Maj.-Gen. Sir George Cathcart falls mortally wounded as he tries to lead his men out of the perilous position into which he had brought them. His ill-judged charge very nearly unhinged the whole of the tenuous British defence of the Inkermann position. *(RMAS)*

13. An 18-pounder gun, similar to those which were to have such a profound effect on the outcome of the battle. Whilst only two were deployed by the British, their range and accuracy caused disproportionately high casualties amongst the Russian guns and gunners. *(RMCS)*

14. The British soldier as he fought at Inkermann. Wearing only the clothes that he had carried since he arrived in the Crimea in September, the weather, constant danger and diminishing numbers meant that every man was deeply fatigued even before the fighting started. *(Wood)*

15. Clearing the dead from the field of Inkermann. French and British troops clear the battlefield despite occasional artillery fire from Sevastopol's outer defences. *(Clifford)*

16. The consequences of the battle as *Punch* saw them! (Punch, 5 November 1854)

Introduction

The battle of Inkermann lasted for less than twelve hours, was one of the bloodiest single engagements in Europe between 1815 and 1914, and saw the hopes of the British, French and Turkish allies for a swift and lasting lesson to the Tsar perish. Now the battle is largely forgotten, despite the fact that in Victorian folklore its memory shone brighter than any of the other engagements of the whole Crimean War. Today 'The Soldiers' Battle' is eclipsed by the Charge of the Light Brigade – a defeat that took less than half an hour and in which the casualties were counted in hundreds rather than thousands – and the memory of a nurse called Florence Nightingale who visited the Crimea only once. It is a battle that almost defies description, fought in fog over deeply broken ground and to no particular plan or strategy, a series of disparate and bitter mêlées rather than a 'battle' proper. To try to piece it together is difficult but fascinating; this probably accounts for the comparatively few accounts that have been written of it. To grasp it, however, the context of the Crimean War as a whole needs to be understood.

To precis the muddled circumstances, the frustrated ambitions and the jingoism that led to the War is almost as difficult as an account of Inkermann. In brief, however, its origins lay in the nineteenth-century developments of industrialism, nationalism and imperialism, changes in the European status quo brought about by the revolutions of 1848-9, British-Russian rivalry, chronic Russo-Turkish hostility, the resurgence of French Bonapartism, and the increasing divergence of Russia and western Europe. The fighting ought to be seen as two separate wars; that between Russia and Turkey around the Danube, which preceded the war fought against Russia by the coalition of France, Britain and Turkey in the Baltic as well as the Crimea.

Britain, France and Russia all had a vital interest in the future of Turkey, the vexed 'Eastern Question', for Turkey's Ottoman Empire bordered Russian territories, was contiguous to France's north African Empire and dominated the overland route to British India and her possessions in the east. Furthermore, Turkey's opposition to Russia suited Britain, for she lay in an ideal position to neutralise any Russian threat to India or Persia, such as the Afghan War of 1839-42.

Austria also had a crucial part to play in the equation, being Turkey's and Russia's most powerful neighbour. However, the Tsar had restored her Hungarian kingdom to Austria's young Emperor, and whilst she looked askance at Russian expansion into Turkish territories across the lower Danube, her debt of gratitude effectively neutralised her. Similarly, whilst Prussia was emerging as a new power, her king was related to the Tsar by marriage and had no direct interest in the Eastern Question. Thus, the Tsar's expansionist ambitions depended principally upon a lack of opposition from Britain and France. Britain, however, stood to gain by any division of Turkish territory and she, like Russia, was alarmed by Louis Napoleon's assumption of near dictatorial powers after the coup of 1851; new Bonapartism was attractive to neither.

Another dimension was added to the Tsar's desire for territory and access to the Mediterranean in the shape of the 13,000,000 Greek Orthodox subjects of the Turks. In 1829 Greece had fought for her independence from Turkey with the aid of Russia, and since then the Tsar had seen himself as the protector of those Christians still under Turkish rule. It was a lever that he could use as much or as little as he chose, and in 1850 when Catholic and Greek Orthodox monks squabbled over matters of precedence in the Holy Land, he chose to listen to the appeals of the latter. The Catholics sought the intercession of Louis Napoleon; the Sultan, meanwhile, within whose territories the Holy Land lay, found in favour of the Catholics in December 1852. Whilst on the surface it seemed to be a matter of no great consequence, the issue infuriated the Tsar and drew France, now as a direct supporter of Turkey, into clear conflict with him.

The Tsar judged that it would now be possible to fan the flames of this dispute and, with tacit British support or, at least, no opposition, the long sought after dismemberment of Turkey could begin in earnest.

In early 1853 he approached London and reminded the Prime Minister of the offer he had made in 1844 when such an arrangement had last been broached, namely that Britain would gain Egypt if she allowed Russia to pick at Turkey unhindered. Misjudging Britain's lukewarm response and being unaware of hardening British opinion, the Tsar despatched Menshikov to Turkey to deliver ultimata. Britain's influential ambassador in Turkey, Redcliffe, gave every assurance to the Sultan that Britain would stand by him and he refused either to restore the Orthodox monks' privileges or to allow the Tsar to establish a pro-tectorate over all of his Christian subjects. A French naval squadron had already been despatched to Turkish waters, and despite its being joined by an equivalent British force, Russian troops marched into the long dis-puted Danubian principalities of Moldavia and Wallachia in July 1853.

Despite Austria's attempts at mediation in Vienna, Turkey declared war on 5 October. Crossing the Danube into Wallachia, the Turks initially enjoyed some successes, but Russian counter-attacks soon occurred, the most notable, in terms of what happened later in the Crimea, being that at Oltenitsa on 4 November. The battle itself was bloody and probably rates as a tactical victory for the Turks. Strategically, however, it marked the turning point in the Turkish advance for having been mauled, they feared the approach of Russian reinforcements and fell back across the Danube. The Russian commander was Gen. P A Dannenberg; one year and one day later he and the remnant of his 8,000 strong division were to see action again, this time against the British at Inkermann.

Success on land was added to at sea on 30 November when Admiral Nachimov (whom we will also meet later in the Crimea) sank a Turkish flotilla at Sinope with almost no loss to himself but killing 4,000 Turks. It was a legitimate act of war, but it served to push the divided British coalition Cabinet over the edge, which until then had allowed the British fleet no more latitude than to remain at anchor off Constantinople. Sinope caused the British to agree to a French plan to move a combined fleet into the Black Sea and to despatch troops to the Mediterranean where they could be better poised. To add weight to this, in March a joint ultimatum was sent to St Petersburg demanding a withdrawal from Moldavia and Wallachia. When this was not forthcoming, both Britain and France declared war.

After a relatively inactive winter, the Russians attacked on the Danube and besieged the fortresses of Silistria and Shumla. Meanwhile, a joint British and French force had landed at Gallipoli, and then in June moved up to the west coast of the Black Sea to Varna, there better to support the fighting on the Danube. The Russians had hoped for a quick and easy series of victories, which would cause the Turks to collapse and sue for peace before the Allies were in a position to do anything constructive. However, not only did the Turks resist well, but, more significantly, the Austrians, much against Russian expectations, moved 50,000 troops up to her borders and jeopardised her neutral status by demanding a Russian withdrawal from the principalities. With Britain and France being much more menacing and business-like than he had anticipated, with the Turks showing much more spirit than they had done in 1853, and with his territorial and diplomatic flanks unexpectedly threatened by Austria, the Tsar capitulated thus instantly removing the *casus belli*.

Too much was at stake, however, for the Allies to withdraw merely because the Russians had capitulated to all demands! Both Britain and France had committed themselves politically and militarily, and the temptation to continue was too great. For France a successful military adventure would solve several issues: first, it would give substance to the new Bonapartism whilst distracting people from difficulties at home; second, it would cement an ever fragile relationship with Britain, and third, it would allow the new France to be seen as a credible player in European affairs. Britain's reasons for continuing were not so very different, but on top came the fact that public opinion was baying for military adventure; the coalition government was too weak to resist it.

All that needed to be decided now was what and where the Allies should attack. Throughout the preceding year, reconnaissances had been made of the north and west coasts of the Black Sea. It had always been assumed that no matter how the fighting around the Danube developed, the Russian Black Sea Fleet would have to be neutralised, and whilst this would be a relatively simple tactical matter at sea, its Sevastopol base would have to be reduced if the threat were ever to be removed completely. Sevastopol was more than just a naval base, it was the jewel in the crown of Russia's influence abroad. Here was concentrated much of the wealth of southern Russia; the Crimea had been populated by native Russians during Peter's time and it had become one of the most advanced and innovative ports and arsenals in the world; destroy it and Russia's ambitions would be badly dented. Accordingly, in mid-September the Allied armada set sail for the Crimea with the destruction of Sevastopol as its aim.

Chapter I

'The bullet is a fool, the bayonet is a hero!'
The Protagonists

'We should have to go far back in history to find the record of a battle so fiercely contested as that of Inkermann. No instance is called to mind, this side of Thermopylae, where an invincible handful so successfully withstood the crushing force of overwhelming numbers. For eight terrible hours, 14,000 of the Allies thrust back, with great slaughter, 60,000 Russians inspired by patriotism, religious fanaticism and the stimulus of intoxication'.[1]

Even allowing for hyperbole, there is much truth in this account of a battle that beggars description. It should also be added that the field over which this contest raged was one of the smallest of its kind measuring some two miles by two. As a result, the slaughter was appalling; as one officer who claimed to have fought in every major engagement in the Peninsula put it,

'never did I witness anything approaching the carnage, the fury, the fiendish deviltry [sic] of that drizzling morning . . . I saw whole ranks with their musket-stocks as men who played at quarter-staff; I saw them hang on each other like gnashing bull-dogs and roll on the ground over and over again stabbing, tearing, cutting and mangling like men who had lost every characteristic of humanity and acquired more than tiger ferocity'.[2]

But why did both sides go at it with such a will? An examination of both armies' composition and fighting spirit may provide an explanation.

THE BRITISH

Alone amidst the combatants, the British Army was an all-volunteer force whose soldiers enlisted for an initial period of ten years in the Infantry or twelve in the Artillery, Cavalry or Engineers. 'Going for a soldier' in mid-Victorian England was still not a respectable thing to do but, as industrialism spread, so there was less need for men on the land and unemployment began to be a factor. Ten years before the Crimea a vast

1

proportion of the Army had been made up of Irishmen, but the potato famines and emigration had sapped this source of recruits who now tended to be found from the rural and industrial working classes. Such men were tough – they had to be in order to survive into manhood – but fewer fit, healthy ploughboys or farm workers were offering themselves as recruits. Despite this, the soldiers generally met with the approval of their officers, 'strong, hardy, well-intentioned fellows whom no nation on earth could match'[3] wrote one Guardsman, whilst a Line officer described the Grenadier company of his regiment as, 'a particularly fine set of men'.[4] An important factor, perhaps, was the fact that volunteers had been called for to make up those regiments that were embarking to full strength. This allowed the sick or feeble to be left behind, thus 95th (the Derbyshire) Regiment, typical of most, received reinforcements from the 6th, 36th, 48th and 82nd Regiments. Furthermore, the average age of the other ranks who embarked for the Crimea was 26 – mature by any army of any era's standards.

The officers are widely assumed to have been wealthy amateurs, scions of the great houses and families of England. Certainly there was an element of just that sort, and the fact that commissions and most subsequent promotions up to lieutenant-colonel (in all arms other than the Artillery and Engineers) still had to be bought confirms that most officers came from monied backgrounds. Much has been written about the iniquities of the purchase system, and indeed it was open to abuse, but it was a system that had been seen to work for several generations and to which few in the Army objected. One of the interesting corollaries of the social changes going on within Victorian England was that more and more middle-class families were now in a position not only to buy a commission for their son, but also chose to. Thus, the bourgeois sneering at the 'children of luxury' was beginning to give way in certain quarters to a desire for the kudos that a commissioned son might bestow on the family. One of the most damaging consequences of this trend, however, was that young men from such backgrounds were frequently the targets of bullying by sons of 'old money'. Public opinion was influenced by a number of scandals, well publicised by *Punch* and similar organs, where young officers' lives had been made intolerable by their peers. The case of Lt Perry of the 46th (South Devon) Regiment was infamous; so mercilessly had he been 'ragged' that his case came to court martial. So much public interest was there in it that the case had to go ahead despite the fact that the 46th were due to embark for the Crimea. So many witnesses were involved in the case that only two companies were able to embark; they were to be centre stage at Inkermann.

The professional standards of the British infantry and cavalry had depended, until the early 1850s, solely on the determination of their commanding officers. With the introduction of rifles in the late 1840s, a school of musketry had been established, and in 1853 manoeuvres on a large scale had started annually at the Chobham Camp of Exercise, but much still rested upon each regiment's internal training regime. With the Artillery and Engineers, however, things were a little more formal. Standards were established and maintained by Woolwich, and both corps were thought to compare well with those of other nations.

The tempo of training, though, depended upon the lessons learned in action. A casual glance at the operations of the British Army in the late 1840s and early 1850s would suggest that most of the Crimean army would have seen action, but this was not the case. Only one infantry battalion, 1st Rifle Brigade, had seen active service in the preceding four years (fighting the Kaffirs in South Africa), though most of the commanders at brigade level and above had a fair measure of experience. The Commander-in-Chief, Lord Raglan, was 66 years old and had lost an arm at Waterloo as one of Wellington's ADCs. There was no question that he was an able staff officer, but he lacked experience of command, was painfully over-sensitive to the feelings of others, and had little of the iron needed to lead in battle. He was to epitomise British lack of drive at the higher levels, for he was the product of a long peace and, like so many of his contemporaries, hidebound by the dead hand of his mentor, Wellington.

The main fighting element of the British Army was its infantry battalions. By the time the army landed in the Crimea, most were about 750–800 strong and consisted of eight companies. One of these companies was styled 'grenadier' and another 'light'; both of them had had different tactical functions in the past, but as most of the regiments had by now been equipped with the rifle and taught skirmishing tactics, their function was little different from that of the other six companies. Each regiment had a territorial title as well as a number. Thus, the 55th were the Westmorland Regiment, but owed little to that border land. In practice, territorial titles had been introduced in the eighteenth century as a recruiting expedient; these titles signified little as most regiments were known by their much-cherished numbers.

The infantry were organised into brigades of three battalions under the command of a brigadier-general, whilst each division, commanded by a major-general, consisted of two such brigades. Four divisions of infantry and one of cavalry embarked for the Crimea attached to each of which were one or two batteries of artillery armed with four 9 pound guns and two 24 pound howitzers. Also, there was a siege train which was to deploy two 18 pound guns at a critical juncture of Inkermann. To think of these divisions and brigades as tactical entities, however, would be a mistake. The component units had been thrown together in Turkey arriving mainly from the English, Irish and Mediterranean garrisons and did very little training above unit level either in Turkey or at Varna because of the pace of events and the occurrence of disease. They had to depend upon the early engagements of the war to forge any sort of tactical coherence.

The British artillery was still muzzle-loading and largely smooth-bored (though there were some rifled Lancaster guns landed from the Fleet), with the same characteristics of the guns that had been used at Waterloo. Round shot and common shell were the staple ordnance for static operations, but shrapnel rounds and canister in particular were to be responsible for most of the casualties at Inkermann. Canister had the same effect as a huge shotgun; a light container packed with iron shot was loaded into the gun-barrel which immediately fanned out from the muzzle when the gun was discharged. With an optimum range of 200–300 yards, against massed infantry it was devastating.

Less well understood, however, were the new rifles of the infantry. The 4th Division still had the old smooth-bore percussion musket which, though quicker to load, lacked the range and the stopping power of the new Minie rifles. Most of the regiments thus equipped had received their weapons whilst on the way to the Crimea in Scutari and did not properly understand the fundamental advantage that they bestowed over the old smooth-bored weapons. Whilst still muzzle-loading and requiring the use of a ramrod, the percussion Minies were capable of accurate fire well over 300 yards and would easily pass through the torso of a man.

There was some opposition to the new weapons on the grounds that a ramrod had to be employed to get the round to the very bottom of the breach in order to achieve the correct compression. Whereas, in extremis, the old smooth-bore could have a round dropped down the barrel, and a sharp tap of the butt on the ground would serve to seat the round sufficiently for it to be lethal. Furthermore, nothing had been done to adapt tactics to this new weapon despite the fact that it had been used with success against the Kaffirs in South Africa and that its characteristics and potential had been studied extensively at the School of Musketry. Thus the range of volley fire was still deemed to be that of the smooth-bore – about 100 paces. Added to which, both smooth-bore and rifle were very susceptible to rain and damp, and many weapons were too soaked to fire on the morning of Inkermann; much reliance, therefore, had to be placed on the bayonet.

One element of British tactics was to have a profound effect on the outcome of the battle, however. The British Infantry had always been taught to fight in line – shoulder to shoulder – rather than in the column common to most European countries. In the Peninsula the British had been renowned for the firmness of their battle discipline which had allowed an apparently weak line to bring most of its muskets to bear. A dense column, whilst it was terribly vulnerable to both musket and artillery fire and only allowed a small proportion of weapons to be used, at least gave those within its ranks the illusion that there was safety in numbers. The

Russian columns were to fall terribly foul of the British lines in the same way that the French had fifty years before.

The renown and battle discipline of the British soldier went some way to make up for the lack of ability of most of his commanders. Raglan and the legacy of the Duke of Wellington have already been mentioned, now Raglan was surrounded by officers of very mixed merit. In command of the 1st Division was the Duke of Cambridge who, at 35, was the youngest general officer by far. He had no operational experience until he commanded his division indifferently at the Alma; at Inkermann he was to fight bravely but with little flair. Sir George De Lacy Evans, 67, commanded the 2nd Division. Having had experience in the Peninsula and during the Carlist wars he was well qualified but elderly. At the Alma he performed well and did a workmanlike job at the dress rehearsal for Inkermann on 26 October. On the day of the great battle, however, he was missing, sick on a ship in Balaklava having been thrown from his horse. In his place was his foul-mouthed, combative brigadier, Pennefather. Another Peninsula veteran, he was enormously popular with his men and had much experience in India having commanded a battalion at the epic battle of Meeanee in Scinde in 1843.

One of the most contentious figures of the early part of the campaign was Sir George Cathcart who, at 60, was commanding the 4th Division. Having just successfully fought the Eighth Kaffir War, he had hastened to the Crimea with a reputation that preceded him. Accordingly, he was given a 'dormant commission', that is, in the event of any mishap befalling Lord Raglan, he was to take command of the Army. Sir George Brown, who commanded the Light Division, however, was his senior and the logical successor to Raglan; lest any friction occur, the appointment was kept secret. This curious way of doing business may go a long way to explain the conduct of Cathcart at the engagements before Inkermann and at the battle itself. Quite what the effect was will never be known, however, for Cathcart was to be killed at the head of his troops during an ill-judged charge.

In spite of all of these disadvantages, the average British soldier fought with great bravery and initiative at Inkermann.

'Where their officers and non-commissioned officers were shot down, the men banded themselves together in twos and threes and twenties – under some natural or self-elected leader – and fought the battle out. Thus in one place were eighteen privates of the 95th fighting on surrounded by upwards of 200 of the enemy . . . nine were killed and not one left the field without a wound; all fought on until their ammunition was expended and their bayonets were red with blood'.[5]

Or as Campbell of the 30th observed, '. . . some wandered and a few might go to the rear, not many, for the men were full of resolution'[6] That resolution probably stemmed from the British experience, up until then, of nothing but victory. Whilst the Alma had been most soldiers' first taste of war – and a bloody one it had been – their enemies had been trounced. Unlike some of the cavalry, none of the infantry present had been mauled at Balaklava, and on 26 October, at the so-called battle of Little Inkermann, victory had been theirs. Similarly, the troops most heavily engaged were the 2nd Division and the Guards, the very men who had triumphed before and who knew the limitations of their adversaries. Despite the appalling conditions involved in their picquet duties before Inkermann, morale was still high and the troops were experienced enough to know what they could and could not do in battle. Their stock of courage was not yet over-taxed. They fought well; they fought for their honour and that of their regiment; they fought for their very survival. Yet the British Army was never to fight like this again in the Crimea; Inkermann was to be the high point for the British Infantry.

Underlying this high level of fighting spirit was a closeness between officers and men that is often misunderstood. For all the officers like Lieutenant John Ross Lewin of the 30th whose father, '. . . a Peninsula veteran, had been in eleven battles and sieges and two of his uncles had also distinguished themselves under the Duke of Wellington',[7] there was a greater proportion of officers commissioned from the ranks than might be supposed. The 47th, for instance had three such officers and several commissions had already been granted to soldiers in recognition of the victory of the Alma. Whatever their social origins, the officers knew their men well, and there were to be many acts of selfless bravery at Inkermann which demonstrated their mutual regard. For instance, Pte Palmer of the 3rd Grenadier Guards was to win the VC for springing to the defence of Sir Charles Russell Bt; similarly, the commanding officer of the 55th was engaged hand-to-hand with a Russian officer when a soldier of the Rifle Brigade ran the Russian through with his bayonet with the cheerful cry, 'There you are, sir!',[8] whilst Maj. Clifford won his VC for sabreing a Russian who was attacking a soldier of the 77th and then despatching another.

Without doubt, Britain's Crimean army had plenty of faults and was, at best, indifferently led. At Inkermann, as the epithet 'The Soldiers' Battle' suggests, however, it was the common infantryman full of grim determination who '. . . held the ground they stood upon as long as life was in them'.[9]

THE RUSSIANS

Every aspect of the Tsar's army was copied from that of the widely admired Prussian Army, though little of it perfectly. Soldiers were conscripted for a minimum of twenty-five years in the Infantry and tended to come from peasant stock. Indeed, such was the despair that a family felt once their son was to be conscripted that a party resembling a wake would be held in his honour. There was little chance of the parents seeing their boy again. Once at a regional depot, any man who showed mechanical or technical aptitude was taken for the artillery or engineers; any who had experience of horses went to the cavalry, and the remainder joined the infantry. Whilst there are plenty of other examples of just this selection procedure going on throughout history, it did mean that the soldier who bore the brunt of the fighting at Inkermann was mostly of the least promising quality.

The popular writings of Tolstoy and the account of the Pole, Hodasevich, who deserted to the British after Inkermann, show the typical Russian officer in a very poor light. Both were writing to their own agenda, the former for political ends, whilst the latter had good reason to stress the indignities which had made him desert. However, no British accounts speak of any lack of courage among the Russian officers, even if there was every sign that tactical sense and initiative were not present in any great measure. The way Russian officers were appointed hardly lent itself to this.

There were three ways in which a commission might be obtained. First, about one fifth of officers were the sons of minor nobility and came via officer cadet schools. Military education at these schools was not well developed and left the cadets scarcely better qualified than the second category, the junkers. They were normally officers' sons who had served in the ranks for a number of years as under-officers and then passed a simple qualifying exam. Third were soldiers who had served for about ten years before passing an even simpler exam; they made up the great bulk of regimental officers.

All of these would have served to make perfectly good officers had their training encouraged any sort of daring or initiative. Suvorov's maxim, 'The bullet is a fool, the bayonet is a hero', still held good at the time of the Crimea and this, linked to a distorted idea of the Prussian system, meant that the Russians relied upon heavily drilled masses wielding weapons little better than spears. Indeed, one general advised the Tsar that his troops were ready for battle because, '. . . the men can march well with their toes pointed and their bodies rigid'.[10] Inflexibility was encouraged by such training; the result was countless instances in the Crimea of Russians gaining a minor success but failing to exploit it, not because of lack of courage but simply for want of initiative by both officers and non-commissioned officers at crucial moments.

Russian minor tactics played into the hands of opponents armed with rifles: a forest of cold steel, delivered by columns which, in the words of the 1848 officers' manual depended for success '. . . on the correct stretching of the toe in the march and the proper number of steps'[11] made an ideal target. There were two types of column used at Inkermann: columns of companies and the so-called column of attack which consisted of a whole battalion arranged in two, parallel columns of sections each of three ranks with a depth of twelve ranks and the frontage of a company. The columns, however, were not trained to maximise their firepower, for their main aim was to deliver a blow with the bayonet, the momentum of which would be impossible to resist. For fire support they depended upon skirmishers who operated as a cloud on either flank and, more importantly, on their artillery.

The Russians were organised along Prussian lines of corps of three divisions each of two brigades both of which had four regiments. Each regiment had four battalions, and every corps had a sapper and a rifle battalion attached. In a division, the first infantry brigade were styled 'musketeers' and the second brigade 'jagers', though the actual difference seems to have extended only to matters of dress. Musketeer and jager regiments were each separately numbered with two regiments – one of musketeers and one of jagers – having the same number. Unlike the British, the numbers mattered little to the Russians for they were often changed; to them it was their territorial title which was the more important.

Each infantry division had an organic artillery brigade which had two, twelve-gun field batteries of six 12 pounders and six 18 pounders as well as two twelve-gun light batteries of eight 6 pounders and four 9 pounders. The guns were all brass smooth-bores mounted on characteristic pea-green carriages which, like their British counterparts, could fire about two rounds per minute. The artillery of both sides was to have a decisive effect on the battle, as we shall see, but the Russian gunners were much more of a match for the Allies than the infantry. Well trained, equipped and led, they were probably the most competent arm of the Russian Army. In a letter to his father after Inkermann, Capt Thomas Davies makes the point that the Russian infantry

> '. . . are not to be feared by British or French troops in anything like equal proportions – say one third to two thirds of them – but their artillery is very formidable. Our loss would have been comparatively nothing on the 5th had it not been for that, which is more powerful than ours, and our guns came up slowly and after firing a few rounds of ammunition fell silent.'[12]

Mention should also be made of the sailors of the Black Sea Fleet. The way that they manned the defences of Sevastopol is well known and much admired, but contemporary British accounts speak with some confusion of columns of 'marines' or 'naval infantry' appearing at Inkermann. The fact is that Russian mariners were trained to act as infantry on land and sailors at sea and uniformed and equipped much like infantrymen with muskets, bayonets and crossbelts but wearing shakoes rather than helmets. Hodasevich speaks of the contempt in which these sailors were held by soldiers proper, but they were used extensively in the infantry role and appear to have acquitted themselves well.

One of the Russians' greatest disadvantages were their small-arms by which both sailors and soldiers were poorly served. For the most part the Russians carried percussion smooth-bores converted in the 1840s from flintlock. Whilst they were quicker to load than the Allied rifles, they had only a fraction of the range and stopping power though there were a number of rifles served out to the infantry regiments which were carried by the skirmishers and company marksmen. In addition, the rifle regiments carried a copy of the Brunswick rifle which was a vastly superior weapon to either the muskets or the smooth-bores of the infantry. As the war progressed, the Russians converted a number of their muskets into rifles and trench raiders often sought the highly prized Allied rifles. When Inkermann was fought, however, the Russians were still largely using the tactics and weapons that they had deployed against Napoleon.

Traditionally, discipline in the Russian Army had been harsh with almost barbaric methods used to perfect the drill which was supposed to bring success in battle but certainly made a splendid spectacle on parade. To that end physical punishment was dealt out by officers and non-commissioned officers alike with great vigour. A fault on parade would merit a slap or a punch, whilst rods or birches were regarded as necessary adjuncts to perfection. Scabbards and drumsticks were used liberally; being struck in the face with such was referred to as receiving the 'toothpick'. Despite this, the Russian infantry seems to have followed its leaders willingly enough, though the Polish deserter, Hodasevich, does stress that a number of officers fell at Inkermann by their own troops' hands. No British accounts mention such behaviour, and many eye witnesses relate how well the Russian officers led from the front and, though their appearance was less distinctive than that of their British counterparts, they made themselves obvious by constant sword-waving and bellowed encouragements. The action of one Russian officer of the Kazan Regiment at the Alma was not untypical. Very tall, he singled himself out to the British troops of the 7th Fusiliers by striding about, oblivious to British bullets, encouraging his men until he became such an object of respect to the British that they were reluctant to shoot at him. Eventually, the Fusiliers' commanding officer had to order him to be shot.

Battle experience amongst the Russians was, for the most part, greater than that of the British; most of that experience, though, had been of defeat. The troops that mounted their attack from Sevastopol had, in most cases, seen action at the Alma, at Balaklava or at Little Inkermann. At the Alma the British had been dubbed the 'Red Devils'[13] by the Russians, who had been told that they could expect the British, a seafaring nation, only to be as expert on land as their own sailors. The artless ferocity of the assault and the number of casualties had stunned the Russians; also, they had tasted Allied artillery and the deadly Minies for the first time. At Balaklava, few infantrymen had been in action, but they had seen first the Heavy Cavalry Brigade defeat a much larger body of their own cavalry and then the Light Cavalry Brigade charge massed artillery with suicidal eagerness. Whilst the Light Brigade had been mauled, their action had left a profound impression on the Russians. Again, those troops in action at Little Inkermann had been roughly handled this time by a handful of picquets which, by the normal conventions of war, should have fallen back rather than fight to the death. In short, the Russians who had already met the British knew that they would be meeting a tough enemy.

Those who marched on Inkermann from the interior of the Crimea had yet to have any experience of fighting in this campaign, but were mostly veterans of the operations on the Danube against the Turks. Dannenberg's drubbing at Oltenitsa has already been mentioned and it is interesting to note that he was initially ordered to attack on 4 November rather than 5 November, that is, precisely one year to the day after his defeat by the Turks. The fact that his troops were told to attack on the very day that they had completed a 250-mile march from Bessarabia was reason enough for the assault to be delayed, but Dannenberg also asked that his troops' superstitions should be respected by not attacking on the first anniversary of a defeat. In other words, most of the Russians at Inkermann had become used to the concept of defeat; they had tasted the bitterness of casualties and retreat, and they had probably passed their fighting prime. This was in stark contrast to the British who had yet to become jaded by war. This was a British impression of their foes at Inkermann:

'The Russian soldiers were infinitely inferior in appearance to those we met at Alma. In all that relates to discipline and courage, our late antagonists were far superior. They were all clean but ragged in the extreme. None had knapsacks but merely a little canvas bag of that disgusting, nauseous-looking stuff they call bread . . . The knapsacks, I presume, were left behind in order that they might scale the heights on our left with greater facility . . . they appear to have been veteran troops as a large number bore the scars of previous wounds. The dead officers, as at the Alma, were with difficulty to be distinguished from the men. Their officers behaved very well . . . It is said that the Russian soldiers had been liberally supplied with liquor previous to the commencement of the attack. Their continued and loud shouting and the impetuosity of their attack render it probable that they were under the influence of some artificial stimulus of the sort. In the canteens of many of the killed on the field was found a mixture of raki and water. The men who have fallen into our hands, though generally of short stature, are of sturdy frames, with broad chests and well-developed, muscular legs.'[14]

It is interesting to note that the British believed their foes to be drunk at Inkermann, whilst the Russians thought that the Light Cavalry Brigade must have been drunk to do what they did at Balaklava. Hodasevich complains, however, that the issue of raki before the attack was particularly meagre being restricted to one measure only. Perhaps all troops who are subjected to frenzied attack feel that their enemies are acting under the influence of something that they wish had been available to them too! Such then were the Russians – brave, stoic, experienced (perhaps too experienced) but lacking intiative and poorly armed. Whatever their relative merits and demerits, their endeavours, as we shall see, were very nearly the undoing of the Allies.

Notes

1. *Complete History of the Russian War*, p78
2. *ibid*, p88
3. Wilson, p38
4. Wylly, p6
5. *ibid*, p55
6. Bannatyne, p419
7. *ibid*, p410
8. Hume, p72
9. Shervinton, p17
10. Thomas, p19
11. Alabin, quoted in Seaton, p14
12. 'I'm Ninety-Five', September 1896, Davies Mss
13. Macdonald, Letter of 20 September 1854
14. *Complete History of the Russian War*, p94

Chapter II
'Never mind forming, for God's sake, come on, come on men!'
The Alma

'How they can resist such a force as ours I know not. Failure seems impossible',[1] wrote Doctor Skelton, the surgeon of the 1st Coldstream Guards, as the Allied fleet set sail from Varna bound for the Crimea on 7 September 1854. He had cause to be optimistic after the dreadful tedium of Varna which had been so beset by disease and indecision. Weeks had passed in Bulgaria as rumours circulated, odd reconnaissances by both land and sea were despatched, and it became clear that the Russians had decamped from the principalities. Cholera had plagued both French and British, and had caused much movement of camps to less 'infectious ground' all to little effect other than that of distracting the troops from training and causing mighty apathy. The news that the troops were to embark caused excitement to spread like wildfire, and the health of the troops, as the surgeons predicted, improved dramatically.

Certainly, the armada was an impressive sight as sail and billowing smoke from the high proportion of steam-driven ships spread across the sunlit Black Sea. The British embarked about 27,000 men, the French about 30,000, and there was a token force of 7,000 Turks as well, but no one was quite sure which rumour to believe about where the landing was to be made. The construction of siege equipment such as gabions (wicker-work baskets that were designed to be filled with earth and from which parapets could be constructed), fascines (bundles of brushwood for filling in ditches), and scaling ladders for weeks before suggested Sevastopol, but Odessa was a hot favourite amongst the troops despite publication by *The Times* before the fleets set sail that Sevastopol was to be attacked.

The French commander-in-chief, the ailing St Arnaud, impatient with the length of time the British were taking to embark their much greater number of horses, left port on board the *Ville de Paris* before Raglan on the *Caradoc*. For them there was no question that Sevastopol was the target, but it had not yet been decided whether to land well north of the great port or to its south. Naval reconnaissance over the last months had indicated that Sevastopol was strongly defended from seaward, but that there were good, deep anchorages to the south of the city from which re-supply might be mounted. This seemed like a straight and speedy direction from which to attack Sevastopol, except that the anchorages were clearly defended, and no one was quite sure how powerful was the portion of the Black Sea Fleet that lay there. Instead it was decided to land to the north of Sevastopol on one of the gently shelving, beached parts of coastline which could be protected by the ships' guns. Initially the French wanted to land well north of Eupatoria, but Raglan prevailed against the rapidly weakening St Arnaud, and a landing about thirty miles north of Sevastopol in Kalamita Bay was agreed upon.

Accordingly, on 14 September the Allies started to land, unopposed by all but a small vedette of cossacks who observed from a distance. The captain of the troopship *Pyrenees* wept to think how few of the troops now going over the side would return from the Crimea, '. . . hardy old salt as he was',[2] and much mirth was had by the sailors at the scramblings of the lubberly soldiery, particularly the kilted Highland troops who responded balefully to their cries of, 'Come-on, girls'![3] But the British were terribly badly prepared. Most of the transport carts and ambulances had been left behind in Varna in an effort to make the disembarkation as speedy as possible and to save space, there being a mistaken belief that native carts, or arabas, and ponies would be readily available. Similarly, each soldier, whilst personally heavily laden with ammunition and camp equipment, carried only a minimum of extra clothing. In an effort to lighten the load, knapsacks were to be left on board ship, and each soldier's blanket and greatcoat were rolled into a makeshift pack which contained extra boots, socks, one shirt and a forage cap. In addition to sixty rounds of ball ammunition, rifle and bayonet, each man carried a canteen of water, three days' rations, cooking kit and some a billhook. All of this looked soldierly enough and was perfectly adequate for a few days, but there was simply nothing more to back it up. Those soldiers who survived disease and bullets were destined not to see their knapsacks again until well after Inkermann.

The French conducted themselves in a very different manner. Their recent experience of active service was manifest, and whilst the British affected to sneer at their constant bugling and over-eagerness to plant tricolours, their business-like approach, excellent administration and soldierly appearance caused a sneaking admiration to spring up. The night before the landings, a buoy had been placed off-shore to indicate which half of the beach should be used by the French and which by the British. On the morning of the 14th, it was found to have moved south, giving the French a capacious beach upon which to land and leaving the British facing a sandstone cliff. As the French bustled ashore most efficiently, the British had to move south to another beach automatically

14

delaying disembarkation and allowing the French to be ashore first. Many saw this as deliberate and a sign of things to come.

After more delays the Allies moved off south towards Sevastopol hugging the shore in the lee of the fleets' guns. The French, having no cavalry with them, marched nearer the sea whilst the British were farther inland with their meagre cavalry force guarding the eastern or inland flank of the whole Allied force. The lack of cavalry for reconnaissance and flank protection and the dependence on the protection of the ships' guns was to warp Allied tactical thinking in the clash with the Russians which they knew to be inevitable as they marched south. The Bulganak, Alma, Katcha and Belbek rivers ran east to west to the sea directly hampering the Allies' advance. One or more was going to be held, and unless the Allies moved inland using their cavalry and horse artillery aggressively and forsaking the protection of the ships, they were going to face a frontal assault on at least one, pre-prepared river position. There was an inconclusive cavalry skirmish at the Bulganak, but on the evening of 19 September the Allies bivouacked on the north side of the Alma, looking straight at the entrenched positions of the Russians on the other side into the teeth of which, unless some semblance of tactical sense were to be shown, they would attack the next day.

The Russians had prepared the Alma position tolerably well, but only after months of dithering and making very poor use of the time they had to prepare for the Allied invasion which many believed to be inevitable. Much of the indecision must be attributed to Menshikov who had been appointed commander-in-chief of the Western Crimea region and commander of the Black Sea Fleet after his return from Constantinople as the Tsar's envoy. Whilst he was immensely well connected, wealthy, clever and cultured, he had almost no understanding of military matters having been a diplomat and courtier all his life. It is difficult to assess just how much of a threat Menshikov thought the Allies were to the Crimea for, whilst he exuded calm confidence and made a joke of the Allies' presence across the Black Sea: in June he wrote to his superior, Gortchakoff (at that stage commanding the Army of the Danube), complaining that the enemy might land 60,000 troops; to oppose them he could only find 22,700 infantry, 1,100 cavalry and thirty-six guns. Similarly, in July he wrote to the Tsar telling him that he expected '. . . an attempt against Sevastopol and the Black Sea Fleet'.[4]

Some were impressed by Menshikov's calm self-assurance but others, such as Miliutin (later to be war minister) were aghast at his '. . . apathy and irresponsibility . . . distrust of his subordinates and lack of attention to the troops.'[5] Certainly, the fact that he failed to form a coherent headquarters, preferring to surround himself with a loose collection of officers to whom he referred in diplomatic terms as a 'chancellery', did not inspire much confidence. Furthermore, despite giving the appearance of concern in some quarters, he could also appear dismissive of threats to his command. Thus, on 12 September he wrote, 'my assumption that the enemy will never dare to land has been proved entirely correct'; he concluded 'with the lateness of the season, a landing is no longer possible'.[6]

Others saw the Allies' intentions rather differently. First, *The Times* of London had made it quite clear that the target of the fleet setting sail from Varna could only be Sevastopol; second, on 18 May craft had been noted by the Russians taking soundings off beaches to the north of Sevastopol and there had been further sightings in June and July. Third, when the siege of Silistria had been lifted in June, it became increasingly clear that the Allies' objective would be Sevastopol; and, lastly, once the fleet had set sail, its course at first could have been Odessa but by 13 September observers in Sevastopol could see the smoke of a distant and numerous fleet above the horizon and that evening the coastal semaphore sited near the mouth of the Alma signalled that about one hundred enemy vessels were moving in a north-easterly direction towards Eupatoria, forty-five miles north of Sevastopol.

Fortunately for the Russians, there were in Sevastopol some men of real ability who were sufficiently perceptive to have identified Menshikov's inadequacies and to have gone ahead with preparations for the defence of the port. We have already met Vice-Admiral Nachimov, the victor of Sinope; he was the de facto commander of the Black Sea Fleet. A much-beloved leader and man of deeds, he was matched by the more reserved but equally able Kornilov the chief-of-staff of the Fleet. Kornilov had been pressing since 1852 for the introduction of steam screw vessels into the Russian Navy and for the extensive fortification of Sevastopol. Public funds had proved impossible to get so he had petitioned private individuals for subscriptions and drawn up a substantial list which he presented to Menshikov for his approval. At first the scheme was rejected by the complacent Menshikov, but eventually he relented and allowed Kornilov to go ahead and use funds donated by a wealthy contractor to build the Volokhov fort which was completed two days before the Allies landed and was instrumental in holding off Allied ships during the first bombardment. Seaward, therefore, Sevastopol was relatively well defended, but landward few fortifications existed.

As can be seen from the map, Sevastopol is divided north and south by a deep fjord known as the Roadstead. The military facilities of the port were sited on both sides, but most of the yards, the dock used for laying down and refurbishing keels and the like, were concentrated on the south bank. An attack from landward could logically come from either side (or both if the enemy was powerful enough), so an extensive chain of defences was necessary. Conscious that Menshikov would need all the engineering help he could get both with the defences of Sevastopol and with the construction of fortifications for delaying battles, Gorchakov sent his own engineer advisor, Lieutenant-Colonel Todleban, to Menshikov in August. Todleban was at first sent back by Menshikov with the words, 'Prince Gorchakov . . . has apparently forgotten that I have my own sapper battalion',[7] but was eventually allowed to stay although he was not actively employed until after the Alma. He was to emerge as the real genius behind the construction of Sevastopol's defences, a talented leader and a hero of the siege. Furthermore, he was to play an important part in the final stages of Inkermann.

Whatever Menshikov's beliefs, the rapidly deteriorating situation and the entry of Britain and France into the war caused the Tsar not only to replace those troops of the Crimean garrison who had gone to support the forces on the Danube, but also to reinforce them. By 10 September, therefore, there were a total of thirty-four battalions in Sevastopol with another eight marching to it, a total of 38,000 troops and 18,000 seamen. But there was a crucial deficiency in warships with only fourteen men-of-war and seven frigates, all sail-driven, holed up in Sevastopol. This paucity of naval craft was important; intelligence on Allied directions and speed whilst at sea would have allowed an earlier confirmation of their intentions; secondly, no matter how well armed, Russian craft could not hope to out manoeuvre the steam-driven ships of the Allies, and thirdly, Russian land forces would be almost powerless to stop an Allied landing as it would be conducted under the protection of their ships' guns which Russian ships would be equally powerless to engage.

Whilst the failure of the Russians to oppose the landings at first seems odd, the lack of naval strength goes some way to explain it, as does the perception that such a landing could be a feint. Certainly, Todleban's memoirs show that it was generally thought that the Allies would land, carry out a raid and then sail away; he also believed that the speed of the Allied fleet would allow them to land, draw a Russian force north, re-embark and then speedily move to another landing site close to a Sevastopol destitute of defenders before the army could march to its succour. Accordingly, the Alma was selected as the site for the first defensive battle lying, as it did, sufficiently north of Sevastopol for the Allies to be smashed before the city was threatened directly and south enough of the expected landing site for Allied intentions to have become clear. Furthermore, the folds of the terrain were thought to provide a screen to protect the defenders from the fleets' guns, and the cliffs to seaward were also considered to be unassailable.

With no staff to speak of, Menshikov chose to do all the planning and siting of the forthcoming battle himself. The position that he chose on the south bank of the Alma was good in general terms. It allowed him to use his strongest arm, his artillery, to best advantage in that the high ground gave good, clear fields-of-fire across the river Alma and into the village of Bourliouk on the north bank and dominated the one bridge which carried the Sevastopol to the Eupatoria highway across the river. His left or west flank was protected by the cliffs, whilst in the centre, out of range of the Allied ships, he built the earthwork which the Allies were to know as the Great Redoubt. He sealed his right flank with another fort, dubbed the Lesser Redoubt.

By 20 September Menshikov had been considerably reinforced with a total of 35,000 troops made up of forty-two infantry battalions, sixteen squadrons of light cavalry, eleven squadrons of cossacks and eighty-four guns in ten batteries in a splendid, natural, defensive position ready to meet the Allies. The force was divided into two parts – the right wing and centre under Prince P D Gorchakov (brother of Prince M D Gorchakov then commanding the Army of the Danube) consisting of 16 Infantry Division and the left wing made up of 17 Infantry Division under the command of Lieutenant-General Kiriakov. Menshikov was confident that he would bring the Allies to battle here and that his linear formation, with little depth but some reserves concealed in the rolling hillocks to the rear of the redoubts, would be strong enough to resist the frontal assault across the river which was the only tactic that he expected the enemy to use. With his left, he believed, protected by the cliffs and his right screened by a strong body of cavalry, he presumably felt secure enough not to have bothered with any more elaborate entrenchments than those of the two redoubts. With no experience of the potency of the Allies' rifles, he was content to leave much of his artillery and infantry unprotected on forward slopes. Similarly, he had yet to appreciate that rifles had equal if not greater range than his artillery; he was soon to be disabused.

Whilst he was aware that the Allies might seek to outflank him to the east in an attempt to by-pass the Alma position, he rightly assumed that they would be reluctant to operate outside the umbrella of the ships' guns. Accordingly, the only contingency plan he had for such an eventuality was that his forces would withdraw to Sevastopol; no other delaying positions had been prepared. The plan was simple and relied upon attrition being inflicted by the guns and then an infantry *coup de grâce* against the shattered remnants. In the words of Prince P D Gorchakov,

'It was the intention of Menshikov to hold the ground in front of the river only as long as it suited him, and then to fight the main battle preferably when the enemy was crossing the river. With this in mind he sited eighteen light guns near the main road at about 700 yards from the bridge so that both the bridge and the road were enfiladed, and twelve field guns farther to the right in the epaulement to engage the area of the bridge and ford with roundshot and case-shot. Near this battery stood the composite naval battalion, the Kazan Regiment, the Vladimir

Regiment and the Sousdal Regiment, and all except the Sousdal stood in column of attack ready to counter-attack. The purpose was to exploit the inevitable confusion of the enemy when he crossed the river and, striking him a swift blow, drive him back. All this was laid down quite clearly by Prince Menshikov and was repeatedly brought to the attention of unit commanders by me.'[8]

The plan, however, was badly flawed; it lacked any understanding of the enemy's weapons and depended upon his being as rudimentary a tactician as Menshikov. Menshikov's assumption was very nearly correct and the Allies were to pay for their poor tactics in blood that their forces could ill afford to shed.

On the morning of 20 September the French were ready to march at daybreak, but at nine o'clock stood down and made coffee as the British were still not prepared for the advance. It took another two hours of French impatience and grumbling before the British finally moved off, and the whole array plodded down towards the sluggish Alma. Inland lay the British, with their cavalry covering the whole of the Allies' eastern flank, facing the main Russian positions on the Kourgane hill on the other side of the Alma. They were deployed with two divisions leading, Sir George Brown's Light Division on the left and Sir George De Lacy Evans's 2nd Division on the right straddling the Sevastopol-to-Eupatoria road. They were supported by the Duke of Cambridge's 1st Division on the left and Sir Richard England's 3rd Division on the right. To the left and rear was that part of Sir George Cathcart's 4th Division which had not been left to clear the landing beaches and to act as a rearguard. The fact that they were to play no part in the forthcoming battle was to have a significant influence on future events and is a subject to which we will return.

The French took the position of honour on the right flank. Whilst this may have been decided merely by precedent, it had many practical advantages for the left flank was secured by the British, the right by the sea and by the guns of the fleets, and opposite it lay a much smaller portion of the Russians than the British had to face. Its major disadvantage was the amount of ground upon which the French had to deploy for they were constrained on both flanks. Thus, as Bosquet's Division aligned themselves next to the sea, so the French 1st and 3rd Divisions found themselves short of space and began to jostle the British who, in turn, were extending into line on their left. The British began to give ground to their left and quickly found that the left regiments of the 2nd Division were beginning to overlap the right regiments of the Light Division in the very area that was covered most effectively by the Russian artillery.

As the Allies deployed so the Russians began to open fire at extreme range. Although the vineyards to the south of the Alma had not been cleared to give the gunners the best fields-of-fire that could have been created, the Russian gunners knew their business and had, indeed, knocked in posts on the south bank at precisely measured ranges to allow the gunners to adjust their fire to a nicety. With enemy fire beginning to tell, it was time for the Allies to put their design for battle into practice. No such design, however, existed. The night before, St Arnaud had ridden to Raglan's headquarters and suggested that the French should attack first, ascend the high ground on the Russians' left and hold their attention whilst the British assaulted their centre and turned their right flank. Quite simply, the French would roll the Russians up from seaward and beat them against the British. Raglan, who had already decided to make no plan until he knew the dispositions of the enemy, politely declined to contribute to the discussion, simply telling St Arnaud that he could rely on the full cooperation of the British without making any useful contribution at all. Despite the fact that St Arnaud had no clear idea what the British intended to do beyond support him, he remained bouyant and was confident enough to ask the 88th Regiment the next day: 'I hope you will fight well today', and to receive the reply from the quick-tongued Irishmen, 'Sure, your honour, we will; and don't we always fight well?'[9]

Shortly before one o'clock St Arnaud was again seen in conference with Raglan on a knoll from which both inspected the Russian deployments opposite. Sir George Brown heard St Arnaud say: 'Do you intend to turn their flank or attack in front?'[10] as he snapped his spy-glass shut. Raglan would not commit himself beyond saying that a flank march would take too much out of his men and leave his left, with the few cavalry that he had, vulnerable. With that the Frenchman rode away with no clear idea of what the British were going to do beyond make a plan as the battle unfolded. As the British came closer to the river it became clear that more time was needed for the French on the right to get across the river and up the high ground on the Russian left and for themselves to sort out the confusion that their overlapping regiments were causing. Accordingly, one of the most testing periods of the battle began as the British, now under increasingly severe fire, lay down and waited for the French. It was a severe trial enlightened only by incidents such as the Coldstream drummers' pet Maltese terrier, Toby, gallantly chasing round shot; but for others, such as Morgan of the 95th, '. . . fragments of shakoes, blankets, clothes and human flesh' being 'carried up in the air' was '. . . a horrid sight but many similar were occurring every minute'.[11]

Amongst the artillery fire rifle bullets from Russian skirmishers had also started to whizz. As these troops fell back, they torched the village of Bourliouk which had been pre-prepared to act as a giant, blazing impediment to the Allies' advance. An impediment it certainly was, but to both sides, for whilst it would cause Evans's 2nd Division to split either side, more or less by brigades, adding further to the confusion and the lack of space, the smoke also drifted south-east, partially masking Russian fields-of-fire and certainly making it more difficult for the Russians to assess Allied intentions.

First into action on the right were Bosquet's division followed by the Turkish contingent. Supported by fire from French ships, the Minsk Regiment was driven off and French artillery was brought up to fire onto the Russian flank in very short order. Menshikov was appalled that his apparently secure left was the first position from which he should be threatened and ordered up seven battalions, four batteries and four squadrons of hussars to counter it. The French artillery, however was being handled most excellently and making itself felt against the forty or so guns with which Kiriakov was replying. The French began to get the better of the duel and Menshikov, realising that his infantry was impotent against such a threat, marched the seven battalions back to the Kourgane position leaving Bosquet firing with deadly effect into his left flank. With greater daring, Bosquet might usefully have advanced his infantry at this point and distracted the Russians further from their task of punishing the British opposite their centre. Again at Inkermann, Bosquet was to err on the side of caution; at the Alma he remained where he was, awaiting reinforcements.

With Bosquet held up, St Arnaud abdicated responsibility in magnificent style. His orders to Canrobert commanding the 1st Division and to Prince Napoleon in command of the 3rd were simply, 'With men such as you I have no orders to give. I have but to point to the enemy.'[12] Canrobert moved forward, scaled the cliffs opposite with difficulty, but found that he could not get his guns onto the high ground to support his advance. One of the tenets of French tactics was that no advance should be attempted without artillery support; accordingly, the 1st Division ground to a halt. Similarly, Prince Napoleon found that advancing under heavy fire through vineyards, and then attempting to get guns and infantry across the river, was too much for him. Canrobert's men got some protection from the slopes leading up to the plateau, but their rearmost troops came under stinging fire from Telegraph Heights to the west of Kourgane. The 3rd Division were subject to the fire from a mixture of batteries opposite and clung to the cover of the walls and pits of the vineyards. As the French jibbed, messages began to arrive with Raglan asking for help. An ADC delivered a message that asked for British help to relieve the pressure on Bosquet lest he should be 'compromised'. When asked to explain himself in plain French, the ADC admitted that this really meant 'retreat'.

At this Raglan turned to Airey, his quartermaster-general, and spoke a few words; Airey's face brightened perceptibly and moments later

Captain Nolan, an ADC, galloped away with orders for the troops to advance. The orders were simple and were to be the death warrant of many good soldiers whom Raglan could ill afford to lose: the infantry were to cross the Alma and attack the Russian redoubts frontally. No rapid arrangements were made for a concentration of artillery fire; there was to be no feint, no volley fire from the rifles of one division whilst another moved, and definitely no flanking attack. The British were playing right into the hands of the Russians and allowing their enemy to make maximum use of the one arm in which they were expert, artillery.

On the left the Light Division surged forward and into the Alma; some crossed easily enough whilst others sank into deeper parts of the river emerging only after all their ammunition had been soaked. To the right the 2nd Division's cramped deployment had been exacerbated by the blazing village which caused most of Adams's brigade to go to the right, whilst the rest of the Division became even further entangled with Codrington's brigade of the Light Division. Under a hail of well directed fire, the regiments became very mixed, and control was lost as the troops plunged into the river and then sought cover on a narrow strip of land that was protected by the steep southern bank of the river. On the extreme left Buller became mesmerised by what he thought was Russian cavalry threatening his flank, and he ordered his brigade to halt, even causing the 88th to form square despite the concentrated target which they presented. Seeing the lack of logic in halting, the 19th broke away from their brigade and attached themselves to Codrington's brigade which was making straight for the Great Redoubt. Similarly, most of the 95th from Pennefather's brigade of the 2nd Division, having become inextricably mixed with the 7th Fusiliers, also attached themselves to the knots of troops storming towards the Russian guns. All semblance of order had been lost by troops faced with the crossing of a difficult obstacle under deadly fire. The commanding officer of the 7th Fusiliers was heard to utter an order that ought to have been unthinkable, 'Never mind forming, for God's sake . . . come on, come on, men! Come on anyhow!'[13] With every tactical practice they understood abandoned, without their officers and non-commissioned officers in the places to which they had become accustomed, these untried troops might have been expected not to go forward. Certainly, the walls of the vineyards and the bank of the Alma provided tempting cover, but advance they did with little hesitation.

The 23rd Fusiliers, 33rd, 7th Fusiliers, 19th and errant 95th approached the Great Redoubt firing as steadily as their advance would let them. Casualties were appalling but as they neared their objective, the Russian guns fell silent, horses and drivers approached and most of the 32 pound howitzers were dragged to the rear with great dexterity. Two gun teams were too slow, however. Captain Bell of the 23rd Fusiliers ran at one driver as he struggled to get the gun's wheels out of a rut; pointing his pistol at the Russian he signalled that the gun should be turned around and taken down the slope. Similarly, Captain Heyland, commanding the 95th's No 6 Company, despite having received a wound that was to cost him his arm, drove off a number of Russians from the other gun and scratched '95' on its carriage with the point of his sword. Once in the Redoubt, however, it became clear that supports were too far away, for the Duke of Cambridge's 1st Division was only now crossing the river rather than being close up behind Codrington's men in a position to exploit their gains. Nervously the troops looked over their shoulders as the 7th Fusiliers stuck grimly to a fire-fight with the massed columns of the Kazan Regiment on the right and the Vladimir Regiment began a ponderous, down hill counter-attack.

'The column is French, don't fire men! For God's sake don't fire'[14] came the cry from a never identified staff officer as the Russians approached. Simultaneously, bugles took up the calls 'Cease fire' and 'Retire' and the cry, 'Fusiliers, retire!'[15] was also heard. It was too much to bear; all of the impetus that had taken the troops up the slope had gone; the men had been given time to reflect on the danger of their position and their fragile hold broke. With over 900 dead and wounded around them and overwhelming numbers bearing down upon them, the mixed bag of regiments, clustering around their colours, began to fall back from the prize that they had so bloodily gained.

Russian accounts of the charge of the Vladimir Regiment vary. Prince P D Gortchakoff claims that he led the charge personally and that his troops not only ousted the British from the epaulement but chased them down to the river where they were brought under stinging rifle and artillery fire and found British reinforcements advancing towards them in unequal numbers. Certainly, a noble bronze statue was erected to the dead of the Vladimir in the area of the Great Redoubt on the fiftieth anniversary of the battle, and their bayonet charge became one of the most celebrated feats of arms of the whole war, but the facts seem to be rather less glamorous. No Allied eye-witnesses speak of the Vladimir going any farther forward than the Great Redoubt; rather, having followed up Codrington's men, they seem to have been content to remain within the earthwork clustered around the one 32 pounder that remained there, and doing their best to stay under cover from French fire and that of two British 9 pounders that were now enfilading them. The presence of these two guns is significant, for they mark the only clear influence that Raglan exercised once battle was joined. Having ridden much too far forward once across the river and placed himself on a knoll to the west of the road that, by some miracle, was not swept by Russian fire, he ordered up guns to fire into the flank of the Great Redoubt. Their arrival was timely, for they saved Codrington's men from further punishment.

On the right flank the French advance had halted and would have been the target of a Russian counter-attack had the Russians themselves not halted due to lack of artillery support and the crossing of the river in the area west of the bridge by Adams's Brigade and some of Pennefather's with the 3rd Division following. The Kazan Regiment had stuck to its ground to the west of the Great Redoubt and continued its fight with the 7th Fusiliers, but could not be persuaded to charge Lacy Yea's depleted battalion. The arrival of Warren's 55th, however, who wheeled and began firing into the flank of the Russian battalions with almost peace-time precision, sealed the Kazan's fate; they began to give way.

Simultaneously, events were developing fast at the Great Redoubt. The chronology of exactly what happened and the proximity of the opposing troops is very difficult to establish. Certainly, the Vladimir reached the Great Redoubt and may have gone beyond; certainly, the remnants of Codrington's troops withdrew to the river line and there rallied, but quite what happened to the advancing Brigade of Guards is difficult to ascertain. Stung by requests to support Codrington, the Duke of Cambridge ceased to dither and urged his Division forward. The 1st Bn Scots Fusilier Guards were the first guardsmen to cross the river and on the south bank, instead of waiting for the other two guards battalions to cross and form-up on their flanks, they went at the Great Redoubt with the same impulsiveness as Codrington's men. They were met, however, not just by a storm of artillery and musket fire, but also by the tangled mass of the regiments falling back from the Redoubt. Thrown into chaos by these men and hearing the same calls of 'Fusiliers, retire' that may have caused the initial confusion in the Redoubt, the Scots Fusilier Guards faltered. Certainly, there were acts of great gallantry; Robert Lindsay won the first Victoria Cross of the campaign by holding his ground with the colour party, but the battalion was new to war like so many others and they met a mixture of terrible fire and total confusion to which a fair measure of general panic was added by those around them. Afterwards there was much talk about their conduct; one Grenadier officer's view was '. . . they retired, causing our men, who were in line on their right, to cry out "Shame!", saying at the same time that they wished the Queen could see the favourites now.'[16]

The 1st Coldstream and 3rd Grenadiers took a more deliberate approach. They crossed the river, took their dressing under fire, and then advanced deliberately, firing as they moved. The gap between them was plugged by the rapidly reformed Scots Fusilier Guards; the remnants of the 23rd Fusiliers, 33rd and the 19th re-grouped and went back into the attack, whilst the colour party and a substantial body of the 95th attached themselves to the Grenadiers. With the Kazan melting fast on their left and faced by the Guards, the Vladimir began to give way. The arrival of Sir Colin Campbell's Highland Brigade on their right flank completed the ruin. All three Highland battalions arrived on the Russian position in quick succession, tearing into their opponents with drilled rifle fire delivered in volleys. Under plunging artillery fire, and with fresh British troops arriving in good order, the Russian right and centre began to give. The left was already crumbling as more French guns came into action from the plateau, and British gains were exploited. Soon the whole of Menshikov's force was in retreat, streaming towards Sevastopol.

Now was the time for the victory to be turned into a rout. No further positions had been prepared by the Russians and a scant, rapidly formed rearguard stood according to Hodasevich, '. . . trembling with fear as we saw the enemy's cavalry coming forward to cut off retreating stragglers'.[17] But no pursuit was allowed. The British cavalry moved forward, had begun to take prisoners, and were just beginning to exploit their advantage when the order came to halt. The French would not advance without their guns forward to cover their infantry, and they lacked the cavalry that they would normally have used to protect their guns. Furthermore, their infantry needed time to collect their knapsacks and, despite some protestations to the contrary, the British seem to have been so stunned by the effects of what was, for most, their first battle that there was little enthusiasm to chase their enemies. The fault, however, was a bad one; as one Russian survivor observed:

'He then sat there rejoicing at his victory over what he imagined to be the advanced guard of our army; his mistake saved us and Sevastopol . . . It is frightful to think what might have happened had it not been for this cardinal error of the enemy's.'[18]

It had been a bloody battle. The French claimed to have lost 1,351, though it was generally accepted that this number reflected all of their casualties from both disease and battle, and that at the Alma a more accurate estimate would have been '560 at the most'.[19] The British lost 2,002 and the Russians 5,709 which included the unusually high proportion of 1,801 killed. The official Russian historian notes: 'Neither Inkermann nor the battle of the Tchernaya nor even the final assault and the fall of Sevastopol, though this latter event was far more important than the Alma, produced a more depressing effect'.

As an afternote to the battle, the fortunes of the 4th Division are worthy of mention for they were to have a most important bearing on Cathcart's later conduct at both Balaklava and Inkermann. Torrens's depleted brigade had been left behind to clear the beach landing site and to act as a rearguard. Cathcart had marched with the remnant of the division as a reserve leaving instructions to Torrens to join him as soon as possible. Torrens set off as soon as his task was complete, but for some unaccountable reason, he took the road to Simferopol instead of the road due south towards Sevastopol. Only after some several miles was the mistake realised and the brigade turned back to retrace its steps. A mounted staff officer eventually found the column and delivered the message that all haste was to be made to the Alma for a battle was to be fought, but Torrens arrived just too late to be of any use and apologised to Raglan for his tardiness. Whether their lack of numbers prevented Cathcart's division being used in the battle or not is open to debate, but the fact is that the divisional commander with the most recent operational experience was not called upon to fire a shot and one of his brigades had made an elementary error which reflected badly on the whole division. Whilst others had been gaining laurels, the 4th Division with its renowned leader had either sat and watched or blundered about as the victims of poor navigation. The scorn of those who had fought for those who had not can be imagined; one wonders if the apparent slur on Cathcart at the Alma and his subsequent actions at Balaklava account for his impulsiveness at Inkermann.

Notes

1. Skelton letter of 7 September 1854, quoted in Hibbert
2. Wylly, p6
3. *ibid*, p7
4. Menshikov, quoted in Seaton, p24
5. Miliutin, quoted in Seaton, p24
6. Menshikov, quoted in Seaton, p25
7. *ibid*, p26
8. Gorchakov, quoted in Seaton, p27
9. Gowing, p16
10. Kinglake, vol III, p34
11. *Journal of the Society for Army Historical Research*, vol 44
12. Kinglake, vol III, p67
13. *ibid*, p205
14. *ibid*, p151
15. *ibid*, p152
16. Neville Letters, 28 September 1854
17. Hodasevich, p74
18. Russell, p67
19. Kinglake, vol III, p154

Chapter III
'Raglan and Canrobert were donkeys!'
Balaklava

Many of the Allies believed that the path to Sevastopol now lay open as Menshikov's broken army streamed southward after the Alma, and in many ways that was true, for the defences of the city were by no means ready to repel an attack and the defenders were few. The seaward defences had been strengthened during the spring of 1854, and by May there were 610 guns mounted in a series of batteries. Furthermore, on 23 September, despite arguments to the contrary from Kornilov and Nachimov, Menshikov gave the order for the Black Sea Fleet to be used in the defence of Sevastopol with seven ships being scuttled in the mouth of the harbour and ten men-of-war being anchored in positions to bring their fire to bear on the north side of the roadstead. All remaining ships were to be made ready to be scuttled in the event of the city's falling to the Allies, whilst the crews of the sunken ships were moved to the land batteries. There was much debate in the Russian press about whether these craft should have been used in this way or have put to sea, but given the Allies' weight of numbers and preponderance of steam-driven craft, the decision was probably right.

From landward the picture was considerably less healthy for the Russians. A chain of defences had been started during Alexander's reign, and there had been a further project to put a series of redoubts around the whole of the main town and the Korabelnaya suburb in 1834. But only about one fifth of the town had any defences completed. In the summer of 1854 the Navy had been charged with the construction of many further defences, but little was achieved due to a lack of money, resources, skilled labour and, above all else, any impetus from Menshikov who, as we have seen, was still not convinced that the Allies intended to land at all.

One important asset had been added to Sevastopol's defences which was to be critical in the fighting that lay ahead. In April the sapper battalion from 6 Corps had built a new road that linked the city with the interior of the Crimea. It ran from the Korabelnaya suburb over the mouth of the Careenage ravine along the shore of the roadstead to the Inkermann bridge where it linked up with the main roads from the interior. It was never severed by the Allies; it proved to be the lifeline of the city throughout the siege. It skirted the base of the position occupied by the British 2nd Division once the siege was established, and a casual assessment leads one to conclude that it had to be cut if the siege was to be a success. The fact that it was allowed to continue to function is, therefore, hard to understand. However, two facts determined its survival. First, the Allies did not have enough men to prosecute the siege properly, the British being particularly weak on the right flank in the area of Inkermann. Second, always moored in the bay were warships, most notably *Vladimir* and *Chersonese*, whose fire and that of the guns in the Korabelnaya dominated not only the road but the high ground at the extreme right of the Allied position which, as a direct reflection of the accuracy of this fire, became known as 'Shell Hill'. The British seem to have accepted that the Sapper road was unassailable, despite all of its implications for the survival of Sevastopol, and this probably explains why little mention is made of it in contemporary accounts. A grasp of its significance, however, is fundamental to a proper understanding of the battle of Inkermann.

The city was further weakened by Menshikov's decision to march the majority of his troops out of Sevastopol on 23 September with a view to leaving them free to manoeuvre inland rather than being besieged. His reasoning was simple: with no troops outside the city the Allies would be free to interfere with lines of communication and dominate as far eastwards as Bakchisarai, forbidding reinforcements, and re-supply from mainland Russia. Furthermore, he answered Kornilov's protests that the city's defences would be utterly denuded by his withdrawal by pointing out that the Allies would not be able to mount an attack sufficiently forceful to take Sevastopol with their flanks and rear threatened by a mobile force. How much he was motivated by these tactical considerations is questionable, for there had been scenes of disgraceful indiscipline by the troops who had been beaten at the Alma and mutiny was in the air. The last thing that soldiers in such a state needed was to be kept cooped up in a town where a confrontation with the troops who had just beaten them was inevitable.

Thus, on the next day an advanced guard of 13,000 men led 6 Corps under Prince P D Gortchakoff and Kiriakov's 17 Division eastward out of Sevastopol. A series of mishaps occurred with Kiriakov straying far beyond the Mackenzie heights, where he was supposed to halt and wait for Gortchakoff, and overtaking the advanced guard. The confusion that this subsequently caused for Gortchakoff meant that the artillery train following in his wake was delayed and fell into the hands of the leading British units who, unbeknown to the Russians, were hurrying south in an attempt to cut off Sevastopol from the east and south. In the overall scheme of things, however, these errors were unimportant, for Menshikov's presence to the rear of the Allies served to distract them and prevent them from pitting all their strength against a highly vulnerable Sevastopol; had they been able to concentrate, the city might have been taken and the campaign concluded in very short order.

The Allied decision to march to the south of Sevastopol was a convoluted one. Originally it had been intended to land well to the north of Sevastopol then march along the coast and attack the city from its northern shore, the Severnaia. Intelligence was poor, however, and once ashore the only further news the Allies got was that the Star Fort, the major fortification that covered the Severnaia, was ready to repel any attacks made upon it, and that the scuttling of the ships in the harbour would prevent Allied ships from entering the roadstead. It was thought that a crossfire from land forces to the north and ships to the south was the only way that such a fortress would be reduced and, further, with the roadstead blocked, that it would be impossible to get troops across to the southern bank to attack the rest of the city. Furthermore, the Allied commanders believed that all logistic traffic would have to be landed on the shelving beaches somewhere to the north of Sevastopol which would be difficult to defend from Menshikov's field army and easily disrupted by autumn and winter storms.

The Allies were probably right about the beaches, knowing that there were deep-water, useful and defendable ports to the south of Sevastopol which would be better protected from the ravages of the weather. But they took little account of the fact that Balaklava, the port chosen by the British, was defended with forts and a garrison. Also, the lines of communication from Balaklava to the site of any siege works would be just as vulnerable to Menshikov as those from the beaches to the north of the city. The greater error was, however, the Allies' over-estimation of the state of the garrisons to the north of Sevastopol for the Star Fort was only partially in use and badly under-manned, whilst there were too few troops in the Severnaia's guard force and their morale was very shaky after the defeat of 20 September.

So it was that the Allies, after unconscionable delays following the Alma, set off on a march that was certainly bold but ran directly against the logic of landing some distance north of Sevastopol in the first place. Had an attack from the south of the city been planned initially, it is perfectly possible that the battle of the Alma could have been avoided and that a far faster and more deadly blow struck against Sevastopol which would not have signalled Allied intentions as obviously as the landing at Kalamita did. In the event, the Flank March, as it became known, was a success. Despite the fact that the two armies, as we have seen, blundered into one another, and that Raglan's cavalry seemed to be incapable of either proper navigation or reconnaissance work, the British and French arrived to the south of their objective without major incident.

The defences around Balaklava capitulated almost at once, and the port initially became the beachhead for both French and British. It soon became obvious, however, that Balaklava was too small for the whole force and the French headed farther west into the Chersonese peninsula and took two smaller ports. They made a good choice as the two ports had a greater overall capacity, despite the fact that the French had a smaller fleet. Much more importantly, as in the march south and at the Alma, both French flanks were secure; their west flank lay against the sea whilst the British protected the east. Furthermore, the French lines of communication to their besieging troops were much shorter than those of the British.

The British appeared to have drawn the short straw again as it soon became obvious that with Menshikov at large considerable numbers of men would have to be dedicated to the protection not only of the Allied eastern flank but also the rear of the besieging forces; manpower would be at a premium. Meanwhile, the garrison of Sevastopol had been split up into three virtually independent commands by Menshikov before he departed. The Severnaia had been put under the command of Kornilov, with Nachimov commanding the main town south of the roadstead, whilst Lieutenant-General Moller, the commander of 14 Division, was put in charge of all the army personnel in the garrison. Such an arrangement could never hope to work, and a military council was soon formed in which Moller was marginalised and the two admirals took the decisions. The Russians believed that the Allies would not delay, but would attempt to storm the port off the line of march as they came south and hooked westward. Accordingly, every effort was bent to the further construction of trenches, earthworks and the improvement of existing forts. Sailors and soldiers worked around the clock ably assisted by civilian volunteers and urged by both Nachimov and Kornilov who appreciated how quickly the months of lassitude had to be overcome if the city were not to fall. Todleban's genius came to the fore, and under his guidance a ring of defences soon began to take shape, but the strength of the garrison was remarkably low. As the Allies wheeled around the outskirts of Sevastopol on 27 September, there were only 3,500 troops on the north bank and 16,000 in the south, with 3,000 sailors on board ship. On 2 October, however, 10,000 reinforcements reached Menshikov but none of them was sent to the increasingly beleaguered Sevastopol.

The time was ripe for the Allies to strike a swift and final blow at the city and make up for the opportunity that had been lost after the Alma. The French, however, now commanded by Canrobert whose excellent record both in the fighting in Algeria and of loyalty during Napoleon's coup d'état had caused him to be appointed to command the French army after St Arnaud had succumbed to disease, were against an immediate assault. Similarly, General Burgoyne, Raglan's chief engineer, advised against it; he agreed with the French believing that the developing

Russian defences were already too powerful and that no attack could succeed without earlier softening-up by siege artillery that had not yet been landed. But there were those who disagreed, most notably Cathcart who, since the Alma, riding high on a reputation that had yet to be tested in the Crimea, had been declaring the enemy all but beaten and that Sevastopol would fall with ease. Looking down on the Russians from the high ground that the 4th Division occupied, he told Raglan, '. . . the place is only enclosed by a thing like a low park wall, not in good repair . . . I am sure that I could walk into it with scarcely the loss of a man at night or an hour before daybreak'.[1] The decision not to assault incensed him, and with an irritation born of the anomalous 'dormant commission', he remonstrated with Raglan on 28 September, 'Land the siege-trains! But, my dear Lord Raglan, what the devil is there to knock down?'.[2]

The Russians remained convinced that the city would be taken by storm despite the feverish work on the defences which were becoming, according to Kornilov in his Diary for 3 October, '. . . more and more impressive to look at'.[3] Hodasevich believed that

'. . . the best kind of defence against a regular attack consists of earthworks, that can so easily be changed, altered, and increased to meet the attacks. The batteries at Sevastopol were at first nothing but earth, loosely thrown up with the shovel, the embrasures were plastered with moistened clay, but when it was discovered that this was not enough, they were faced with stout wicker-work. Then fascines were introduced, and finally gabions were employed. The batteries were frequently found not to bear upon the principal point, or the embrasures were not made so as to enable the guns to be pointed in the right direction. Whenever a discovery of this sort was made, the whole was changed during the night.'[4]

Despite this, on 10 October there was considerable relief when the Allies' saps and trenches could be made out slowly edging towards the outer defences; the Allies were digging in for a form of warfare that the Russians understood well where artillery, their best arm, would decide the day. Allied fears of Menshikov's force and a misappreciation of the lethality and readiness of the defending artillery had bought the Russians just what they needed: time. It was to be another bad mistake by the Allies, for as Todleban later told Canrobert, if an assault had been mounted in early October, 'they would have taken it easily'.[5] Nachimov's views were more pungent: when he heard of his enemies' intentions to besiege rather than to storm he observed that, 'Raglan and Canrobert were donkeys'.[6]

Sevastopol is a fjord surrounded by a plateau riven by deep ravines. The deepest of these, which climbs south-eastwards from Sevastopol's South

Bay, was to mark the boundary between the Allies' siege works. To the west were the French, and to the east were the British whose five infantry divisions were deployed in a half-moon as far north-east as the ground south of the Sapper road, Shell Hill. Immediately to the right of the French were the 3rd Division with the 4th Division to their right whose flank lay on the edge of the next ravine, the Careenage, to the north-east of which and up as far as Shell Hill, lay the 2nd Division. Southwards was the 1st Division, whose right rested on the Sapoune ridge, and two divisions of French under Bosquet, the so-called 'Army of Observation', whose job it was to guard the Allied rear by looking down onto the Balaklava plain. It was from these positions that the Allies prepared to bombard Sevastopol before assaulting it.

On 17 October the long awaited barrage started after many delays caused by getting guns of sufficient calibre up from the ports and into position. Fire was to be brought to bear on all points of the Russian defences on the landward side, whilst the fleets pummelled the seaward fortresses. The damage caused by the ships was surprisingly slight, however, but their casualties were heavy. There had been 520 sailors injured and killed and over 50,000 rounds fired, not without effect, but without the crippling damage that was expected; at last light the ships withdrew. Hodasevich noted, 'It was extraordinary how small an amount of damage was done to the sea-batteries by the allied fleet; but I suppose this was because the ships were stationed at too great a distance from them to do them any harm'.[7]

On land the British guns had been noticeably more effective than those of the French whose fire ceased when the second of two magazines exploded. The British artillery persevered against the bulk of the Russian guns inflicting considerable casualties; just over 1,100 of which Kornilov was one. He had spent the day under shot and shell, inspiring his men at the guns and, despite being begged not to come into the hard-pressed Malakhov redoubt, he insisted and paid dearly for his gallantry, being struck by a British round from which he died a little later.

The important point was that the expected Allied assault had not been made. A Sevastopol denuded of manpower and sheltering behind largely improvised defences had withstood all that the French and British could throw at them. It was evident that as long as re-supply continued to come into the city either from along the Sapper road or directly into the Severnaia, then they might hold out. Thus, that night the defences were repaired under cover of darkness in preparation for the next day's bombardment which started at first light but with only the British firing. Two days later the French joined in again, and so it went on for a week; fire, destruction and counter-fire all day, then rapid repairs and even improvement to the defences at night.

As the weather worsened and Sevastopol's defences appeared as good as new each morning, so optimism evaporated amongst the Allies as it became apparent that the opportunity for a swift assault was slipping away. After a week's intermittent bombardment it became clear to Raglan that he did not have the resources to carry on with his share of the siege, whilst at the same time guarding the west flank and rear. To make matters worse, by 24 October reports had been received that a reinforced mass of Russians was gathering in order to raise the siege. Little seems to have been made of these reports despite the fact that during the first three weeks of October Liprandi's 12 Infantry Division, consisting of twenty-four battalions, had arrived from Bessarabia, and the cavalry force had also been considerably augmented. This gave Menshikov 65,000 troops, and there were another 25,000 men on the way in the shape of 10 and 11 Infantry Divisions. With no more than 75-80,000 Allied troops in total, of whom many were ineluctably tied up in siege operations, the balance had swung towards the Russians. The only decision that now remained for Menshikov to make was whether an attack should be mounted immediately or whether he should wait for the next two divisions to arrive.

Menshikov elected to attack sooner rather than later due not, as might be supposed, to a careful tactical analysis of the situation but rather to the pressure that he was being subjected to by the Tsar, and to his own, apparent pessimism. After the Alma there had been constant missives from the Tsar urging Menshikov to go onto the offensive before French and British reinforcements could be landed. Perhaps equally significantly, Menshikov appears to have lost any faith in his army to win. As Miliutin put it, '. . . the Commander-in-Chief regarded the situation with the greatest of pessimism and despaired of holding on to Sevastopol. But the sovereign would not entertain the thought of giving it up.'[8] In this frame of mind, Menshikov decided to attack the port of Balaklava with a view to cutting the British lines of communication and re-supply and getting between the sea and the main body of the Allies on the Sapoune. The Russians were encouraged in their plan by the fact that the outer ring of defences around Balaklava were manned by Turkish troops overseen by a few British non-commissioned officers. Furthermore, the Russians knew that the Turks they were going to face here were not of the stamp of those they had fought on the Danube; they were second-rate colonial troops, mainly Tunisians, whom the French had recently used as porters and for other menial tasks.

The port of Balaklava is a deep-water anchorage sheltered on three sides by steep slopes with the entrance angled south-eastwards to make a perfect harbour. The hills are crowned by ancient fortifications which had been improved by the Russians and were now manned by guns and men of the Royal Marines. The road that approaches the port was dominated by the village of Kadikoi which, in turn, stood at the mouth of a funnel-shaped plain bounded to the west by the Sapoune ridge and to the north by a series of rolling heights known as the Fedioukine Hills. The main road route from Sevastopol to the interior, the Woronzoff road, ran along a series of hillocks that effectively divided the plain into two smaller plains known to the Allies as the North and South valleys. There were several vantage points from which the whole of the Balaklava plain could be seen laid out below almost like a table-top model. From the east a good view could be had from the hills to the east of the Baidar valley and from the largest of the hillocks, dubbed Canrobert's Hill by the Allies. The hills above the port allowed it to be seen from the south, whilst the Fedioukine heights afforded an equally good view from the north. Perhaps the most comprehensive view, however, could be had from the Sapoune ridge, the vantage point from which Raglan chose to direct the battle. Crucially, however, the spine of hillocks running across the plain prevented anyone in North valley from knowing what was going on in South valley and vice-versa. Not even a mounted man standing in his stirrups could see beyond the confines of the valley in which he found himself, and this was to mean that events separated by only a few hundred yards were entirely hidden from the view of anyone who was not perched on high ground.

Steps had been taken to protect the port from exactly the sort of attack that the Russians were now planning. First, an inner ring of defences had been built 500-600 yards from Balaklava in the shape of several batteries linked by a line of earthworks. Rather less than a mile farther inland, running along the hillocks, were six redoubts numbered consecutively from the one on Canrobert's Hill in the east, the remains of which can still be seen today. Numbers 5 and 6 were neither finished nor manned, but the rest had two or three British 12 pound guns in them supervised by a Royal Artillery non-commissioned officer and a garrison of about 250 Turkish Tunisians. Whilst each of the redoubts could support at least one other position, more could have been done to strengthen them and to improve fields-of-fire, and the Russians did not feel that they posed much of a threat most particularly because of the quality of the garrisons. Command of all these defences was entrusted to the experienced leader of the Highland Brigade, Sir Colin Campbell, who had performed so coolly at the Alma. The only formed body of infantry that he had at his disposal, however, were the 93rd Highlanders from his own brigade. Realising that the defences were widely spread and weakly manned, Raglan had stationed Lord Lucan's Cavalry Division outside Balaklava to give some mobile support to the infantry and gunners.

The Russian plan of attack was simple. Early on 25 October a force of seventeen battalions, twenty squadrons, ten cossack *sotni* (about eighty horsemen) and sixty-four guns under the command of General Liprandi, commander of 12 Infantry Division, was to move against Balaklava and seize it. Simultaneously, a column of 5,000 troops, commanded by Major-General Zhabokritsky, was to march onto the Fedioukine Hills in order to give flank protection from any Allied troops who might attempt to interfere from the Sapoune. Whilst the main artillery force opened fire upon the redoubts, the infantry was to move in and take them; then the cavalry was to be unleashed against the British cavalry and the inner line of defences. Accordingly, with Zhabokritsky already moving into position, at six o'clock the Russian guns opened fire on the redoubts which, having received no information from their outlying picquets about a Russian advance, were thrown into confusion. No 1 Redoubt was taken, the garrisons of 2 and 3 fled having hardly fired a shot, and the troops in No 4 waited for the Odessa Regiment to deploy into attack formation before decamping in the wake of their comrades. By half-past seven the outer line of defences were in Liprandi's hands and the way seemed clear for his cavalry to sweep to Balaklava itself.

Liprandi's orders to Ryzhov, the leader of the Russian cavalry, were somewhat less than precise, for all he was told was to take a mixed force of hussars and cossacks and mount an attack 'against the enemy camp'. This was interpreted in a number of different ways; a staff officer in Liprandi's headquarters believed that the target was the British transport lines; others thought that his objective was the artillery park; Ryzhov himself was clear that he had been given the hazardous task of attacking '. . . infantry and all the English cavalry in a fortified position with an understrength hussar brigade'.[9] Whether anyone was entirely clear about what Liprandi wanted was not, in the event, to matter, for as Ryzhov's force moved off westward along North valley, so the British Heavy Cavalry Brigade, under the command of Brigadier-General Sir James Scarlett, who had been moving eastward along South valley to support the withdrawing Turks, caught sight of them and wheeled left to intercept.

Simultaneously, Ryzhov had ordered four squadrons of hussars to attack the infantry force which had been drawn up north of Kadikoi to resist any direct threat to Balaklava. With horse artillery in support, Campbell had moved the 93rd (Sutherland) Highlanders with a mixed bag of Turks of roughly battalion strength to their right into a blocking position. What followed was to be vastly embroidered by the press of the time and dubbed the 'Thin Red Line', but amounted to nothing more than some effective artillery and rifle fire delivered with great firmness. As the Russian cavalry cleared the causeway (as the chain of hillocks has become known to the British), in the area of Redoubt No 4, they came under canister fire from the horse artillery but pressed on. The 93rd fired one volley, probably at too great a range, for it seemed to have little effect, reloaded and fired another. Probably another followed; whatever, the Russians sheered off and crossed the rise back into North valley where they reformed. One Russian eye-witness described the rifle fire as 'murderous', but Liprandi, in his official despatch, made little of this affair. The comments of a British officer not actually involved in the battle make interesting reading:

> 'The newspapers got hold of it and made great business out of it . . . A lot of cossacks advanced towards them and at about 500 yards the Highlanders fired an ill-directed volley. They then got the order to retire which was done . . . leaving 15 or 20 horses and about half the number of men on the field'.[10]

Whether the affair was actually glorious or whether it was simply made to sound so by the sweep of a journalist's pen, is actually irrelevant. The facts were that well disciplined infantry, supported by artillery, had met cavalry in line, a formation that was usually judged to be most unwise, and foiled a direct threat to the port.

Coming slowly to the aid of the Cavalry Division were the Duke of Cambridge's 1st Division and Sir George Cathcart's 4th Division from the Sapoune. The cavalry had stood to at the western end of South valley from where Scarlett moved off, as we have seen, to attempt to protect the running Turks who were providing sport for Russian lancers, and to poise himself for a counter-attack against the fallen redoubts. His decision to wheel north was taken as the lance tips of Ryzhov's men were seen over the causeway and what followed was to be one of history's best examples of a spoiling attack. Scarlett was neither an experienced cavalryman nor soldier but he seized his opportunity. As the Russian cavalry came over the ridge they were confronted by a broad line of British cavalry who were clearly preparing themselves to attack. Simultaneously, they began to receive fire from the various British batteries dotted around South valley and they jangled to a halt. Scarlett set off well in front of his five, weak regiments who were outnumbered by at least three-to-one and crashed into the Russian column hacking left and right. The Inniskilling Dragoons and the Scots Greys were hard behind him; following them were the 5th Dragoon Guards and the Royal Dragoons all of whom buried themselves in the face of the Russian column. The 4th Dragoon Guards charged home on the north-west flank of the Russian host which began to give way. The work was close and vicious with most of the damage being done with sabres rather than lance or pistol as two tightly wedged bodies of men fought for supremacy. The Russians were wearing greatcoats which resisted all but the most energetic of cuts, and their sword-play was considerably less rigid than that of the British. One trooper when asked after the fight how he had come by an ugly gash to the head replied, 'Well, I had just cut five [a cut to the body] and the damned fool never guarded at all but hit me over the head'![11]

The Russian cavalry crumbled under the sheer vigour of the British attack leaving about 270 men on the field, three times the number of their enemies' casualties. Helped on their way by the British guns, Ryzhov's broken force streamed back into North valley before eventually rallying at the eastern end under the shelter of Zhabokritsky's men on the Fedioukine Hills. The Heavy Cavalry Brigade pursued until they came under fire from the Russian guns in North valley, and then retired leaving South valley clear, but another opportunity had been lost to turn a Russian defeat into a disaster, for Cardigan's Light Cavalry Brigade had been waiting some way north and west of Scarlett's Brigade and could have taken the Russian cavalry in the flank and rear as they tumbled back over the causeway. In all too short a time, Cardigan was to regret that he had allowed yet more Russians to concentrate in North valley.

The tensions that existed between Cardigan and his divisional commander, his brother-in-law Lord Lucan; the animus between both of these senior officers and Captain Nolan, Lord Cardigan's aide-de-camp who delivered the fatal message to charge; and the rivalry between the Light and Heavy Cavalry Brigades are too well known to need to be repeated here. It is worth noting, however, that from the span of over a hundred years the actions of the Light Cavalry Brigade seem scarcely believable until one pauses to think about the lie of the land and some of the pressures under which their commanders found themselves. It has already been mentioned that from the top of the Sapoune everything below in both valleys could be clearly seen, but from the north-west of No 4 Redoubt, even on top of a horse, little could be observed. Certainly, Zhabokritsky's men on the Fedioukine Hills could be seen, as could some of the Russian infantry in the captured redoubts, but the force which was drawn up at the east end of North valley would have been quite invisible to the British cavalry who were grouped on a little plateau from the edge of which the valley floor slopes gently downwards for about a mile and a half towards the east. In the valley, obscured by the edge of this plateau, was the 3 Don Field Battery with a lancer regiment in support in the area of No 2 Redoubt. Effectively, therefore, North valley was surrounded on three sides by artillery and small-arms that could produce a devastating crossfire; it was clear to anyone perched on the several vantage points that any cavalry moving into this killing-ground would be massacred. Such a conclusion, however, was far from clear to Cardigan and Lucan. A highly volatile atmosphere existed between them; already animated by his dislike of Lucan, Cardigan must have been additionally incensed by the success that the Heavy Cavalry Brigade had just enjoyed, and even the slightest spark would have caused him to make one sort of impulsive gesture or another.

That spark came when it became clear to Raglan that the Russians were beginning to make off with the guns captured in the redoubts; until then it was possible to believe that battle had finished for the day. The Russians had fallen back and were consolidating, and the British infantry that Raglan had ordered forward were taking an impossibly long time to arrive. There had been a suggestion that the Cavalry Division should move eastwards and threaten the captured redoubts, but Lucan preferred to wait until infantry support was available. Here the matter might have rested had it not been for the enlivening sight of guns being removed. This was too much for Raglan whose mentor, Wellington, it was claimed, had never lost a gun to the enemy. An order that was crystal clear to anyone sitting on a high ridgeline and looking down onto a battlefield like a chess-board was sent to Lucan with a qualifying verbal message in the hands of Nolan: he was to prevent the enemy carrying off the guns and could expect horse artillery and infantry support. On the valley floor the message was less than clear; neither the guns in redoubts nor those of the Don battery could be seen; and no infantry was obvious to Lucan save Cathcart's troops who had taken leisurely possession of the unoccupied Redoubts No 6 and 5, but who were showing little inclination to advance. The order had to be obeyed; Scarlett's men had enjoyed a considerable triumph and dithering would not allow the Light Cavalry Brigade a chance to equal their success.

Accordingly, Cardigan led his men forward with no real idea of what he was to attack. As they moved eastwards the valley began to slope and gravity would have lent momentum to troops and horses already hopelessly over-excited. The batteries on the Fedioukine and in the redoubts opened fire as did the Don battery shortly afterwards. Perhaps Nolan knew what was meant by the order or perhaps he was attempting to divert the Brigade when one of the first enemy rounds to be fired killed him quite dead. By this time, however, it was probably too late, for the Brigade had no battle experience to speak of, a mass of guns was firing at them, and the noise of explosions and drumming hooves would have made communication impossible. The ground lent itself to a full blooded charge, and the troops' overarching desire must have been to ride out of the storm of shot and close with those who were firing at them.

Despite heavy casualties the five under-strength regiments reached the end of the valley and put their tormentors to the sword. But it did not end there, for the decimated brigade had to endure a similar ordeal as largely leaderless, disjointed knots of mounted and dismounted troopers alike made their way back up the valley, run down and picked at by Russian lancers the while. The retreating British were helped enormously, however, by the actions of d'Allonville's 4th Regiment of Chasseurs à Cheval. These colonial light horsemen attacked Zhabokritsky's artillery uphill over the broken ground of the Fedioukine Hills, broke through two battalions of the Vladimir Regiment and silenced all fourteen guns, giving tremendous succour to the retreating British below. The Vladimir, already mauled at the Alma, eventually rallied and ejected the French colonials at the point of the bayonet, but not before much damage had been done. Kozhukhov, an officer of 12 Artillery Brigade, sums up events well:

'It is difficult, if not impossible, to do justice to the feat of these mad cavalry, for, having lost a quarter of their number and being apparently impervious to new dangers and further losses, they quickly reformed their squadrons to return over the same ground littered with their dead and dying. With such desperate courage these valiant lunatics set off again, and not one living, even the wounded, surrendered.'[12]

With the destruction of half of the Allies' cavalry, the battle came to a close. It was decided that the outer ring of Balaklava's defences would remain in the hands of the Russians for whom the battle must be rated as a victory. It was not without cost, however, for the Russians had lost 238 killed and 312 wounded, whilst the British lost 360, the French 38 and the Turks 260. The most serious consequence of the battle was the loss to the British of the use of the Woronzoff road from Balaklava to the siege lines; in future a longer route over broken tracks would have to be taken which would have dire consequences once the ground deteriorated with the onset of winter proper. Furthermore, the Allies were even more constrained on their eastern flank; further resources would have to be dedicated to keeping it secure. The question must be asked, of course, had Menshikov not surrendered to the pressure of the Tsar, and waited for reinforcements in the shape of the two extra divisions, would he have been able to take Balaklava? On balance, the answer is probably yes; had Balaklava fallen, it is difficult to see how the siege could have continued.

There is one, final footnote to the battle which makes an interesting study, as it goes some way to explain later events at Inkermann. In the same way that Sir George Cathcart had taken no part in the battle of the Alma, he and his division made very little contribution at Balaklava. The crucial difference was, however, that at the Alma his force was depleted and he was not called upon, whilst at Balaklava he had most of his troops with him and he was ordered to act in a determined and resolute manner which, had he chosen to interpret his orders properly, could have materially affected the outcome of the battle in favour of the British. As has already been seen, Sir George's behaviour during and after the flank march was sulky and high-handed; he was at pains to make it obvious to anyone who cared to listen that he was the tactician and soldier of experience whose opinion and advice should be sought on all matters strategic and tactical; 'We hear that Cathcart is very angry at the way things are going on and at his never being consulted,'[13] wrote one officer to his wife.

On the morning of 25 October, Raglan sent word to the 1st and 4th Divisions as soon as it became obvious that the Russians were going to attack. Whilst the 1st Division moved off promptly, the staff officer who delivered the message to headquarters of the 4th Division met a blank refusal to move from Sir George. 'My orders are to request that you will move your division immediately to the assistance of Sir Colin Campbell. I feel sure that every moment is of consequence. Sir Colin Campbell has only the 93rd Highlanders with him. I saw the Turks in full flight,' said the galloper. 'Well, sir, if you will not sit down and have breakfast, you may as well go back to Lord Raglan and tell him that I cannot move my division,' was the retort, apparently because the 4th Division had only recently returned from a night in the trenches. The staff officer was not to be put off, however, and a further entreaty met with the reluctant reply, 'Very well, sir, I will consult with my staff officers and see if anything can be done.'[14] In due course and without hurry, the division moved off from the Sapoune towards a battle that was already joined.

Cathcart arrived only after the Heavy Cavalry Brigade had charged, and he was ordered to move forward and recapture the redoubts. Having deployed his troops with exasperating precision, he moved up to the nearest redoubts, first No 6 and then No 5, and occupied them. Both were empty, however, and everyone assumed that the division was simply taking them to act as a secure foothold from which to launch an attack on the others; but there Cathcart stalled. Some skirmishers were thrown out and guns moved into action to fire on the other redoubts, but the range was too great; nothing else was done. His lack of action and the fact that the 1st Division was still too far away to be of any use caused Raglan to chivvy the Cavalry Division into action essentially unsupported by any infantry.

Slightly less than an hour later, during which time Cathcart had moved not an inch, not even trying to push his guns forward into range, the Light Cavalry Brigade moved off down North valley. As they advanced, the Russians in all but one of the remaining redoubts forsook the earthworks and formed square, the standard infantry formation to resist cavalry. The Russians had divined Lord Raglan's intent quite correctly; they saw that the logical thing for the British to do was to attack with a joint force of cavalry and infantry supported by guns and, indeed, the British had shown every sign of preparing for such an attack by moving their infantry forward into a secure attacking position. Cardigan and Cathcart did not understand their leader as well as their enemies, however, for the former had been committed to a suicidal attack devoid of tactical sense, and the latter simply refused to take an opportunity that was offered him. Had Cathcart moved with speed, properly supported by his own batteries, he could have rolled the Russians up the Woronzoff road as the Light Cavalry Brigade outflanked them from South valley. In fact he failed to do anything; he neither consulted with Lucan or Cardigan, nor did he use his initiative. As a result, the battle was an ignominious defeat of which Cathcart was one of the principal architects.

The furore of the Light Cavalry Brigade's débâcle, and the acrimonious avoidance of blame that followed amongst the cavalry commanders meant that Cathcart's contribution to the failure was largely ignored. One cannot help but speculate what effect his inaction at the Alma, his frustrations and obvious discontent over the conduct of the siege and his lethargy at Balaklava would have had upon him. The lack of laurels for a renowed warrior such as he would not have been easy to bear. Similarly, as one of the only officers present with recent experience of active operations, it is tempting to believe that he was one of the few who realised what he might have achieved had he displayed the qualities that his reputation attributed to him. After Balaklava he must have been looking for every opportunity to burnish his fast tarnishing reputation.

Notes

1. Kinglake, vol IV, pp174–5
2. *ibid*, p189
3. Kornilov, quoted in Seaton, p125
4. Hodasevich, p42
5. Todleban, p122
6. Nachimov, quoted in Seaton, p123
7. Hodasevich, p146
8. Miliutin, quoted in Seaton, p139
9. Rhyzov, quoted in Seaton, p144
10. *Journal of the Society for Army Historical Research*, vol 44
11. Wood, quoted in Hibbert, p122
12. Kozhukov, quoted in Seaton, p151
13. Paget, quoted in Hibbert, p128
14. Kinglake, vol III, p69

Chapter IV

'An hour of the best training that any good troops could have!'
Little Inkermann, 26 October 1854

The day after Balaklava the Russians attacked the British 2nd Division as they guarded the Allies' exposed north-eastern flank. It proved to be a dress rehearsal for a much more serious attack, but no account of the fighting around the position which the Allies came to call Mount Inkermann would be understandable without a description of the ground over which it took place. First, the term 'Inkermann' is a misnomer for the old town of Inkermann lies on the other side of the Tchernaya valley some two miles distant from the edge of the plateau for which the Allies chose the same name. The old buildings, churches and caves of Inkermann proper were easily visible from the British position and were used by the Russians as a forming-up point for their assault, but they would never have regarded the ground that they were to attack as 'Inkermann'. Lying to the south of the eastern extremity of the roadstead, where the harbour narrows to the mouth of the Tchernaya river, the whole position is as remarkable for its size as it is for its ruggedness. From sea level precipitous hills, sheer cliffs in places, rise to a rolling plateau that is deeply fissured by gullies and ravines the sides of which are just as steep as the slopes that mark the edge of the plateau. The whole arena, however, is surprisingly compact. From Sevastopol to the centre of the position is only about two and a half miles, whilst the area in which the fighting occurred is no more than one and a half miles in both width and length. Thus, from the centre of the British position on Home Ridge to the centre of the Russian gun-line on Shell Hill is no more than three-quarters of a mile, and the two main British defences, the Barrier and the Sandbag Battery, were less than five hundred yards apart.

In 1854 the whole of the position was thick with stunted oak and thorn bushes that made both movement and observation difficult. Whilst little had been done to clear fields-of-fire through the brush, many tracks had been worn by both local people and, more particularly, the infantry who traversed it daily on picquet duty. Most contemporary accounts make mention of the brush but few dwell on it as much as it perhaps deserves, for those who fought there must have accepted it as a not very remarkable feature. It is important to realise, however, just how significant it was, for in places it made bodies of men who were very close to one another practically invisible. It greatly impeded the cohesion of the solid Russian columns, and lent itself to the skirmishing tactics of the British whilst hiding the paucity of their numbers. Protruding from the ground were outcrops and boulders of lime which meant that when scrambling up slopes every step had to be watched. Furthermore, there were slopes everywhere which were sometimes bare and craggy, sometimes gently wooded glens, and sometimes miniature jungles. In short, it was a piece of ground that made command and control almost impossible, particularly when, to make matters additionally difficult, it was covered in a thick blanket of fog.

In more detail, starting from the north-west corner of the battlefield, that closest to Sevastopol, the Sapper road headed east from the city along the plateau before dipping north-east down St George's Ravine. From there it continued along the southern shore of the roadstead before joining the Post road just before the Traktir bridge over the Tchernaya. Looking south from the Sapper road the plateau looms above riven by two, deep ravines. The more easterly one, the Volovia gorge, culminates in a shelf of flat ground which then rises into another knoll which was known both as Cossack Mountain and Shell Hill which was to be the centre of Russian operations on both 26 October and 5 November. Spreading out either side of Shell Hill were two shoulders known as West Jut and East Jut; the latter falls away to its south-east into a major landmark of the battle, Quarry Ravine. Half way down the slope of East Jut ran the so-called Post road whilst on the floor of Quarry Ravine a rougher track ran which joined the Post road just below the British positions.

Moving farther east and south from Quarry Ravine, a mighty finger of land, sheer for its last two hundred yards, points north-east: this is Inkermann Spur. No one who went to the extremities of this spur could leave other than by retracing their steps or abseiling off the side. The south-eastern face of the spur was bounded by the verdant St Clement's ravine which culminates in another shelf known as the Kitspur. Some of the most savage fighting on 5 November was to occur in and around this ravine and the earthwork known as the Sandbag Battery at the top of it, so it may be worth pausing for a while to look at the implications of assaulting up a slope such as this. The incline is steep and the ground loose and rocky underfoot, the most exhausting sort of ground to climb. Whilst the slope is not quite steep enough to require one to grasp at the brush for hand-holds, a fit man would have found it a stiff climb from the base to the edge of the rocky shelf above. When such a man was encumbered with thirty-or-so pounds of ammunition and equipment, carrying a musket and bayonet and with adrenalin born of fear pumping around his system, the climb would have been exhausting. Once the attacking Russians reached the lip above, that is, when they were at their most breathless, it was here that they would have been faced by the defending British, which may go some way to explain why the Russians always hung back as they breasted this rise; the British attributed it to the intimidating power of their defence; doubtless this was partially true but their breathlessness would also have rendered them particularly vulnerable at this point.

Rising above the Kitspur and Inkermann Spur was the main British position which was shaped like a back-to-front letter L. The north-south spur was referred to as Fore Ridge and the west-east spur as Home Ridge, the whole feature being slightly lower than Shell Hill some three-quarters of a mile to its north-west. Running north-south up and over Home Ridge and being abutted to its west by the finger valleys of the Careenage Ravine was the Post road. The Careenage Ravine ran directly south-east from Sevastopol's roadstead and provided deep and covered access from the city straight into the rear of the British position. At its south-eastern extremity it divided into lesser ravines, the Mikriakoff Glen heading east-south-east and the Wellway leading right up to the Post road itself. The Careenage Ravine was bounded to the south-west by Victoria Ridge at the south-eastern edge of which lay a windmill that was much used by the Russians as a landmark.

So much, then, for the ground over which Russians, British and French were destined to fight, but of crucial significance were the defences which the British had thrown up to protect this open flank. The vulnerability of the Inkermann position had been clearly identified by the British, and a whole infantry division had been stationed there to protect it. However, it is clear that until events after Balaklava unfolded, there were few who fully appreciated how easily the whole of the Allied cause might be unhinged by a determined attack in this quarter. Without doubt, everyone's hopes lay in a quick capitulation of Sevastopol which might be brought about by every effort being bent towards the prosecution of the siege. Accordingly, too few troops were dedicated to the defence of the Inkermann position; the over-stretched and battle-depleted 2nd Division was expected to hold a position which was close to the enemy and required probably twice the number, leaving maximum numbers of troops to get on with siege operations. The effect of demanding too much from the 2nd Division was that they did not have enough men or time to prepare their defences properly – everyone had their work fully cut out providing picquets for the mobile defence of Inkermann as well as finding troops for both carriage of supplies and trench work. Conditions were summed-up by one officer:

'We are all nearly worn out with exposure to the intense November cold, constant fatigues, indifferent food and the loss of nearly every night's rest; three out of four have I been up, and the poor men scarcely

45

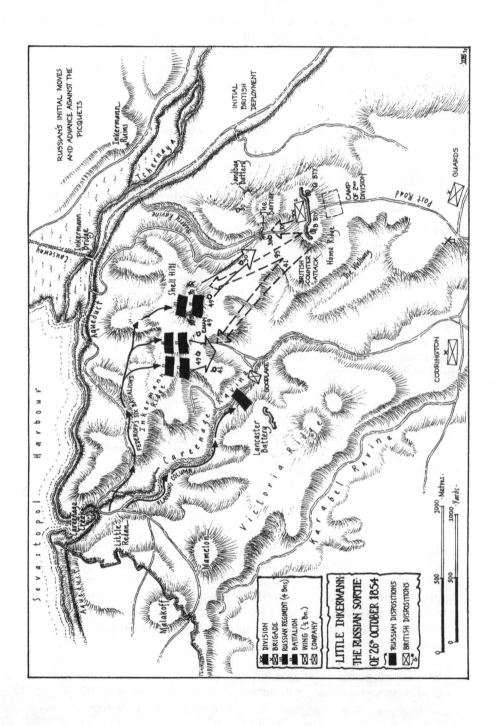

ever get a night in their tents – not bed – for all lie on the ground; we have not taken our clothes off since landing, and even when they have a night all are under arms soon after 4 am and remain standing in the cold some hours till daybreak. Such is our life!'.[1]

Added to the fact that there were not enough men, there was a feeling that there was little point in digging in too deeply as a conclusive assault on Sevastopol was imminent. Accordingly, the earthworks that had been prepared were few. A low wall at the top of Quarry Ravine where the old track in the bottom of the ravine met the Post road had been built which was about four feet high and made out of piled stones and earth but lacked sandbags or revetting. 'The Barrier', as the breastwork came to be known, was to serve as a shelter for the picquets who covered the Post road, the road itself having been dug up and made impassable to wheeled vehicles some distance farther down the ravine. The camp of the 2nd Division lay just south of Home Ridge out of sight of Shell Hill but well within gun shot. It was a tented camp with no protective walls or trenches which was to suffer badly from Russian overshoots from Shell Hill.

The crest of Home Ridge had another low, loose wall built upon it which had been prepared with a view to giving some protection to the Divisional artillery should it be brought into action there. One face of the wall looked directly north, but it had been angled on its western side to face north-west, directly at Shell Hill; this portion had embrasures for three guns and was several feet thicker than most of the rest of the wall but only, apparently, two or three feet high. The wall was better prepared to the east of the Post road than to the west and various officers took it upon themselves irregularly to improve parts of it, usually earning that part which had been laboured upon the epithet of 'Folly' with the officer's name appended! Whether or not it was mocked, this rude defence was to prove itself time and again in the ensuing fighting, for not only did it protect both guns and infantry much better than might have been expected, it was also found to be an invaluable rallying point for disordered units and individuals.

Lying less than five hundred yards to the east of the Barrier was a curious structure that was to assume a significance out of all proportion to its real importance. It was observed that an earthwork was being prepared by the Russians to house a number of guns near the old town of Inkermann with a view, it was assessed, to harassing the positions on Home and Fore Ridge, and possibly as a supporting position for the forthcoming assault. It was decided, therefore, to destroy the position before it could make a nuisance of itself, the most effective tools for which were thought to be a pair of 18 pound guns from the Siege Train. Before the guns were brought into place an eight or nine feet high palisade was built out of spoil faced with sandbags at the top of the Kitspur; two embrasures were made in it and it was wide enough for both guns. In due course the guns came into action, knocked their target to bits and were withdrawn as they were too far forward to be easily protected. But the earthwork remained in place.

Obvious as it was, it remained there to dissuade the Russians from any attempts at long-range sniping and soon became a recognised gathering place for the out-lying picquets for whom it provided much sought after protection from the easterly wind. Christened the 'Sandbag Battery', it was never intended to be defended as it served no tactical purpose; to that end, there was no firestep built inside and infantry who wanted to fire from it either had to peer around the tapering ends or leap into the gun embrasures. Whether it was tactically important or not, however, is irrelevant, for on 5 November the Russians came to regard it as a much valued prize, a tangible sign of success, and equally perversely, the British defended it tooth-and-nail, endangering the whole of their north-eastern flank in the process. The French found themselves drawn to it by the same fatal magnetism and after 5 November they produced a new name for it, 'L'Abattoir'.

The only fully prepared and armed earthwork lay not in the area that was to prove to be at the eye of the forthcoming storm, but half way along the Victoria Ridge facing north-west. Here had been built a battery position for Lancaster guns manned by the Royal Navy facing towards Sevastopol and covering the Careenage Ravine. Whilst never attacked by infantry on either 26 October or 5 November, it was severly shot at on both occasions being well sited to observe the western approach to Shell Hill. Protected by picquets of the Light Division, it was to be another landmark in the fighting that lay ahead.

As has already been explained, the whole of this sector was the responsibility of De Lacy Evans's 2nd Division. The Division's camp had capacity for about 3,000 infantry, and stationed with them were the twelve guns of B and G Batteries Royal Artillery. Divided into two brigades of three battalions each, the Division furnished about 400 men for trench duty with the balance of those troops, who were not resting or administering themselves finding the picquets to which allusion has already been made. The ground was watched by a chain of these picquets that started on Victoria Ridge with Codrington's Brigade of the Light Division, moved across the ravine into 2nd Division territory with Adam's Brigade being responsible for the left sector of West Jut and Shell Hill, and then to Pennefather's Brigade's sector on the right which included the heads of Quarry and St Clement's Ravines, the Kitspur and as far south as a point to the rear of the Divisional camp. From there responsibility devolved on to the Guards Brigade of the 1st Division whose camp lay rather more than half a mile south of that of the 2nd Division.

It is worth looking at the tactics and methods of these picquets in some detail for they were fundamental to the engagements of both 26 October and 5 November. Each day a brigade of the 2nd Division would have to find four picquets each of company size (which by this stage was probably no more than about sixty or seventy men). Sometimes all of the picquets would be found from one battalion, and at other times from two or more, their duty lasting for twenty-four hours. The duty of the picquet was to observe the enemy and give early warning of his approach whilst buying time by harassing him with rifle fire and, perhaps, local counter-attacks. This would be achieved by a chain of paired sentries being thrown out in front of the main body of the picquet sufficiently far for them to be able to listen without being distracted by the noises of their own people, yet close enough to be easily reached. To supplement this and to check that they remained alert an officer-led patrol would roam around visiting periodically. On the approach of the enemy the outlying sentries would signal with shots or simply by firing at them; one man would then run in to the main body of the picquet whilst the other stood his ground with those to his right and left to gain time for the main body to stand to. The main body was allowed to rest with their arms piled, but once the alarm was given they would stand-to-arms in their pairs, each pair being some six paces from the next pair, and load and fire alternately.

This process would continue until the picquet could no longer hold its ground; it would then fall back by pairs to another position at which a further stand could be made, or until it was ordered in by the rest of the battalion or brigade. In the Peninsula, British and French picquets had perfected the way in which they operated, each side understanding perfectly the function of the other to such an extent that one side's picquets would signal to the other's whether a serious attack was being made against which a determined stand was pointless, or whether what was about to happen was merely a skirmish. In the Crimea the picquets had no real depth of experience and their task, simply to buy time before yielding ground, was imperfectly understood. On both 26 October and 5 November the picquets were to fight as if each inch of ground was precious; we shall see how their commanders capitalised upon this attitude.

One further group should be mentioned. Each division was told to find a band of about sixty men who could operate as what would now be known as a fighting patrol. They had to seek the enemy, taking any opportunity to snipe – particularly his gunners – and be prepared to remain hidden near to enemy lines for up to twenty-four hours. Almost every regiment had trained its men in the skirmishing tactics mentioned above, but these roving units required skills more akin to those developed in the bush wars of the Cape than anything learnt on the barrack square in London or Fermoy.

The 1st Division appear to have been the most advanced in forming such a group, and under the command of Captain Goodlake of the

Coldstream they roamed far outside their Division's tactical boundaries. By 26 October they had already been involved in several scrapes including a raid on a Russian picquet in which an officer and several men had been taken prisoner and for which they expected the Russians to seek revenge. Kinglake, the official historian of the campaign, sums up the approach of these men perfectly:

'A narrative of the exploits of this force would make a volume of extraordinary interest; but I imagine that there is no hope that any such will ever appear; for they who do these sort of things are apt to be men of few words . . . by constantly hanging close upon the enemy they gained the opportunities of doing really good services; but they would hardly deny, I believe, that one motive at least, if not the main one, for engaging in these enterprises, was the love of adventure and sport.'2

In Sevastopol the battle of Balaklava was hailed as a great success. Bells were tolled and every opportunity was taken to bolster the troops' morale by making the achievements of 25 October seem to be more significant than they probably were, but what the precise motive was for the adventure of the following day is not entirely clear. Certainly, the Russians believed that Liprandi was vulnerable in front of Balaklava and that the Allies might attempt a counter-attack to remove the threat that he posed to the British lines of communication. Accordingly, if they could be distracted by a sizeable sortie, then more time might be bought for the expected reinforcements to arrive from Bessarabia before the offensive was resumed. It has also been suggested that the sortie that did take place was simply an armed reconnaissance for the full-blown attack that was eventually mounted on 5 November. Whilst that is possible, the troops that took part in the affair of 26 October used precisely the same route and plan that was to be used on 5 November, but they were all carrying entrenching tools and full battle equipment which suggests that they intended to stay rather than simply reconnoitre by fire before with-drawing. It may have been that they intended to dig in on Shell Hill and there construct a redoubt from which fire support could be given during a later attack. Whatever the precise intention, whilst no ground was taken nor earthworks constructed, the Russians were to probe the weakest point of the British flank and gain invaluable intelligence particularly about the siting of their own supporting artillery and the weight of counter-battery fire that the British would bring to bear. The *Illustrated London News*, one of the more xenophobic periodicals, tells us that the Russians were fired-up for the attack by their generals telling them that,

'You are mistaken if you think you are fighting against the English whom you saw at Alma. The troops before you are merely Turks. Our brothers attacked them yesterday in the plain of Balaklava. They beat them all, killed large numbers and plundered the dead . . . You can see they are Turks for they wear grey coats; whereas British soldiers, as you well know, have red coats.'[3]

Whether this was a deliberate attempt to deceive the soldiery who were about to face the British is difficult to say, but the British had for some time been wearing their long, grey greatcoats in the field with scarlet coatees now a relatively rare sight.

Colonel Federoff was placed in command of this endeavour. At his disposal he had six battalions of infantry – four of his own regiment, the Bourtirsk, who had so far seen only siege warfare having arrived in Sevastopol from Kertch in the eastern Crimea on 2 October, two battalions of the more experienced Borodino who had seen action at Alma and within Sevastopol, and four light guns, a total force of about 4,300; marching on his flank was a 700-strong column of sailors in the infantry role. The plan was simple; Federoff's main body was to march out of Sevastopol from the Korabelnaya along the Sapper Road, follow it along the shore of the roadstead until adjacent to the Volovia Gorge and the ravine to its west, turn south off the line of march, deploy straight into battle formation and then ascend Shell Hill. All of this was to be done unseen by the British picquets until the crest of Shell Hill was reached, when the guns would quickly be brought into position and the engagement opened. Simultaneously, the column of sailors would march along the Careenage Ravine and strike at the rear of the British position emerging from the Wellway and the Mikriakoff Glen distracting the defenders and being in a good position to attack their artillery and reserves in the flank.

The morning of 26 October was a particularly beautiful one with bright, warm sunshine and a light breeze. The 2nd Division had been aware that much was going on in Sevastopol due to the tolling of bells and the movement of many bodies of troops, but this was attributed to the general fuss still being made by the Russians over the events of the previous day. About breakfast time the 2nd Division stood to as there was a report that the enemy was advancing, but this proved to be incorrect and they soon stood down. In fact, about midday Federoff set off with his troops from the Korabelnaya reaching the northern slopes of Shell Hill by early afternoon. On the southern side of Shell Hill waited a picquet of the 49th commanded by Lieutenant John Conolly, unaware that the Russians were approaching. The outer sentries were soon in action however, and Conolly shook his company out into skirmishing order as the first of his men came running in to report that a large body of Russians was approaching.

Cavendish-Taylor, a so-called 'Travelling Gentleman' who had served until a few months before the outbreak of war in the 95th, saw the Russians advance and noted that they were almost impossible to see in their long, grey coats and flat forage caps (which they were wearing for the first time rather than the customary high, leather, spiked helmets) against the brushwood. Hume of the 55th was standing on the breastworks on Home Ridge trying to get a view of Sevastopol when he was alerted by rifle fire from the picquets. He knew the area well having been relieved that morning by Captain Atcherley and his company of the 30th, and was astonished to see Russian artillery come galloping over the crest of Shell Hill with columns of infantry hard behind. 'Green Guns, by Jove,'[4] said Daubeney, his commanding officer with whom he was standing, referring to the characteristic pea-green painted carriages of Russian field guns, and off they ran to stand their men to arms. The same sight was being watched in minute detail by the Light Division's picquet on Victoria Ridge which probably spotted it before the first rounds were fired. Hibbert of the 7th Fusiliers wasted no time in telling his brigadier who passed the message to the 2nd Division as fast as his aide's horse could carry it.

Conolly's men met their assailants with a hail of rifle fire which temporarily checked them but did not prevent them from closing in. The usual practice would have been for the picquet to fall back firing as they went, but in Kinglake's words:

> 'Ill-brooking that coercion by numbers which old campaigners accept, they, many of them, took offence, as it were, at the notion of being pressed back, grew savage against their assailants, and fought on with an obstinacy that could hardly have been exceeded if, instead of this outpost duty, they had had to defend to the last some only-remaining stronghold.'

Aided by his sergeant, Owens,

> 'Conolly fought throwing off his grey coat – so that all might distinguish him from the enemy – and flinging himself into a clump of Russians, where he felled one man with his field-glass, whilst he cut down another with his sword'.[5]

Eventually the weight of Russian numbers began to tell and Conolly, now wounded, had to fall back on the remainder of the 2nd Brigade's picquets on his left.

Meanwhile, on the right, Maj. Champion, Senior Major of the 95th, who was in charge of the three companies forming the 1st Brigade's picquets, saw the danger that faced the picquets to his left and deployed his men just to the south of the brow of Shell Hill to '. . . await the attack which was to be expected so soon as the picquet of the 49th was forced back'.[6] Champion did not have long to wait; despite the actions of the stalwart

Colour-Sergeant Sullivan of the 95th who looped around the flank of the advancing Russians to snipe at the following gun teams, his three companies were soon hard pressed but they continued to resist long enough for the British artillery to get into position on Home Ridge. Their job done, now was the time for Champion to retire his men slowly, firing and moving by pairs.

That was far too easy a course to follow, however. Instead they contested every inch of the ground but could not stop the Russians pushing them back off Shell Hill and getting their guns into position. By fighting so stubbornly, Champion effectively masked the fire from his own guns on Home Ridge which dared not open fire for fear of hitting the greatcoat-clad British now closely mixed with the Russians and indistinguishable from them at any but the shortest of ranges. Yet Champion was encouraged in his stance by Evans's principal staff officer, Colonel Percy Herbert, '. . . Colonel Herbert . . . had told me, in case of the 49th being driven in, to hold the position as long as possible.'[7] Herbert now saw Champion obeying his orders with enthusiasm; in a fighting ecstasy much at odds with the deeply religious, high-minded tone of his letters to his wife, Champion strode amongst his men bellowing, 'Slate them, my boys, slate them!'.[8] De Lacy Evans, however, when asked by Herbert to send a battalion forward to support the picquets gave his famous reply, 'Not a man',[9] for he intended to fight this battle from the strong position on Home Ridge dealing with his enemy with artillery from a respectable range rather than committing yet more infantry to a scrimmage that was bound to be costly.

Evans's eighteen 9-pounders were now in position and ready to answer the flimsy fire of the Russians with interest had it not been for the tenacity of the picquets who continued to block any direct fire support. Suddenly things changed, however. The Russians were begining to turn Champion's flank by virtue of their superiority of numbers when, according to Todleban, the picquets fell back in confusion. The British version was different; Champion was told that his right was threatened by a mass of Russians coming up Quarry Ravine; if they overwhelmed the company that he had left there then there would be nothing to stop them pushing up on to Home Ridge. Accordingly, the picquets rushed back pell-mell, breaking their engagement with the Russians by a series of ragged volleys and then falling back on the barrier at the top of Quarry Ravine. There they found an overspill of Russians who had wound their way down the slope of East Jut and were feeling their way forward up Quarry Ravine trying to find the path of least resistance.

By the time Champion organised himself at the barrier he had the better part of four companies at his disposal, about 240 men, to defend nothing more than a drystone wall against hordes of Russians. He describes events graphically:

'. . . we met the enemy boldly pitching into his artillery until it was sufficiently advanced to play upon us; then I retired the picquets behind the crest, and fought their foot soldiers until the artillery could be brought up, by which time all my picquets were concentrating towards me, and we made a general rush to the barrier of our main picquet, where we defended ourselves vigorously against the swarms of Russians now appearing everywhere but in our rear. We stood with artillery and rifles until all our ammunition was at the last ebb. I knew that succour must come shortly, and sent to say how hard we were pressed. Then I told the men that supports were coming up to us, and I made them fix bayonets, which daunted the Russians, who had nearly driven us out by turning one flank. I tried to get up a charge but it was too much for human nature and the few men I had with me; but they advanced a little, firing a few shots, and the Russians fell back. Then came the cheering sound of our guns crowning the hill behind us, and pouring showers of grape. The Division, all formed up in battle order, came up . . .'[10]

Against this band the raw Boutirsk Regiment dashed themselves. The officers waved their men on against the British, the young Ensign Koudriazeff falling at the head of his men as one of the many assaults was driven back.

Whilst the action was heaviest on the slopes of Shell Hill, the column of sailors had been making good progress up the Careenage Ravine. Hidden by the depth of the ravine and its many bends, the sailors were approaching undetected by the sixty or so guardsmen of Goodlake's sharpshooters who were waiting for events to develop. Fearing just the sort of enterprise upon which the Russians were now engaged, Goodlake and one of his sergeants, Ashton, scouted forward down the ravine towards some caves out of sight of his main body. The troops remained where they were, lining the bed of the ravine and extending a little way up either bank facing down the chasm and expecting to see their officer and sergeant return at any moment. Instead, the Russians were suddenly upon them. The guardsmen had time to note that their attackers wore black belts and peaked caps with red bands, unlike any that they had seen before, and that there were about six to eight hundred of them before they opened fire and began to fall back up the ravine without their leaders.

Goodlake and Ashton, meanwhile, had been involved in the sort of adventure that only this campaign could have brought about. They took cover in the caves as the column began to pass, but were seen and fired at from very close range but without effect. Ashton, referring to their most recent escapade, told Goodlake that 'They would kill us over that picquet job',[11] and both concluded that any attempt to surrender was pointless.

Deciding to sell their lives dearly, the pair fired their rifles into the nearest knot of Russians and then set to with their butt-ends stoving in heads and hewing a path into the throng. Having made their way into the midst of a column they were amazed to find that they were not seized. Their grey coats and field caps must have made them inconspicuous to the Russian sailors who had, in all probability, never seen British troops before; in any event, remarkably, they were swept along by the Russians for almost half a mile with little notice being taken and no harm befalling them.

Eventually the Russian column came to a halt in front of Goodlake's men who were making a stand at a shallow trench that had been dug below the junction of the Mikriakoff Glen and the Wellway. The column paused allowing Goodlake and Ashton to sprint across the intervening gap and rejoin their men. With their leaders now back in charge, the Guards held the far stronger Russian column in the bottom of the ravine stopping them, just in time, from being able to influence the course of events on the ground above them. They had so nearly achieved their goal; had they done so they would have been able to flood into the flank of Evans's reserves now forming behind Home Ridge and his artillery, all of whose attention was focussed on the battle to their front. Instead, despite valiant efforts by their leader to generate enough momentum to overcome the little group of guardsmen, the Russians were held in check. Eventually, reinforcements arrived in the shape of Captain Markham and a number of his men from 2nd Battalion Rifle Brigade from Buller's brigade of the Light Division. Sharp little combats occurred with the Rifles alone having five wounded, but many more of the enemy were killed, wounded and taken prisoner before the Russians gave way. The fighting in the Careenage Ravine started at about the same time that the first shots were fired on Shell Hill and was hard fought for all of the three hours that the main fight lasted. However, the fighting on and around Shell Hill ebbed and flowed whilst that in the ravine never ceased. This little group of men frustrated a potentially decisive move from the Russians and Goodlake richly deserved the Victoria Cross which he was awarded for this, and other, brilliant skirmishes.

We left the picquets down to their last rounds and fighting manfully against superior odds. The crucial part of the engagement was about to take place for Federoff now elected to support his leading troops by successive waves of reinforcements; but against these fresh men De Lacy Evans's tactics were to pay off handsomely. Seeing that the picquets had fallen back as far as he needed them to, and realising that Champion's men on the right and Major Eman's men on the left were holding the Russians conveniently at the base of Shell Hill, he slightly relaxed his stance on reinforcements and sent two companies forward, a company of the 30th under Captain Paget Bayly went to the barrier whilst the 41st's Light Company went to Eman's men on the left. Whether these men had stripped off their greatcoats or whether the forward picquets had removed theirs the more easily to wield their weapons is not clear, but the forward line of British troops were now much more visible to those on Home Ridge by virtue of the scattering of red coats amongst the Russians.

So, with his field-of-fire now clear of his own men and his forces poised, Evans was able to implement his plan as he wished. His own guns had been reinforced by H Battery from the Guards Brigade and E Battery had been despatched from the Light Division on Victoria Ridge; the Duke of Cambridge had marched his brigade up to support the 2nd Division's right flank and Evans had the bulk of the 30th and 95th in cover behind the ridge. Sergeant Bloomfield on the 95th was there:

> As soon as we were formed up we got the order to lie down and remain so until the enemy got within 200 yards of us, and we had orders not to expose ourselves as we were lying in brush-wood at the time. The enemy were still coming on, firing and driving our picquets back to where we lay. I was the left-hand man of the Regiment, and my rear rank man, whose name was Charles Carter, was the only man in the Regiment that lost his life this day. This poor fellow rose on his elbow to see the columns of the enemy advancing towards us, when a round shot struck him on the chest and killed him dead on the spot. He fell across my legs behind me.'[12]

Against this array the first Russian column approached and the guns crashed out unobstructed by their own men. The first rounds were wide; mighty must have been the relief of the advancing battalion of the Bourtirsk as the shot whistled harmlessly overhead. Quickly, however, the British gunners got the range and soon great furrows began to be carved through the marching Russians. Hume of the 55th, who were in reserve close to the Divisional camp, was watching:

> 'It was splendid to see our gunners at work. One, a red-haired man, was greatly excited, and used very strong language when he found one of the ammunition boxes could not be opened; he soon knocked the hasp off with a stone'.[13]

The first column broke and ran forward into Quarry Ravine for cover, but there they continued to be harassed by the rifles of Champion's men at the barrier above them. A second, strong wave advanced over precisely the same ground and met precisely the same storm of fire except that this time there were no wasted rounds; they reeled, checked and then broke, streaming back the way that they had come. A third wave was sent forward; exactly the same fate awaited them. Cavendish-Taylor, the travelling gentleman, relates: 'They lost their formation – the columns broke before they retired. I saw them.'[14] Meanwhile, the men of the first column were trying to get away by moving back up the north-western slope of East Jut towards Shell Hill but they came under the combined fire, once again, of the guns and the rifles of Champion's troops; about this time Federoff was gravely wounded and what spirit there was left in the attack was snuffed out.

The Russians had never managed to get all of their slender number of guns into action despite the rapidity with which they initially got them into fire positions. Now, galled by the accurate fire from Home Ridge, seeing their broken infantry swarming back around them and with their leader stricken, they began to limber up and make good their escape. The picquets followed up as quickly as they could, snapping at the Russians' heels and trying to bring down as many of the artillery horses as possible, but they were kept at bay in most areas by disciplined rearguard actions fought mainly by the Russian skirmishers with whom they had tussled at the beginning of the fight. Now Evans judged the time right to unleash his reserves to complete the work that the picquets had begun. Under Colonel Percy Herbert, four companies of the 41st went forward to support their picquets on the left, which were commanded by Eman, and the remaining four companies of the 30th and seven companies of the 95th swept forward up Shell Hill. There most of them were halted under the lee of the hill lest they should come under the fire of the guns in the Korabelnaya and the ships in the roadstead. Despite being in cover they continued to come under fire from the retreating Russians; one soldier was badly wounded and was being attended to by Dr Clarke, the 95th's surgeon, when Major Hume of the 95th said to him, 'Sir, you are very slow'. The doctor replied, 'I am doing my best'. Hardly had he said the words when a second round struck the wounded man and finished him. Rising resignedly from his charge Clarke said to Hume, 'I can do no more for him now'.[15]

Everywhere the Russians were now in retreat. One or two companies were allowed forward to harry them, the 95th's Light Company particularly relishing the task, so much so that it was only when the guns from the town and the ships opened fire, the very guns about which Evans had been so rightly cautious, that they could be restrained. As trophies they brought back on the ends of their bayonets loaves of the coarse black bread favoured by the Russians. Some of the last and most effective shots of the engagement, however, came from the very point from which the Russian advance had first been seen. Midshipman Hewett, the youthful naval officer commanding the Lancaster gun on Victoria Ridge, saw his opportunity and, slewing his gun around at right angles from the arc that it had originally been designed to cover whilst breaking down the breastwork that would have obstructed the barrel, he opened a punishing fire on the remaining Russian guns and infantry. For this and for other acts of gallantry that day, Hewitt was to be decorated with the Victoria Cross.

With Federoff being carried off the field on a litter, with the infantry and guns making for Sevastopol as fast as they could and the sailors in the Careenage Ravine also in flight, the fight came to an end. Cavendish Taylor noted the state of the dead '. . . most had been killed by our Minie rifles. Our heavy conical balls cause frightful wounds; wherever they touch limb, they smash the bone.'[16] For three hours the Russians had been subjected to such projectiles; they lost 270 killed and wounded and eighty prisoners; the British suffered twelve killed and seventy-seven wounded with no prisoners being taken.

Despite the relatively high number of casualties, the Russians had gained something of immense value: intelligence. They now knew exactly how they might approach the British position undetected, how quickly they could get guns into position and the ranges to the British gun-line, the layout of the defences, the reinforcements that would be brought up and the level of fire that they might expect in return. All this was of course, predicated upon the fact that the British would alter none of their defensive arrangements – which they did not. Quite why nothing was done will be examined later, but it is interesting to note just how obvious to those who took part in the action were the future intentions of the Russians. Lieutenant Morgan, an acting company commander in the heavily mauled 95th, had this to say: 'I do not think [the Russians] intended anything more than a reconnaissance in force; they only came to see the nakedness of the land and, as their subsequent moves showed, they attained their object'.[17] This may have been said with the benefit of hindsight, however, for J R Hume of the 55th observed: 'No one thought that the Russians, after their experience on the 26th October, would attack us again on the same ground'.[18]

If the Russians gained intelligence, however, the British gained an equally powerful asset: moral ascendancy. Whilst the Alma had been a victory, casualties had been heavy; Balaklava had been, at best, a bloody draw, and some were beginning to question the wisdom of their commanders who kept them sitting around a town that many believed could have been taken with ease had some daring been shown. Suddenly, here was an almost bloodless victory over a numerous foe whose bodies now lay thickly strewn around the ground as testimony to the fighting prowess of the British infantry. There can be no doubt that the outcome of the fight was decided by the British guns; it was they who had chewed the Russian columns once the infantry was clear and lobbed rounds amongst them as they retreated, but to the infantryman they must have appeared incidental. In the thick of the fight, eye-to-eye with the enemy, it must have seemed as though fire, steel and pluck answered for everything; as Morgan, an infantryman who had been in the thick of the fighting, said '. . . as always the Minie told with murderous effect';[19] in fact, the guns had caused the majority of the casualties. Nonetheless, the 2nd Division emerged crowing from their victory; they had learnt contempt for an enemy whom they had held with slender numbers on open ground and then tumbled to ruin. Whether it was actually the courage and brawn of these men or the pummelling of the guns that had broken the Russian resolve is unimportant for these same men, both infantry and gunners, were going to need every scrap of self-confidence that they possessed in the much more deadly test that awaited them.

Though some may not have realised that 26 October had exposed a deadly weakness to the Russians and that another attack would be forthcoming in the same or a similar place, common tactical prudence should have dictated that the 2nd Division's position was properly prepared for defence. Looked at a little more closely, however, there were many reasons why it was not. The solution should have lain in the hands of the 2nd Division itself, but it has already been established that this much battered body of men was heavily over-worked. Providing troops for the trenches and picquets for the flank, as well as carrying parties for their own administration, meant that not a man could be found for digging, sapping and the construction of parapets. Furthermore, there were no British troops that could be spared to bolster their numbers. The guards were fully committed, their sparse numbers fully extended guarding the next portion of the Sapoune, and Bosquet simply refused to spare any men from his corps involved as it was in watching over the Balaklava plain.

Lord Raglan was aware that resources were stretched to breaking point, so after the events of 25 October he resolved to find ways of releasing manpower from static duties. The advances of the Russians on Balaklava had made the port's security almost untenable, so he seems to have decided to abandon it with a view to doubling up with the French in the use of their two ports, Kamiesch and Kazatch. This plan, in terms of manpower, would have made great sense for it would have made available to the British the Highland Brigade as well as countless sailors and marines, whilst allowing Vinoy's Brigade and the Turkish auxiliary force, who were charged with the defence of the route leading from the Balaklava plain up to the Sapoune, to be redeployed by Bosquet. Having issued preliminary instructions for the dismantling of the harbour, however, Raglan's mind was changed. Admiral Lysons opposed the plan, but the final decision rested upon the view of the Commissary-General, Filder. Without the port of Balaklava, Mr Filder believed, no guarantee could be given that the British Army would be properly re-supplied. Upon his advice Lord Raglan changed his mind and sought to reinforce the vulnerable port instead.

With marines and sailors holding the inner defences of the port, the only infantry dedicated to its outer defence were the 93rd Highlanders whose musketry had had such a decisive effect on 25 October. To these were added the other two battalions of Highlanders to give the defences a whole brigade, whilst a screw-driven warship was brought permanently into the harbour and more sailors landed to stiffen the inner defences further. Such additions might seem to be considerable until it is remembered that the first defensive plan relied heavily on the manoeuvrability of the Cavalry Division stationed on the plain outside the port. To all intents and purposes, however, the cavalry actions of 25 October meant that the Light Cavalry Brigade had ceased to exist, whilst the Heavy Cavalry Brigade was also considerably less potent. The removal of any men from the prosecution of the siege meant that the already heavy burden of trench work had to be increased further for those who remained.

The reinforcement of the Inkermann position must have been low on the list of priorities for Raglan whose mind was firmly fixed on two other, as he saw them, much more significant issues. The 2nd Division had shown that it could look after itself with practically no reinforcements on 26 October; Raglan knew that he had to press on with the siege if he was to stand any chance first of weakening the defences and then of storming the place before winter started properly and the job of the Allies became immeasurably more difficult. Raglan had served in Russia against the French some thirty-five years before, and he fully understood the implications of operations in such a climate. Furthermore, extra Russian troops were marching into the Crimea daily; the arrival of the 10th and 11th Divisions was imminent. Accordingly, every resource, every effort had to be bent towards an assault as soon as possible.

The progress of the siege was threatened, however, by the weaknesses of the lines of supply. Without the necessary ammunition and *matériel* there could be no assault as all warlike stores had to come through the endangered Balaklava. To focus Lord Raglan's mind even more closely, the Russians manoeuvred daily in great numbers in full view on the heights above the Tchernaya, whilst the outposts and vedettes before Balaklava became bolder and bolder. On 2 November Liprandi, now considerably stronger, feinted against the eastern defences of the port. Picquets were thrown out and some guns were brought up which exchanged fire with those of Balaklava's inner defences, and it was even suggested that an amphibious out-flanking move was in the offing. Whilst nothing came of it, the British were further discomfited and distracted from the point upon which the Russians' real intentions lay.

In the light of what was to happen on 5 November, it is easy to be wise

'AN HOUR OF THE BEST TRAINING . . .!'

about Russian intentions on 26 October, and read into them clear motives for a detailed reconnaissance and, perhaps, the construction of a redoubt on Shell Hill. However, whilst the Russians certainly looked closely at the way in which the British dealt with the sortie, noting, in particular, the movements by the forces on the Sapoune to reinforce Evans's troops, and concluding that any future attack would have to occupy Bosquet's troops fully if the 2nd Division were not to be significantly reinforced, Federoff's attack was one of opportunity rather than something that had been carefully planned. Furthermore, it had been brushed off with remarkably few casualties taken and many inflicted whilst bestowing '. . . an hour of the best training that any good troops could well have'.[20] Raglan had his hands full enough with Balaklava and the siege to worry about a threat that had, apparently, been dealt with very satisfactorily. As he put it in a formal letter to the Secretary of War on 3 November concerning Balaklava, 'I will not conceal from your Grace that I should be more satisfied if I could have occupied the position in considerably greater strength'.[21]

Notes

1. Davis, letter quoted in *Sherwood Foresters' Annual*, 1934, p215
2. Kinglake, vol V, p116
3. *Illustrated London News*, December 1854, p571
4. Hume, p57
5. Kinglake, vol V, p10
6. Wylly, p24
7. *ibid*, p24
8. *ibid*, p25
9. *ibid*, p24
10. *ibid*, p24
11. Kinglake, vol V, p11
12. 'I'm Ninety-Five', November 1896, p38
13. Hume, p38
14. Cavendish-Taylor, p32
15. Wylly, p26
16. Cavendish-Taylor, p33
17. *Journal of the Society for Army Historical Research*, vol 44
18. Hume, p62
19. *Journal of the Society for Army Historical Research*, vol 44
20. Kinglake, vol V, p18
21. *ibid*, p27

Chapter V

'. . . the exemplary chastisement inflicted upon the presumption of the Allies!'

Interlude

The pace of events between Little Inkermann and 5 November was hectic developing, as it did, into a race between the Russians to reinforce themselves and launch an attack, and the Allies to assault the city before the Russians increased their strength. These affairs will be examined in detail, but before that the circumstances surrounding Sir George Cathcart and his 'Dormant Commission' should be looked at as they were to have a direct effect on the frame of mind in which he was to fight (and almost brought about a collapse of the British defence) on 5 November.

The action of 26 October had been another chance for glory that was missed by Sir George. It must have been particularly galling for him, the man whose experience and reputation as a great soldier had caused him to be singled out by the government to succeed Lord Raglan over the heads of his seniors, not only to see the renown of others growing, but also to miss another opportunity to rub out the misfortunes and mistakes that had caused him not to take any useful part in the battles of either the Alma or Balaklava.

On the very day that Evans and the 2nd Division added to their laurels, however, Raglan received a letter from the Duke of Newcastle, the Secretary of War, directing him to rescind Cathcart's commission. The reasons given by the government were seen by Kinglake as '. . . they felt that the step they had taken in secret was one which, if known, would have been cruelly mortifying to Sir George Brown'.[1] Furthermore, the energy that Brown had shown in his day-to-day conduct of operations and his great personal gallantry at the Alma had decided the government to reverse their decision. Certainly, the situation in which Cathcart had been put was uncomfortable; he might feel that he enjoyed a privileged position where his opinion should count for more than that of his peers, but he was unable to underscore his authority by letting the trust that the government had placed in him be known. A private letter he wrote to Raglan on 4 October demonstrates his frustration:

'My Dear Lord Raglan, finding that I am not admitted to your

63

confidence, and that Sir George Brown and M[ajor] G[eneral] Airey appear to act in your name, without your knowledge, in the conduct and management of military details at this most serious crisis of the campaign in the Crimea; also that I have scarcely had an opportunity, except at Varna, on my landing, of an interview on business, or received a single communication, verbally or otherwise, on the subject of the state of affairs from you; considering also that the circumstances of my present position, known only to yourself, the Duke of Cambridge, and myself in this country, and to H. M.'s Govt. at home, my duty to my sovereign demands that I should request an interview at the time most convenient to you, without delay, at your headquarters.'[2]

When the commission was withdrawn Raglan lost no time in telling Cathcart, who replied that same evening:

'My Dear Lord Raglan, you have known me long enough, and I hope well enough, to believe me when I say that your communication this moment received is the most gratifying to myself that I could possibly receive, and that the Duke of Newcastle does me no more than justice in saying that he well recollects the obvious reluctance with which I accepted the Dormant Commission. The fact is, I considered it a command, and though I did not fail to express my adverse opinion, I felt bound to submit to H. M. commands and obey them, be they what they may . . .'[3]

Raglan's subsequent correspondence with Newcastle shows what a relief it was to him that the anomalous business was at an end and that he could face Sir George Brown without feeling that 'False face must hide what the false heart doth know'[4] any longer.

Compared with the events leading up to Inkermann and with the battle itself, the doings of the Staff and the conduct of one priggish general officer seem like small beer. However, the frustration and lack of judgement that led this same officer to write such imperious notes to his commander was to lead to the death of many fine men, and jeopardised, for a while at least, the whole of the Allied cause.

British accounts of Inkermann suggest that the Russians mounted their attack in overwhelming numbers on a part of the defences that they knew to be weak and from where they could unhinge the whole of the Allied line from east to west. Furthermore, they insist that the Russians knew the ground well but should have learnt from Federoff's failure not to attempt to beard the British again. A degree of self-congratulation after the events of 26 October is understandable, but the truth is probably rather different.

First, it would be a mistake to read too much into Menshikov's ability to reason tactically. No Russian source attributes to him any desire to return to the offensive, nor any faith in his officers and men, whilst they all emphasise that he was under considerable pressure from the Tsar to act before the Allies were reinforced and the Russians lost their new-found numerical advantage. This same pressure had caused Menshikov to attack Balaklava before he had enough men, but with the arrival on 3 and 4 November of two divisions of Dannenberg's 4 Korps, his numbers rose to 107,000, a considerable advantage in both men and guns. Pauloff's 11 Infantry Division was held back with Menshikov's headquarters, which had recently moved to the heights above the village of Inkermann, whilst Soimonoff's 10 Infantry Division was marched into Sevastopol along the Sapper Road. But Tsar Nicholas knew that the French intended to move another three divisions into the Crimea and that it was faster for Allied troops to sail from western Europe to the Crimea than it was for his troops to march there from central or southern Russia. Furthermore, the French siege lines were very close to No 4 Bastion at the south-west end of Sevastopol's ring of defences, and a French deserter had brought news to the garrison that an assault was imminent. The Tsar appreciated that Menshikov would have to attack soon if he was both to capitalise upon his advantages and not allow the French to break into the city.

Second, whilst it is clear that the Russians had found a new respect for their British adversaries, the Alma and Balaklava having disabused the likes of Hodasevich's men of the idea that Britons could only fight at sea, they still believed that the smaller and more battered British Army, whose lines of supply were now in jeopardy, was a less formidable opponent than the French. Furthermore, Federoff's attack had shown that an approach could be made right up to the British position with total impunity.

Lastly, the ground over which the newly arrived Russian divisions were to attack was largely unknown to them. British accounts always mention the openness of their edge of the Sapoune, the lack of cover and the difficulties of commanding troops thereon. From the Russian point of view, however, the approaches to the British position must have been awesome. Seen from the banks of the Tchernaya, the Kitspur and Inkermann Spur loom hugely above. The Sandbag Battery, though by this stage unarmed, commanded a view right across the valley whilst the barrier blocked the only easy route out of Quarry Ravine onto the plateau. Also, the accuracy of British guns had been seen from the Sandbag Battery and tasted from the pre-prepared positions atop Home Ridge, and there was no comforting redoubt on Shell Hill (the building of which may have been Federoff's intention) to support the assault.

The ground would, in fact, have been much better known to the British who had not only marched to and fro upon it many times, but who also could appreciate over what ranges their rifles and guns would be most effective and where the best cover could be found. Similarly, of all the fifty or so Russian battalions that were to attack on 5 November, only six of them had been on that particular piece of land before; and they, what remained of four battalions of the Bourtirsk and two battalions of the Borodino, had no reason to remember it with much affection!

The physical condition of the British troops was deteriorating and is mentioned by every diarist:

> 'We still worked at the trenches night and day, never getting more than two nights in bed; as soon as we came off trench duty we had to go and dig up roots of trees and dry them the best way we could, and then go about three miles for water, then make a fire and boil the water to make a drop of coffee. Many men did not do this but eat their salt pork raw with a biscuit, and this was the cause of many a poor fellow dying with dysentery . . . I have been so exhausted coming off trench duty that I have walked some distance asleep and into a ditch.'[5]

If the condition of the British was poor the Russians had not had an easy time either. Those who had been in the city had been under constant fire, lived in insanitary conditions and had seen their wounded comrades neglected for want of proper medical supplies:

> 'The very soldiers were afraid to light their pipes, not to draw down upon themselves the fire of the enemy . . . [the food] reached the men quite cold, with fat swimming in large cakes on the top of the soup. Besides this cause, which was a very powerful one, fear I believe to have caused a great deal of sickness, for many of the men calculated that they would soon be killed, so it was useless to eat, and lived almost entirely upon their brandy, of which double portions were now distributed morning and evening.'[6]

Similarly, the two freshly arrived divisions had just completed a march of over three hundred miles without pause and with poor food. Added to which, it was only by the strenuous efforts of Dannenberg that the troops got any rest at all, for the initial plan was for the attack to be launched on 4 November, the very day that the latter body of troops arrived and the first anniversary of the defeat of Oltenitsa!

The total Allied numbers which stood ready to face the reinforced Russians in the days before Inkermann were not impressive. Even when augmented by sailors and marines, the Allies could only muster about 65,000 combatants of which the French had 31,000 infantry and the British a paltry 16,000. Attached to both armies, however, were a number of Turks, about 11,000, whose employment bears closer attention. The French made use of them in static defences above Balaklava, but after their abandonment of the redoubts on the morning of 25 October, the British seem to have lost any faith in them whatsoever. Whilst the quality of the troops that fled before Liprandi's men was certainly dubious, it has to be remembered that the Turks had beaten the Russians soundly on the Danube and that the British press had been quick to lionize both their soldiery and their commanders. Many regiments had detached officers to serve with the Turks, a duty that was viewed initially as exotic and for which there were many volunteers. Balaklava had ruined their reputation in the eyes of Raglan and his staff, however, to such an extent that when Omar Pasha, the Turkish commander, offered Raglan the garrison of Varna as well as further troops from Shumla in late October, he declined. When the pressures on the British troops are borne in mind, and the fact that there were no men to improve the defences of the 2nd Division above Inkermann, then this narrow-mindedness seems criminal. Whilst the British may have viewed the Turks' fighting prowess with contempt, they must have been good enough to wield picks and shovels.

Short of numbers and in an exposed position which had few entrench-ments to which almost no improvements had been made after 26 October, the 2nd Division was very vulnerable. With rather fewer than 3,000 men available for duty, the Division was relieved of one of its tasks, that of furnishing trench parties. This came as a blessed relief for Evans's troops who, at full stretch, had been providing two shifts of picquets, one on watch and another going to relieve it, as well as a full complement of men in the trenches. This had caused Evans to note '. . . I have but 600 men on this front position. The troops are completely worn out with fatigue . . . This is most serious.'[7] The numbers thus added certainly helped, but in the event of an attack reinforcements would have to come from somewhere.

The most convenient source of extra troops was the Brigade of Guards who had similarly just been relieved from trench duty and who lay to the south-west of the 2nd Division along the edge of the Sapoune about three-quarters of a mile to their rear. The Guards now had two tasks, the observation of the northern extremity of the Balaklava plain where it approached the Sapoune, and the reinforcement of the 2nd Division which had been fully rehearsed on 26 October. The Brigade commander, Brig.-Gen. Henry Bentinck, had seen action at the Alma and had been present at Balaklava and 26 October, but the divisional commander, the Duke of Cambridge, chose to remain with this part of his division in person.

Further British reinforcements would have to come from the troops whose principal task was the day-to-day prosecution of the siege. Sir Richard England's 3rd Division was the most distant, being about three miles from Evans's men. Cathcart's 4th Division was closer, about two and a half miles, whilst Buller's Brigade of Brown's Light Division was about a mile and a half away. The other brigade of the Light Division, Codrington's, had a more complex task. Encamped on Victoria Ridge, the Brigade had to furnish a quota of men for trench duty whilst maintaining picquets to watch the open approaches adjacent to the Careenage Ravine. In the event of an attack on the 2nd Division, however, Codrington was meant simply to hold his position on Victoria Ridge and guard the rear of Evans's men. This had been fully put into practice on 26 October, but on 5 November he was to find himself faced with an infinitely more dangerous situation.

The stronger French had been asked to provide a permanent body of extra troops for the Inkermann position but had, so far, not done so. Any such troops would have come from Bosquet's 'Army of Observation' which had a front of over two and a half miles to cover, and which extended right along the edge of the Sapoune from the south-western point of the Guards' picquet. Their task was, from well prepared positions, to oversee the Balaklava plain and prevent any Russian incursion from it up onto the plateau above and into the rear of the Allies. To do this Bosquet had three brigades commanded by Generals Espinasse, d'Autemarre and Bourbaki; the troops nearest to the 2nd Division were Bourbaki's north-easterly battalions which were about two miles away. As the name suggests, however, Bosquet's Army was intended to observe, so any Russian movement below them on the plain was bound to hold their attention. Thus, their first duty was to secure the heights rather than move to the assistance of others; of necessity, therefore, Bosquet was particularly susceptible to feints on the plain below. Whilst he had marched to assist Evans on 26 October, he had only moved once he was completely certain that there was no threat developing to his front; but that movement had been noted by the Russians who now knew that they had only to manoeuvre in full view in order to tie him down.

The steady progress of the French towards No 4 Bastion had caused Canrobert and Raglan to meet on 4 November with a view to finalising plans for an assault on the 7th. Having discussed the general outline of how the attack would be conducted they agreed to meet the next day to tie up the final details with their principal officers. Interestingly, Raglan had intended to have Burgoyne, his chief sapper, and the two divisional commanders whose troops were most intact with him, England commanding the 3rd Division, and the untried Cathcart. The meeting would, doubtless, have been eventful but it was never to happen for the Russians had been doing some planning of their own, and 5 November was to see those plans come to fruition.

The Russian plan of attack was simple in its concept and, essentially, followed the same outline as Federoff's sortie of 26 October but on a massive scale. The principal difference in the two plans, however, was that, based on what the Russians had seen on 26 October, they did not intend to allow the 2nd Division to be reinforced. As a less than promising start to the venture, however, in the same way as cohesive units had been re-grouped into an almost ad hoc formation at the Alma, Menshikov once again changed the organisation of his forces on the eve of battle. First, General P D Gortchakoff was to take Liprandi's 12 Infantry Division under command as well as fifty-two cavalry squadrons and ten Cossack *sotni*, in total a force of 22,000 men supported by eighty-eight guns. They were to demonstrate on the Balaklava plain in sight of Bosquet, thus preventing the French from going to the assistance of the British. Gortchakoff was to '. . . support the general attack, distracting the enemy's forces and drawing them on itself, trying to secure the approach to the Sapoune. Also, the dragoons must be ready to scale the heights at the first opportunity.'[8]

Such orders seem unequivocal, directing Gortchakoff actually to attack rather than merely feint, seizing a path up onto the Sapoune and cutting deep into the British flank and rear as the rest of the assault was pressed home from the north-east. This was not to happen, however, for Gortchakoff was to do nothing more than manoeuvre and Kinglake believes that this was deliberate,

'. . . considering what might be possibly discovered and reported by an efficient spy or deserter, it seems not improbable that the difference between the orders ostensibly given to Gortchakoff and the task which was really assigned to him may have been intentional.'[9]

From Sevastopol Lieutenant-General Moller was '. . . to switch to the attack, covering with his batteries the right flank of those troops ordered to attack and, should there be confusion in the enemy's batteries, to storm those batteries'.[10] Further to this, a strong sortie was to be mounted from Bastion No 6 against the extreme left flank of the French near the sea.

So, with the besieging troops pinned in place and the attention of the French on the Sapoune held, details for the attack on the 2nd Division were outlined. First, a strong column would issue from Sevastopol out of the Korabelnaya along the same route that Federoff had followed. Commanded by Lieutenant-General Soimonoff, the commander of 10 Infantry Division, the column would consist of three of his own regiments under Major-General Vil'boi and another brigade under the command of Major-General Zhabokritsky made up of three regiments of 16 Infantry Division and one of 17 Infantry Division, about 19,000 men and thirty-eight guns. Soimonoff received only these orders: 'The field army-korps at Sevastopol . . . after having previously moved out from the line of fortifications, will march . . . from the Careenage Ravine at six o'clock in the morning.'

Meanwhile, Lieutenant-General Pauloff with his own 11 Infantry Division and a brigade of 17 Infantry Division, about 16,000 men and ninety-six guns, would leave the area above Inkermann village and

> '. . . at six o'clock in the morning, restore Inkermann bridge, and push on vigorously to meet and join the corps of Lieutenant-General Soimonoff. With this detachment will be General de Dannenberg, commander of the 4th Infantry Corps, who is to take the paramount command of the two corps as soon as they shall have effected this juncture.'[11]

So, only after the assaulting troops had been launched and completed their approach march to the place from which they were to attack, would Menshikov hand over the command of Soimonoff and Pauloff to Dannenberg. A change of command in the face of the enemy can never be a sound principal of war and it will be remembered that Dannenberg had already shown a distinct reluctance to attack on the first anniversary of his mauling at Oltenitsa. That earlier battle on the Danube had shown Dannenberg's lack of tactical guile and a fatal tendency to dither when under pressure; Inkermann was to be a much greater challenge for him. Furthermore, his initial orders served only to confuse the meagre and ill-designed ones that Menshikov had already given.

Soimonoff received his orders, then wrote his own and despatched copies to both Menshikov and Dannenberg. In them he was quite clear that he was to follow the appointed route out of Sevastopol, across the Careenage Ravine and then south-west along the Sapper Road before ascending Shell Hill. Nowhere did he mention the possibility of turning off before crossing the Careenage Ravine and moving along the Victoria Ridge into the centre of the British rear, although he did specify that a column of troops led by riflemen should advance up the bed of the Careenage Ravine in order to protect his right flank in precisely the same way that Federoff had used a column of sailors on 26 October. Dannenberg, however, ignoring the fact that he was not in command of the whole venture until both columns were assembled on Shell Hill, began to countermand Menshikov's orders late on the evening of 4 November. First he wrote to Menshikov telling him that he believed that the separation of Soimonoff's and Pauloff's forces caused by the Careenage Ravine was undesirable and that '. . . it seems to me indispensible that we should attack on both sides of the ravine'.[12] The letter required no reply but should have sounded an alarm bell in Menshikov's headquarters for it was followed by further orders that completely overturned those written by the Commander-in-Chief and made a nonsense of the subsidiary orders already written and sent out by both Pauloff and Soimonoff.

Despite having recommended that Soimonoff should advance along the Victoria Ridge, and having taken his leave saying that he would see Soimonoff on the crest of that same ridge the next day, Dannenberg's orders stated:

'Lieutenant-General Soimonoff will depart from the Grafsky Dock at 0200 hours, under the guidance of Staff-Captain Iakovlev, to the place from where it will be possible to cover the crossing of the Tchernaya by Pauloff's troops . . . As soon as 10 Infantry Division have covered the crossing places, then Lieutenant-General Pauloff's troops will cross the Tchernaya by a bridge put in place by the navy, and should continue by the road recently constructed along the bay under the guidance of Staff-Captain Cherniaev'.[13]

Details for the order of march of Soimonoff's regiments then followed which included the disposition for the covering of Pauloff's crossing. Pauloff was ordered to cross the Tchernaya and then deploy into three columns the right one of which was to move along the Sapper Road '. . . in the interval left free between 10 and 16 Infantry Divisions of Soimonoff's forces'.[14] In other words, Dannenberg was asking troops who did not know the ground carefully to synchronise their movements with other units with whom they were totally unfamiliar, whilst close to the enemy and at night! At best the plan was naive to the point of foolishness; at worst it was the work of a man who was totally unsuited to command troops in action.

Luckily, the plans either did not reach Pauloff or Soimonoff in time or they were ignored. But not content with written plans, as Soimonoff's troops were moving along the Sapper Road in the early hours of 5 November under the guidance of Staff-Captain Iakovlev and two other officers of Menshilov's staff, a verbal message arrived from Dannenberg. Soimonoff was to change direction; he was not to move across the Careenage Ravine; he was to turn off before he got there and make his way along the south-west side of the gully and up onto Victoria ridge. Yet again, Dannenberg had had a change of heart and was trying to alter things once the advance had already started. The order was received only when the steep climb up the northern side of Shell Hill was underway; it, too, was ignored.

So, if all went according to plan, and the vagaries of Dannenberg's over-heated mind were ignored, the British were about to be put under severe pressure. Denuded of all reinforcements by virtue of diversionary tactics elsewhere, two powerful columns, well supported by numerous guns, would come together pincer-like at the point where the defences were weakest. Rolling down from Shell Hill, Dannenberg would push all before him and as he did so, Gortchakoff would lance into the French flank and join up with him on the flat ground at the top of the plateau. If fortune continued in their favour, the Russians might unhinge the whole of the Allied operation making it impossible for the siege to continue or, better still, forcing the Allies to take to their ships. In Menshikov's final words: 'Future times, I am confident, will preserve the remembrance of the exemplary chastisement inflicted upon the presumption of the Allies.'[15]

With plans made and orders given, there only remained the need to fire up the Russian soldiery for the fight. For this very purpose the Tsar's two sons, the Grand Dukes Nicholas and Michael, had been sent to the front to add the blessing of their father to his troops' endeavours. They chose to ride in a distinctive yellow carriage which had been spotted by the British picquets reviewing the troops paraded on the Inkermann heights opposite the 2nd Division's position and this, with other tell-tale signs, began to arouse the suspicions of the British.

Religion was also used to fan the flames of battle. At the beginning of the siege some French troops had pillaged the church of Saint Vladimir near Quarantine Bay, and had been seen by Russian sentries within Sevastopol removing their spoils. This was now widely quoted by the Russian priests as evidence of the heretical nature of their enemies, and was to prove highly contentious when the mistreatment of British wounded was excused by the Russians on the grounds that their troops fought to avenge this outrage. What is more, religious zeal seems to have overcome tactical considerations, for in the early hours of Sunday 5 November the church bells of Sevastopol rang out as the troops were shriven. Clearly audible to the British picquets, this was another indication that all was not well.

Furthermore, it was widely supposed by the British that the Russians were encouraged to fight by the liberal application of liquor. Certainly, many accounts speak of the Russians behaving as if drunk and coming on with wild shouts and stupefied expressions. Hodasevich complains, however, that he and his men of the Taroutine Regiment were given the unusually small draught of only one tot of spirits before the battle when they could have done with more!

In the British lines the eve of Inkermann was marked by a steady fall of drizzle that made the ground more slippery than usual, and by early afternoon was showing signs of turning into mist. That day half of the 2nd Division's picquets were found by the 95th Regiment, the rest coming from Adams's Brigade and a damp time they were having of it. Lieutenant Carmichael was on duty:

'Before the battle it was not customary . . . to send patrols or scouts any distance in front of the chain of sentries as doubtless ought to have been done. So that, without lacking in vigilance, our outposts, posted as they were, could not very well be cognisant of any concentrations of force made in the valley below, so long as it took place under cover of darkness and with ordinary precautions.'[16]

The Brigade Commander, the popular and pugnacious Pennefather, came to visit the picquets and saw the yellow carriage on the heights opposite and the gathering of troops. What was more, it was noted that

'. . . there had been a review in the course of the day and it was remarked to him [Pennefather] that the enemy were in skirmishing order, advanced with fixed bayonets, which was entirely opposite to the practice of the British Army'.[17]

So concerned was Pennefather that he detailed Major Grant of the 49th to send Carmichael forward to the Inkermann Spur half an hour before dark in order to '. . . report in person to the General in camp any fresh appearance of movements or alteration of position on the part of the enemy'. The Spur was well known to Carmichael as a spot upon which an appearance was usually greeted by the Russians with a round shot or two from across the valley, and this time he was glad when Major Grant insisted that he come with him as

'. . . he was an officer much senior to me, and who had seen field service before the Crimea, and had there been any indications of the enemy's plans, he would probably have observed them whereas I might, from inexperience, have failed to discover them.'[18]

They were much relieved not to be shot at and noted that a body of cavalry had moved down to the area of the bridge, and that a large flock of sheep had been driven onto the pasture near the ruins of Inkermann '. . . presumably to be at hand for the troops that should carry our positions the following day.'[19]

The rest of the night passed uncomfortably but uneventfully for the picquets. The mist that followed the drizzle, however, was beginning to turn into a thick fog, and the sentries behind the barrier were surprised when the picquets from the top of Shell Hill blundered into their position halfway through the night. The field officer in charge of these troops, Major Goodwyn of the 41st, had decided that the fog was too thick for them to be able to achieve anything and they should withdraw to the base of the hill because there was '. . . an instruction in the Field Exercise Book . . . the idea being that the enemy would, in foggy weather, be better observed on the skyline from the base, than from the top of the hill'.[20] In the dark the picquets had lost their way and headed downhill until they met the road before following it towards the Barrier. Such action was judged by Captain Vialls, who was serving under Goodwyn to be '. . . wholly inappropriate'[21] in the dark and the knowledge that there were now no other troops to their front did little to make the men at the barrier feel any more secure.

Other incidents occurred to unsettle the picquets. A shot was fired which caused the whole line to stand-to-arms, but it was found to be Pte Simmonds of No 3 Company of the 95th who had discharged his rifle accidentally, wounding himself in the hand. As the drizzle continued fitfully and the fog began to swirl thicker and thicker, unusual noises were heard

'. . . the clang of the church bells in the town, and the rumble of wheels in the valley, but the latter noise raised no suspicion in my mind, as it was a nightly occurrence and had been reported previously, and it was well known to all, that the enemy used the road during the night'[22]

What Carmichael of the 95th did not find suspicious, however, Captain Sargent of the same regiment found very unsettling. In fact, the fog seemed to him to present such an ideal opportunity for an attack that he had ordered his men to draw the wetted charges from their weapons; in so doing, it was one of his soldiers who had fired his rifle accidentally. Adding to Sargent's suspicions was the rumbling of wheels in the distance which Carmichael had noted as nothing unusual. Sargent reported the noise to the field officer on duty, Major Grant, but neither was to know that what they were actually hearing were not supply wagons but the guns and limbers of Pauloff's artillery which had started to move at 2am.

An hour before dawn the new picquets arrived. The normal practice was for both bodies to remain in place until daylight had broken before the old picquets marched back to camp, but the night had been so unpleasant and the soldiers so thoroughly soaked that the old picquets were allowed to make their own way back to camp piecemeal. On arrival at the camp Carmichael found

'. . . that the 2nd Division, which was always under arms for an hour before daylight, had been dismissed, and the wood, and water parties had been sent out – the day had however barely broke, and the mist and fog hung thick over the camp.'[23]

Under the pressure of great shortages of manpower, an increasingly heavy burden of work and foul weather, sound tactical practices were beginning to be ignored and corners were starting to be cut.

So, as dawn tried to break across the sodden, brush-clad glens and the fog lay heavy in the gullies and hollows undisturbed by any wind, the new picquets took post on what they expected to be just another Sunday.

The picquets of Pennefather's Brigade were all from the 55th Regiment and occupied the barrier, the Sandbag Battery and the other posts on the Division's right; they were under the command of Lieutenant-Colonel Carpenter of the 41st. On the left the guard was found by companies from the 41st, 47th and 49th. Back in camp, the old picquets started to prepare food and hot drinks before they set about the tedious business of drawing the charges from their rifles which, in all probability, were now soaked and ruined by the night's rain. There was no hurry to make their weapons serviceable for the night had passed quietly; food, warmth and dry clothes were needed first.

Notes

1. Kinglake, vol V, p21
2. *ibid*, p21
3. *ibid*, p23
4. *ibid*, p24
5. Higginson, p34
6. Hodasevich, p42
7. Kinglake, vol V, p28
8. Seaton, p162
9. Kinglake, vol V, p59
10. *ibid*, p491
11. *ibid*, p492
12. *ibid*, p492
13. *ibid*, p493
14. *ibid*, p493
15. Seaton, p163
16. Wylly, p30
17. Carmichael Mss, p9, Author
18. *ibid*, p10
19. *ibid*, p10
20. *ibid*, p11
21. 'I'm Ninety-Five', November 1896, p42
22. Carmichael Mss, p11, Author
23. *ibid*, p12

Chapter VI
'. . . forward with the bayonet!'
The Opening Shots

'At six o'clock General Soimonoff's detachment had mounted on the plateau and began to form in order of battle. In the first line were two regiments, the Tomsk on the right flank and the Kolivansk on the left; the Katherinberg was in reserve. Twenty-two guns of position were placed in line of battle and two companies of the 6th Rifle Battalion were thrown out as skirmishers . . . Having done so, General Soimonoff began to advance parallel with the Careenage Ravine. A thick fog and the grey colour of our soldiers' greatcoats concealed their line from the enemy's outposts, and permitted them to advance, without being remarked, almost up to them. A picquet of the Light Division of General Brown was almost immediately surrounded and taken. Then commenced a musketry fire, which was the signal of a general alert in the enemy's camp'[1]

So Todleban recounts the Russians' opening moves as Soimonoff reached Shell Hill, saw no sign of Pauloff, and without waiting for him, launched into the attack quite against the plans of either Menshikov or Dannenberg.

The first rounds to hit the Russians were fired by the enterprising body of sharpshooters under Goodlake of the Coldstream Guards who had rendered such useful service on 26 October. Posted well down Careenage Ravine, past West Jut and up onto the shoulder of the next spur, Goodlake became aware that columns of infantry were moving up the plateau towards Shell Hill. He at once despatched a soldier to run into camp to warn the British forces but this man chose to move onto the high ground rather than sticking to the bed of the ravine and was captured by a Russian column on its way towards Shell Hill. Goodlake opened fire, however, and these alerted General Codrington to the presence of the enemy and he immediately got his men ready to move towards the camp of the 2nd Division.

The picquet that was overcome came from the 23rd Fusiliers, but the 'musketry fire' was delivered by the most advanced picquet of the 2nd Division, men of the Grenadier Company of the 41st commanded by Captain Hugh Rowlands and Lieutenant William Allen. Rowlands takes up the story:

'On the morning of the 5th, I and the company were for outlying picquet. Colonel Haly of the 47th was Field Officer of the day and he gave me my choice. I selected Cossack Hill (alias Funk Point) . . . on arriving at Cossack Hill, I halted the company about half way up and went out to plant sentries 150 yards over the hill. Having done so, I returned to the company which had just piled arms and ordered the men to take off packs, when the sentries commenced firing in a most determined way.

'I ran up to enquire the cause when one shouted out that there were columns of Russians close to them. I stood to my arms and advanced in extended order, thinking it was a sortie something like that of the 26th. On getting to the top of the hill I found myself close upon, very truly, thousands of Russians. I immediately gave an order to retire, which was done for about 200 yards, when I halted on the next high bit of ground and lay down quietly waiting for them. Fitzroy (Lieutenant G) who was in support of me then came up with the Light Company. His men I likewise extended to support my own.

'When we retired the Russians came on with the most fiendish yells you can imagine. We commenced firing. To my dismay, I found that half the firelocks missed fire, which dispirited the men. At this period the Russian columns opened with their field pieces, pouring in grape and shell. We then got some reinforcements from the 55th and the 30th but were gradually obliged to retire. I begged and entreated Colonel Haly to allow me to charge, which he did. After a little hand-to-hand work we turned them and drove them back about 500 yards, when we were met by a fresh column and compelled to retire.'[2]

During the action Haly was dragged from his horse and surrounded by Russians. Rowlands dashed in amongst them, hacking left and right with his sword where he was joined by Private McDermond of the 47th. Between them they rescued Haly: both were duly decorated with the Victoria Cross for their valour.

The picquets held the crest ably for about half an hour before the Russians were able to get their guns into position and open fire through the patchy fog onto Home Ridge. Here some time had been bought by the picquets for the food and fuel parties to come running in, the 2nd Division to fall in and, most importantly, the guns to get into position. Two guns were kept close at hand 'which were always horsed, and in readiness on the road day and night';[3] they were soon in action followed by the remaining ten guns, Captain Pennecuick's battery on the right of the Post Road and Captain John Turner's to the left. Colonel Percy Herbert, the Divisional Assistant Adjutant General, urged the guns not to remain silent but to fire blindly, if necessary, at the Russian guns shrouded by the fog. Whilst this fire was mostly instinctive, it seems to have been more accurate than might have been expected. A non-commissioned officer of the Taroutine witnessed its effect: '. . . shells were knocking out our guns, for the enemy, apparently firing from a single epaulement, although economical with his fire, used it with great effect'.[4] It would seem that the Russians were replying less accurately for most of their rounds were flying well over the heads of the troops on Shell Hill and into the divisional camp beyond. Whether this was intended to break up any reserves forming there, or whether the Russians were simply firing high is not clear. The mounted adjutant of the 49th, Lieutenant Arthur Armstrong, was unlucky enough to be killed whilst atop Home Ridge by a round that left the troops around him quite unharmed.

The regiments in camp were soon under arms and striking their tents as the rounds began to plough through their lines. Carmichael took his company with the rest of the 95th to a position just short of the crest of Home Ridge; the British gunners

'. . . fired, I should judge, at the flashes of the enemy's guns on Shell Hill, and drew soon a heavy fire on themselves in return – some of these men fell and we also suffered, altho' we had been ordered to lie down to obtain what shelter we could from the ridge. One round shot, I remember, tore into my company severing the left arm and both legs of a man in the front rank and killed the rear rank man without any perceptible wound . . . The guns . . . came into action short handed and were firing as fast as they could load, and each successive discharge and recoil brought them closer to our line . . . we assisted the gunners to run the guns into their first position and some men also aided in carrying ammunition.'[5]

De Lacy Evans had fallen heavily from his horse and was on board a ship in Balaklava harbour; thus, the command of the 2nd Division now fell upon the shoulders of Pennefather his senior brigadier. Had Evans been present, he would probably have chosen to fight this battle in the same way that he had fought that of 26 October, that is, picquets well forward to buy time, then Home and Fore Ridge held by the mass of the Division ready to meet the Russians with artillery support. Pennefather chose the opposite. 'Old Blood and 'Ounds' as he was known to the men in recognition of the profanities with which he littered his speech, was going to fight his enemy well out to the front, contesting every scrap of ground in recognition of the fact that once Home Ridge was crossed there were no pre-prepared positions on which to stand again, and once the enemy succeeded in advancing his guns from Shell Hill to Home Ridge then all would be lost. Further to which, the fog could be used to his advantage. Such defensive positions as there were in front of Home Ridge confronted the Russians as they emerged from one taxing ascent or another. A mass

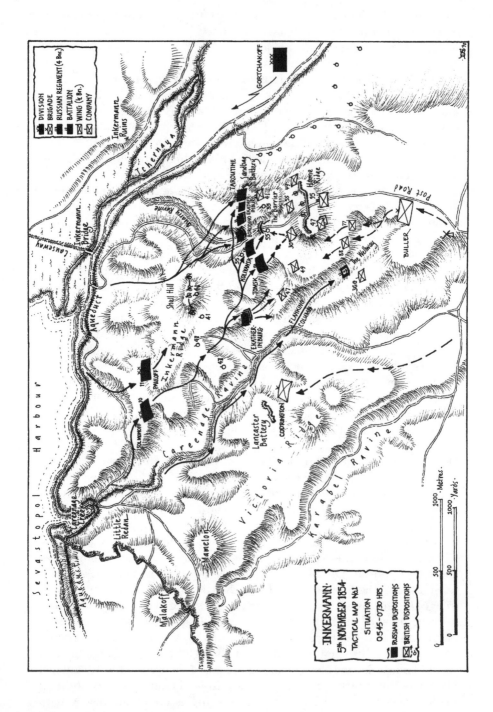

of troops here would catch the enemy at his most vulnerable point whilst the fog would conceal the almost total lack of reserves.

It was a very risky plan, however, for should the forward line be pierced then there was very little to stop the Russians from having a free run all the way up to Home Ridge and beyond. Moreover, it depended upon the junior officers, non-commissioned officers and each and every soldier fighting his hardest and taking every opportunity to use his initiative; Pennefather was not to be disappointed.

So Pennefather launched his troops to a pattern that would dictate the rest of the course of the battle. To him ground was everything so he elected to 'feed the picquets' and fight the enemy well forward whilst he waited for reinforcements to come up. Accordingly, one wing of the 30th, about 300 strong under Lieutenant-Colonel Mauleverer, were sent forward to bolster the barrier whilst the other wing, under Major Patullo, was sent to assist Haly's picquets who were being pushed back down Shell Hill. Those of the 41st not on picquet were sent towards the Kitspur under Brigadier-General Adams with one wing of the 49th under Captain Bellairs following them with orders to halt on the right side of Home Ridge. The other wing of the 49th under Major Dalton and a wing of the 47th commanded by Major Fordyce were sent to the left side of the field to hold the head of the Mikriakoff Glen. The 95th, as we have seen, waited in reserve for a while behind Home Ridge before being pushed forward as two wings. The left, under Major Hume, went towards the barrier whilst the other under Major Champion was to be sent off towards the Sandbag Battery. So, within an hour or so of the first rounds having been fired, say about 6.45 am, the only troops left in the camp of the 2nd Division were a few companies of the 47th and a few of the 55th, no more than about 500 men: Pennefather had used most of his reserve almost immediately.

So far the attack was being fended off perfectly adequately by Pennefather with whose control Raglan did not choose to interfere. Alerted by the firing, Raglan had been quickly into the saddle and riding for the scene of the action, but on arrival he saw no reason to take control out of the hands of an experienced and able brigadier who knew the ground well. On surveying the scene, however, he made one decision that was to be crucial: he ordered two 18 pound guns to be brought up from the Siege Train for he immediately appreciated the numbers and calibre of the guns that the Russians had brought up to Shell Hill. Knowing that artillery would be the key to this fight, he sent for guns that would outreach those of the Russians and which, in tandem, could deliver a volume of fire that would be telling.

The order was intended to go to Colonel Gambier, the officer commanding the Siege Train but, as so often happens in battle, it went to Fitzmayer who was commanding the two batteries defending Home Ridge. Fitzmayer took the order to mean that he should leave the heat of the battle, go to the Siege Train, replace the competent Gambier and arrange for the two guns to be dragged up. His reply to the order was a simple, and entirely correct 'impossible', which was transmitted to Raglan by the unhappy galloper who had been entrusted with the task. With great coolness Raglan unscrambled the mistake and despatched the order to the correct destination, but vital minutes had been lost. Once it was received there was no delay. Two such guns had already been dragged up to a similar position when they were needed for the cross-valley shoot for which the Sandbag Battery had been built, so the route and ground were well known, but the heavy guns had to be moved about two and a half miles, and would not be in a position to influence the battle for some little while.

Despite the lively skirmishing going on to his front, it seems that Soimonoff might have intended to hold the main bulk of his force on Shell Hill and wait for Pauloff, as the original plan dictated, had it not been for an incident on his right front. A column had been pushed forward to reconnoitre and had got well down the hill and towards the upper reaches of the Mikriakoff Glen when it encountered the wing of the 49th that had just arrived there. Its commander, Major Dalton, had already been struck down and it was now being commanded by Major Thornton Grant. At a distance of only a few yards, the Russians broke through the mist and confronted the 49th. 'Give them a volley and charge!'[6] was Grant's order and the 49th did so in grand style. To the foot of Shell Hill they chased them, then up it and even into the gun-line on top! This was too much for Soimonoff who, already in action and being drawn forward when he should have been waiting patiently and quietly for Pauloff on the north side of the hill, launched a general attack.

So far, everything that the British had experienced had been containable. Certainly, the slender number of reserves had been very quickly deployed into the all-engulfing fog, but the Russians were being held. Now Soimonoff intended to use the majority of his troops against what he believed to be meagre forces upon which his artillery in particular was inflicting considerable casualties. The skirmishers from the 6th Rifles led the advance with over 9,000 troops in twelve battalion columns following hard behind. Forming up on the saddle to the west of Shell Hill, Soimonoff intended to advance on a narrow front of two battalions with the third regiment, of four battalions, following as a reserve. The first line was to consist of one battalion each of the Tomsk and the Kolivansk Regiments with the other three battalions of each regiment following in echelon to their rear. In fact, as the troops moved off, the reserve regiment, the Katherinberg, moved rather faster than it should have done and, with the exception of one of its battalions, came level with the leading elements of the other two regiments so that Soimonoff's force quickly sprawled across

1. Lt-Gen Soimonoff commanded the X Division and the combined XVI/XVII Division at Inkermann. Without waiting for Pauloff's forces, he attacked the British picquets and pushed hard against the British left and centre. As the initial Russian attacks failed, so he fell.

2. Lt-Gen Pauloff commanded his own XI Division and elements of XVII Division at Inkermann. Having marched from the interior of the Crimea, his troops were delayed crossing the Tchernaya but were to be amongst the most severely mauled.

3. Gen Dannenberg led 4 Corps into the Crimea from Bessarabia to reinforce Sevastopol's garrison. Ordered to take command of the attack on the Allies on 4 November, he objected as it was the first anniversary of 4 Corp's defeat at Oltenitsa at the hands of the Turks. This bought him only one day's grace – he attacked on 5 November!

4. Brigadier-General Pennefather, the commander of 1st Bde, 2nd Division, was actually in command of the whole of 2nd Division on 5 November. 'Old blood and 'ounds' as the men called him, he, de facto, commanded the whole of the British defence throughout the day.

5. Lt J A Connolly, 49th (Hertfordshire) Regt was to receive the Victoria Cross for his gallantry at 'Little Inkermann' on 26 October. His picquet was engaged very early and he fought the Russians first with his sword and then with his telescope wielded like a club!

6. The Russian infantry, throughout the day, fought in dense columns. Not only were these terribly vulnerable to artillery and rifle fire, they soon lost their coherence amongst the scrub, fog and smoke.

7. Six Russian battalions under Federoff were driven off with comparative ease on 26 October at 'Little Inkermann'. Whilst the Russians suffered heavily, they had, however, bought vital intelligence about the British positions and carried out a thorough, armed reconnaissance.

8. East Jut and the Quarry Ravine today seen from the area of the Barrier. Note the line of the Post Road at the base of East Jut.

9. St Clement's Ravine today seen from the Russians' perspective. The Sandbag Battery lies within the scrub slightly to the right of the peak of the Kitspur.

10. The fight for the Sandbag Battery. The Footguards re-capture the Battery once again, driving the Russian infantry from the tactically worthless but highly prized landmark.

11. Sgt Walker of the 55th (Westmorland) Regt counter-attacks the Iakoutsk Regt as the centre of the British position on Home Ridge is threatened.

12. Maj-Gen Sir George Cathcart falls mortally wounded as he tries to lead his men out of the perilous position into which he had brought them. His ill-judged charge very nearly unhinged the whole of the tenuous British defence of the Inkermann position.

13. An 18-pounder gun, similar to those which were to have such a profound effect on the outcome of the battle. Whilst only two were deployed by the British, their range and accuracy caused disproportionately high casualties amongst the Russian guns and gunners.

14. The British soldier as he fought at Inkermann. Wearing only the clothes that he had carried since he arrived in the Crimea in September, the weather, constant danger and diminishing numbers meant that every man was deeply fatigued even before the fighting started.

15. Clearing the dead from the field of Inkermann. French and British troops clear the battlefield despite occasional artillery fire from Sevastopol's outer defences.

16. The consequences of the battle as Punch saw them!

PUNCH, OR THE LONDON CHARIVARI.

THE CZAR TO HIS CUBS.

Czar. "WELCOME, MY CHILDREN; INKERMANN IS A GLORIOUS VICTORY FOR YOU."
Cubs. "AH SIRE, IF THAT IS VICTORY, WE SHOULD LIKE TO HAVE A DEFEAT THE NEXT TIME!"

a broad front extending from the north-eastern edge of the Mikriakoff Glen right across the lower slopes of Shell Hill. The fourth battalion of the Katherinberg, meanwhile, split away to the left of the whole column and began to head for the Quarry Ravine. This was the first taste of open warfare that these regiments had had, their experience so far having been limited to the confines of a besieged Sevastopol; thus, their keenness to close with their enemies is, perhaps, more easily understood.

As Soimonoff's men advanced they began to receive fire from Home Ridge and they gradually bent away to their right, downhill, seeking the cover of the brushwood around the Mikriakoff Glen. Leading the host in person was Soimonoff, who saw his neatly arranged columns losing order in the fog and bush, but continued to make ground whilst pushing Grant's troops in front of him. The 49th fell back steadily firing, moving and dodging amongst the brushwood. Most of the drenched rifles had now been cleared by the expedient of unscrewing the nipples of the damp weapons' locks with the tool that each sergeant carried in his pouch, then sprinkling powder from a cartridge onto the wet charge, replacing the nipple and putting on a fresh percussion cap and then attempting to fire. Never a simple procedure, under the pressure of battle it must have been much more difficult, but it was done and a stinging fire allowed more time to be bought. Moreover, the 49th had good reason to control the retirement for they had taken several prisoners during their first dash and they were not letting such trophies go free. Sergeant Mackie, a true Scot, stuck to his prisoners as watchful as '. . . any grim constable in the old town of Edinburgh',[7] jealously guarding his prizes.

These twelve battalions were not the only forces that were falling upon the British, however. Parallel to Soimonoff's main body coming down off the slopes above, the column of riflemen and sailors was making good, unopposed progress up the Careenage Ravine. Kinglake, the authoritative British source on the battle, interprets the movement of what he calls the 'Under-road Column' as an attempt to turn the British left by virtue of the column's issuing from the glen into the flank and rear of the Home Ridge positions. In fact, this column had only been intended to act as flank protection for Soimonoff's main force probably as a result of what the Russians had discovered on 26 October – that there was always a picquet guarding the head of the Careenage Ravine where it divided into the Mikriakoff Glen and the Wellway. Soimonoff would have had no wish for such a force to be able to interfere with his flank, and as he and his men angled off towards the upper part of the Mikriakoff Glen, the 'Under-road Column' was, in fact, already slightly in front of his leading troops.

With the British left occupied by Soimonoff, the first battalions of Pauloff's force were beginning to appear on the battlefield; they were to bring another eight battalions, almost 6,000 men, to bear against the right and centre. Two of the Chasseur regiments, the Borodino and the

Taroutine, had moved up the Volovia Gorge instead of St George's Ravine farther west which was the designated approach route of the rest of Pauloff's force, and found themselves in the thick of the battle very much before the head of the remainder of their force had even drawn near. Both of these regiments were experienced, having seen action at the Alma and in Sevastopol during the siege, but this did not stop them from ignoring orders. These troops had been ordered to halt on Shell Hill in order to cover the approach of the artillery, but Lieutenant-Colonel Smelkoff, commanding the 4th Battalion of the Taroutine, saw the Katherinberg battalion veering across his front and down to the left and told his men 'To the left!'. The colonel commanding the Taroutine demanded to know who had given the order to advance to the left since

> 'General Dannenberg had ordered him to crown the heights and wait
> for orders ". . . besides, don't you see the artillery is coming up the
> hill, and we are placed here to cover its advance?" But no one listened
> to his remonstrances, and the 3rd and 4th battalions began to descend
> the hill towards the road with loud hurrahs! When the commander of
> our battalion asked of the Colonel what we were to do, he said "Oh
> go!" with an angry wave of the hand.'[8]

The Taroutine pushed down into Quarry Ravine where many of them abandoned their knapsacks, greatcoats and digging tools in an endeavour to lighten their loads which were making progress on the steep and slippery slopes even more arduous. The men of the 3rd and 4th battalions were leading the regiment and they, through the fog, caught sight of the Sandbag Battery as they emerged from the Quarry Ravine. Their actions were to set the pattern for the rest of the day, for despite its uselessness, the Sandbag Battery seemed to be a symbol of victory, its capture would be a tangible achievement. Accordingly, the Taroutine attacked.

> '. . . the men of the 3rd and 4th battalions were standing before a small
> battery shouting hurrah! and waving their caps for us to come on; the
> buglers continually played the advance, and several of my men broke
> from the ranks at a run . . . As we got higher up the hill we began to
> hear the whistle of rifle balls about us, and some of the men began to
> remonstrate with me that we should be too late, that the battle would
> be over before we could get up . . . Around the Battery there was a
> crowd of soldiers in disorder . . . to the right was part of the regiment
> of Borodino, the rest of which, like ourselves, was still advancing. The
> regiment of Katherinberg was to the right of us . . . formed in a second
> line in the rear, and a little below the regiment of Borodino and our
> own. I brought my company to within forty yards of the battery, and

> . . . I perceived a great many people on the spur [across the valley above the village of Inkermann]; I took them for the Grand Dukes with Prince Menshikov . . . I said to the men ". . . mind you don't disgrace yourselves in their sight! . . . forward with the bayonet!"'[9]

The enemy which the Taroutine had to charge were, in fact, very small. The picquet of the night before had been posted within the battery itself, but the new picquet under the direction of Lieutenant-Colonel Carpenter and commanded by Lieutenant Barnston of the 55th, '. . . did not occupy the battery, but a small hill a few paces from it overlooking it' with only six men within the sandbag emplacement. Hodasevich continues the story

> '. . . with a loud hurrah my company of about 120 men rushed at the battery . . . I scrambled up the barbette of the battery, and saw by the red coats that we were engaged with Englishmen . . . they retired about 400 yards and opened a fire of rifles upon us . . . several soldiers went into the battery and began to look for plunder. Close to me stood a young ensign of the name of Protopopoff, and, seeing that he looked dull, I asked him what was the matter. "Ah!" said he, "tell my uncle to write home, and say that I was killed at the battle of Inkermann". His uncle was in our regiment. I told him that he ought not to joke like that, "for don't you see the day is ours?" I had hardly time to pronounce these words before he was struck in the left side by a rifle-ball and died almost immediately'.[10]

That ball was probably fired by Barnston's picquet which kept up a galling fire on the Taroutine and mounted a few rushes against the enemy's skirmishers that served to make them hold back. Barnston '. . . saw a Russian officer on a pony leading his men most gallantly . . . [he] pointed him out to Private Bell, 55th Regiment, who knocked him over with the first shot',[11] though Barnston himself was dangerously wounded a few moments later.

With the four battalions of the Borodino having now completed their ascent out of the Quarry Ravine and the one battalion of the Katherinberg Regiment close behind, the 6,000 Russians extended from south of the Sandbag Battery right the way across to the Post Road and almost up to the Barrier. On the right Soimonoff's attack was still developing, the whole venture, therefore, consisting of eleven battalions in the first assaulting wave with nine battalions immediately to their rear moving as two great pincers on the British left and right. In the centre the Russians hung back, for here the British artillery continued to duel with their counterparts on Shell Hill where thirty-eight guns were now in position with a further sixteen battalions coming up the northern, sheltered slopes in support.

To face this onslaught, Pennefather had received some slender reinforce-ments from the Light Division whose movement forward to support the 2nd Division had not been entirely without incident. Townsend's battery of six guns and 650 infantry had been despatched by Codrington and were approaching from the left and rear of the fight through thick mist when they came upon Soimonoff's men heading obliquely down the slopes of West Jut and Shell Hill. Five companies of the 88th Connaught Rangers blundered into a heavy column of Russians at the head of the Mikriakoff Glen. For once, the Russians took the initiative, delivered a sharp volley and a swift charge and drove a wedge through the surprised Irishmen. The Grenadier and No 5 Companies on the right fell back in disorder, but the Light and No 7 Companies rallied, replied with a telling volley and then chased the Russians right back up the southern slopes of West Jut until they came to a dry-stone wall about five feet high. Captain Crosse leading, sixteen Connaught Rangers plunged over this wall straight at a numerous enemy now safely back on ground of their choosing. Captain Crosse

'. . . shot four; a fifth bayoneted Captain C in the leg, and fell over him, bending the bayonet in the wound and pulling Captain C on top of him; a sixth charged him but, with his sword, he was enabled to cut along the Russian's firelock to his hands. Captain C got up and made off, but was again attacked by this Russian and again drove him back; he then fell in with Privates Samuel Price, John Gascoigne and Pat Daly who had come to look for [him]'[12]

In the same part of the field, Townsend's battery was advancing through thick brushwood in column, two guns leading. In command of these guns was Lieutenant Miller; he unlimbered the guns, a third one soon coming up to join the others, and rode forward to reconnoitre the next leg of the journey. Visibility was poor, the ground was difficult and there was no infantry support; the gunners were being justifiably cautious and had their leading guns in a position where they could give immediate fire-support. Suddenly, out of the mist poured Grant's men who were stubbornly falling back in the face of heavy odds. Miller ordered these men to halt and give immediate protection to his guns, but knowing the numbers of Russians that were now pouring down on this flank the men who had already been battling hard against infinitely superior numbers continued to withdraw. There were neither horses nor limbers with which to withdraw the guns; the choice was stark: fight and try to prevent the guns being over-run, or spike them and get away.

There could be only one choice for the men of P Battery as two mighty columns of the 2nd and 3rd battalions of the Katherinberg Regiment emerged from the fog not ten yards to their front. 'Fire case' was the order but only one round was discharged before the enemy were upon them. Without hesitation Lieutenant Miller ordered his men to draw swords and charge and they fell upon their foes

> '. . . finding vent for some part of their rage in curses and shouts of defiance, but wildly striving besides to beat back the throng from their beloved guns with swords, with rammers, with sponge-staves, nay even, one may say, with clenched fists'[13]

whilst he waded in on horseback slashing with his sword at his opponents' heads. Eventually the guns were lost, but Miller lived to receive the Victoria Cross.

Moving slightly behind the 88th came their brigade commander, Buller, with four companies, about 250 men, of the 77th under their commanding officer, Lieutenant-Colonel Egerton. As the 88th shook out to the right and headed off into the fog, so the 77th moved off into the upper reaches of the Wellway guided by the sounds of battle rather than by any particular orders. In company with Buller was his young aide-de-camp, Lieutenant Henry Clifford of the Rifles. Despite his relative youth, Clifford had seen active service in the Cape and had been in the thick of the fighting at the Alma. On reaching the top of the Wellway Clifford,

> '. . . saw the enemy in great numbers in our front, about 15 yards from us; it was a moment or two before I could make General Buller believe that they were Russians. "In God's name," I said, "fix bayonets and charge!" He gave the order and in another moment we were hand to hand with them. Our line was not long enough to prevent the Russians out-flanking our left, which was unperceived by the 77th, who rushed on, with the exception of about a dozen, who, struck by the force on our left and who saw me taking out my revolver, halted with me. "Come on," I said, "my lads!" and the brave fellows dashed in amongst the astonished Russians, bayoneting them in every direction. One of the bullets of my revolver had partly come out and prevented it [sic] revolving and I could not get it off. The Russians fired their pieces off within a few yards of my head, but none touched me. I drew my sword and cut off one man's arm who was in the act of bayoneting me and a second seeing it, turned round and was in the act of running out of my way, when I hit him over the back of the neck and laid him dead at my feet. About 15 of them threw down their arms and gave themselves up and the remainder ran back and fell into the hands of the 77th returning from the splendid charge they had made and were killed or taken prisoner.'[14]

What Clifford, Buller and the 77th were not to know was that they had fallen upon the flank of the so-called 'Under-road Column' who were within a few yards of reaching their target, the left-rear flank of the 2nd Division. They had charged right through the column severing its head from its trunk and rendering it, momentarily at least, insensible. Those Russians in the immediate area of the 77th's attack lost all momentum and stood around in the fog paralysed by indecision before falling back upon their comrades who were still trying to get out of the confines of the Wellway. The decapitated head showed even less fight. Hearing fire, shouts and havoc from their rear, they simply abandoned their weapons and surrendered. There only remained the torso of the Russian column which lingered within the main part of the Careenage Ravine. A picquet of the Grenadier Guards under Captain, Prince Edward of Saxe-Weimar had been pushed out from Bentinck's Guards Brigade to hold a point on the lip of the Careenage Ravine that was known as Quarter-Guard Point. Here was posted a company of about eighty men who, once it had been gathered what was happening, were pulled back some little way from the edge of the ravine, made to lie down and then opened fire in a classic ambush from above and into the flank of a column whose head was already reeling back under the assault from the 77th. Prince Edward pursued his advantage and followed the smitten column into the ravine, firing time and again into the troops who offered little resistance. Prisoners were taken and the column simply ceased to pose a threat. Thus, a highly dangerous body of troops who had so nearly succeeded in their task played no further part in the battle.

As the fighting on the right around the Sandbag Battery continued and the 'Under-road Column' was flung back, so Soimonoff's main assault bore down. On the extreme left Major Fordyce with fewer than 300 of the 47th met Soimonoff's right hand battalion, the 1st Katherinbergers, who had forced themselves forward from the reserve position that they were meant to be occupying. The Russians came down the slopes of the Mikriakoff Glen firing wildly and harmlessly in the air, giving away their progress in the fog to the little band of 47th who awaited them. The 47th opened a steady and well disciplined fire that tore into the cumbersome columns of the Russians, each Minie round causing at least one casualty at ranges of less than fifty yards. The Russian column shuddered, advanced a little, received another volley and then began to crumble back in the direction from which it had come. The brush was thick and the gradient steep and the Russians were falling over themselves to get away from the hard hitting rifles of the 47th. Fordyce controlled his men superbly, however, his thin line extending beyond the sides of the much more numerous enemy column which allowed his fire to pour in from left and right as well as from the front. The Russians gave and Fordyce pursued them as far as he thought safe, eventually stopping just below Shell Hill and getting his men to lie down in the brush far in advance of any other British troops.

He was not to be alone there for long, however. Over to his right Egerton's 260 men, fresh from their trouncing of the sailors and riflemen of the 'Under-road Column', now moved against two battalions of the Tomsk Regiment. These two battalions presented a narrow but dense target screened by a cloud of skirmishers pressing together ever more closely in the brushwood. It would have been impossible for Egerton to see the other battalions of the Katherinberg Regiment that had over-run Townsend's guns and were now threatening his left, nor would he have seen the host which was gathered on his right. Had he done so it is doubtful that he would have attacked with such impulsiveness! Once again, though, his thin line would have extended beyond the flanks of his enemy's column and, in the fog, would have been assumed by the Russians to have every bit as much depth as one of their own formations. On being confronted by Egerton's troops the front ranks of the Tomsk men hesitated and then stopped whilst those in the rear pushed them on. A desultory fire was opened by the Russians but momentum had been lost and Egerton turned to Buller who was riding by his side and asked, 'There are the Russians, General, what shall we do?' Buller's answer was uncharacteristically decisive, 'Charge them,' said he and Egerton obliged with the command 'Prepare to charge – charge!'[15]

With a cheer the 77th fell upon the Tomsk and shot, stabbed and clubbed them back up the slopes. Here a tendency of the Russians was first noticed, for many of them fell to the ground when at close-quarters with the British, feigning death until the fight had passed over their supine forms. Once immediate danger had passed they would spring up again earning the disdainful soubriquet of 'the resurrection boys' from the British troops. So many of these shammers arose, however, that at one time Egerton's men, whilst they were not only pushing back Russians to their front, were also all but engulfed by those who were eagerly pursuing them trying to get through them and back to their own people! Recognising that there were far too many to take prisoner, the 77th ignored them and let them skulk off around the flanks unharmed.

The Tomsk battalions seem to have lost all cohesion under the pummelling that Egerton was giving them, and they recoiled hard back to the position from which they had started their advance and even beyond. What brought the 77th to a halt, however, was Egerton's perception that they were far too far forward, and the beginnings of effective fire from Russian artillery firing blind into the fog from West Jut. Just like Fordyce over to his left, Egerton brought his troops to a halt and ordered them to lie down in the brush and continue firing at the muzzle flashes of the guns on West Jut. Had the fog cleared he would have seen that he was approximately level with Fordyce and that his actions had also helped to bring about the undoing of two more Russian battalions on his left.

Between Fordyce and Egerton we left Grant confronting the 2nd and 3rd Katherinberg battalions who had over-run three of Townsend's guns. These two battalions, however, fired at by Grant from the front, and aware that their left flank was suddenly going to be left totally unsecured by the Tomsk, gave way. They abandoned their trophies unspiked, much to the joy of those gunners who had had to abandon them in the first place, and began to fall back. As they retreated so Grant pressed them hard, and soon they were tumbling back in much the same chaos as their 1st Battalion on their right and the Tomsk to their left. Lieutenant-Colonel Jefferies and his five companies of 88th followed in the wake of Grant, and soon the little force was established on the western slopes of Shell Hill just beyond canister range of the guns on West Jut in rough alignment with Fordyce and Egerton.

So it was that the right of Soimonoff's attack failed. By resolute action and the use of unstinting rifle fire small numbers of British had driven back large numbers of Russians. But one thing was noted by the British; amongst the Russian throng very few had been seen on horseback. Unlike their British opponents whose infantry was studded with mounted officers, the Russians appeared to have few in the saddle that day. One such, however, had been foremost in the fighting, urging his men on and making a target of himself that no one had managed to hit. Now, as the columns trudged back up the hill, that one figure was seen to fall heavily from the saddle and not to remount. Whether this was actually Soimonoff or not will never be known, but what is certain is that at about this time he received a fatal wound and with his demise all spirit went out of the Russian attack in this sector. Had he been less impetuous and waited for Pauloff's forces to appear, their combined weight of numbers would have made the assault very difficult to resist. As it was, what he might have lacked in judgement he made up for by sheer personal courage and drive which was to be sorely missed by his men on the rest of that blood-soaked day.

Farther to the right two battalions of the Tomsk and four of the Kolivansk continued the attack oblivious, in the mist, to the fortunes of the force to their right. Heading towards Home Ridge they drove the handful of picquets in front of them over the level piece of ground between the base of Shell Hill and the gentle rise up to Home Ridge. So far no Russians had dared to cross this space because of the devastating fire of the British guns which they supposed to await them there. Now the picquets were running out of ammunition and were falling back directly in the line of fire of the guns which should now have been sweeping this threat away. Half of Captain John Turner's Battery had its fire masked most effectively by the retiring picquets until Sergeant Conway left Turner's side and bellowed, 'Lie down, men, lie down!'[16] sufficiently loudly for the warning to carry even above the din of musketry. The warning was heeded, however, and the British infantry fell to earth amongst the brush just in time for the guns to belch forth two rounds of canister at very short range into the densely packed Russian columns. The first round brought five of the battalions to a sudden halt; the front ranks collapsed and began to turn and try to claw their way back through the ranks to their rear. The second round brought ruin. Furrows were carved through the densely packed Tomsk and Kolivansk men, and the whole mass turned rapidly into a rabble and streamed back the way they had come. Their left brushed against Egerton's 77th lying in the undergrowth, but they passed unharmed as they were mistaken, in the mist, for advancing British. Only one group remained intact; one of the Kolivansk battalions had detached itself from the others and had forged off towards the bend between Home and Fore Ridge little realising the fate of the rest of the Regiment.

That one battalion's progress was only arrested, however, after a distinct scare had passed through the defenders of Home Ridge. The land levels out and narrows before the gentle slope that leads up to Home Ridge from the north-west, and over this saddle of land the remnants of the picquets and those troops which had been sent forward to support them began to retire with a haste that made Lieutenant-Colonel Percy Herbert, who was watching the scene from behind the breastwork on top of the hill, very uneasy. Out of cartridges, heavily outnumbered and with no support from Pennecuick's guns, which had fallen silent due to ammunition shortages, these men began to run in front of the Kolivansk battalion which was now scenting victory. Herbert saw an emergency unfolding before him, but luckily, there were 180 men of the 49th to hand under Captain Bellairs. As the Russians came closer and closer, Brigadier-General Adams's aide-de-camp arrived from the General and said, 'I think you had better advance, Bellairs'. The response was simple.

'Fix bayonets and advance,' said Bellairs and his men cleared the low wall in a leap and marched steadily at their enemies without firing a round. At forty yards' distance they broke into a dash and went at the Kolivansk battalion with a yell. The Russians did not wait to receive the bayonet but broke and ran, being pursued by the fire of the 49th.

Farther to the east the 6,600 Russians who stretched from the Post Road to beyond the Sandbag Battery had still not made any significant move. Milling around the Battery were the four battalions of the Taroutine whose capture of the emplacement we saw earlier, and slightly to their north remained the errant battalion of the Katherinberg Regiment. Moving hesitantly up Quarry Ravine came four battalions of the Borodino

Regiment; the two which led were spread across the mouth of Quarry Ravine and two more in echelon came some way to their rear. There was little barring the further progress of this powerful force except the remains of the Sandbag Battery picquet which '. . . remained about 400 yards from us, firing, and when in some cases I suppose they ran short of ammunition they came nearer and threw stones'; and 200 or so of one wing of the 30th Regiment under Lieutenant-Colonel Mauleverer who confronted the right part of the Borodino along the line of the Post Road.

Mauleverer brought his men to the present and fired a volley as the Russians emerged to his front through the fog. Most of these men, however, had spent their night on picquet and a lot of the rifles misfired. A tremor went through the 30th; they had come to trust and to depend on their rifles after their experiences at the Alma and on 26 October, and they could see that they were heavily outnumbered. The commanding officer was equal to the moment, however; he pushed himself forward on his charger as an example, and led his men on with the one weapon that he knew would not malfunction – the bayonet. Reaching the barrier he got the troops to lie down behind its scant cover and look to their arms; when the Russians were within a few yards he gave the order to advance, and he and his officers led over the breastwork and went headlong at the Borodino. Cold steel triumphed; the 30th lanced into the first battalion, tore through it and belaboured the flank of the second. Both battalions collapsed in the face of a ferocity that they had not witnessed since 26 October. Indeed, as the two front battalions gave way so did the two to the rear who had scarcely been fired at, let alone been charged by the suicidally brave 30th. Nevertheless, the whole Regiment ceased to have any fighting cohesion and streamed away at first up towards Shell Hill in the hope, presumably, that they would get some cover from the guns thereon, and then sheered off and made their way into the depths of Quarry Ravine.

Prominent in the charge had been the 30th's Adjutant, Lieutenant Mark Walker, who was to receive the Victoria Cross for his part in this action; indeed the heavy number of officers who became casualties, including Mauleverer, speaks for the personal example and leadership that the 30th's officers showed to their men. The fact remains, though, that 200 British wielding rain-soaked weapons that were, at that moment, hardly more effective than spears, put over 2,500 Russian infantry to ignominious flight despite the fact that the Russians were supported by artillery. A brief look at the recent history of the Borodino Regiment may hold some clues to their performance, however. At the Alma first their skirmishers were '. . . cut down like corn'[17] by British rifles, then the whole Regiment suffered heavily from artillery fire and they were one of the first, if not the very first, regiments to start to withdraw from the field. Next, they had been at the eye of the storm throughout the siege occupying some of the hottest bastions and being battered accordingly. Most recently, they had been soundly beaten on 26 October, inflicting few casualties and receiving many. Without detracting from the achievements of the 30th, the Borodino was a regiment which had already suffered more than most and which had tasted nothing but defeat – always at the hands of the British.

Much the same fate awaited the five battalions, four Taroutine and one Katherinberg, which now held the Sandbag Battery. A non-commissioned officer of the Taroutine had the same impression of Barnston's men of the 55th as Captain Hodasevich, also of the Taroutine, '. . . the enemy dare-devils hardly withdrew sixty paces and, seeing that they were not followed, calmly opened fire, picking us off, one by one'.[18] Hodasevich recounted the lack of drive which gripped his men

'. . . the chaos was something extraordinary around the Battery . . . others were shouting for artillery to come up, the buglers constantly played the signal to advance, the drummers beat to the attack, but nobody thought of moving; there we stood like a flock of sheep . . . having gained possession of the Battery nobody thought of pushing on, nor did we know which direction to take'.[19]

The strongest body of British which the Russians had yet to encounter was about to appear, however, for Brigadier-General Adams and seven companies of the 41st, about 525 men in total, were advancing down the Kitspur.

With Lieutenant-Colonel Carpenter elsewhere as the senior field officer of the day, the 41st were under the command of Major Eman, the officer who had so distinguished himself on 26 October. The colours floated out at the head of the Regiment in the hands of Lieutenants Lowry and Stirling, the latter of whom had risen from his sick bed to be with his men. Over 4,000 Russians awaited them, but the 41st halted, fired, reloaded and advanced at a steady pace down the boulder and brush-strewn slope towards their enemies. Hodasevich saw the 41st advance and heard his buglers sound

'. . . To the left about! All turned round and began to run helter-skelter. The officers shouted for the men to halt, but to no avail, for none thought of stopping, but each followed the direction his fancy or his fears prompted . . . During this flight not a few were shot down, as the fire of the rifles increased every minute'.[20]

The Regimental History of the 41st continues:

'The 41st, longing to get in with the bayonet, followed up the enemy, but in the thick undergrowth the regiment was thrown into some confusion. The Brigadier, knowing that that this was not the last of the Russian attacks, would not permit a close pursuit, but ordered pursuit by fire and not with the bayonet'.[21]

Adams and Eman saw the danger of letting the over-eager men chase the Russians too far down the slope, for they realised that, once the men were over the lip of the Kitspur and pelting down the steep slope in pursuit of their quarry, all hope of control would be lost. They were not the last to have to make this decision that day, but they succeeded in exercising an iron discipline on their men which others were not able to achieve; they were to be proved more than correct.

So it was that another host of Russians were ousted by a handful of British. Again, the Taroutine had seen plenty of action already at the Alma and during the siege and had never tasted victory, but they had approached the battle in good spirits and had been keen not to disgrace themselves in the eyes of the young Grand Dukes. Yet when they had had the chance to exploit their gains their officers failed to show the slightest trace of initiative. Thus, with their retreat the last element of Soimonoff's assault failed and twenty battalions left the field to take no further part in the day's fighting. The punishment that they took, however, should not be underestimated. When Soimonoff fell Vil'boi took over and was immediately wounded; Colonel Pristovoitov succeeded him, was wounded and was replaced by Colonel Uvazhnov-Aleksandrov who was rapidly killed. The Katherinberg Regiment '. . . suffered not only a terrible slaughter of its rank and file, but lost all of its battalion commanders besides two-thirds of its other officers', whilst '. . . the Kolivansk battalions, which had gone into action with a strength of more than fourteen hundred men, came out, after less than an hour, in charge of a captain, with only . . . some ten score of men between them'.[22]

So the first phase of the battle ended with Soimonoff's enterprise as dead as its architect and 15,000 Russians beaten from the field. In reserve were still some sixteen battalions on the north side of Shell Hill sheltered from the fire and oblivious to the defeat of their comrades whom they were not in a position to see. For the defenders, however, there was to be no break in the action where they could draw breath, replenish their ammunition, seek some food and drink and organise reinforcements, for no sooner had the grey-clad columns scurried into the shelter of the brush and the ravines than others rolled up the same gullies to challenge them once again. They were not to know that they had inflicted terrible losses on one, major part of the force that opposed them and sent it back to Sevastopol to lick its wounds for, as far as they knew, the columns that were now rolling ineluctably forward, were the same as those whom they had just beaten off. It was half-past seven and even more severe tests were yet to come.

Notes

1. Russell, *Todleban's Defence of Sevastopol*, p175
2. Moore, p37
3. Carmichael Mss, p17
4. Seaton, p165
5. Carmichael, p18
6. Kinglake, vol V, p130
7. *ibid*, p132
8. Hodasevich, p190
9. *ibid*, p192
10. *ibid*, p193
11. Hume, p67
12. Steevens, p92
13. Kinglake, vol V, p140
14. Clifford, p89
15. Kinglake, vol V, p153
16. *ibid*, p160
17. Seaton, p89
18. *ibid*, p169
19. Hodasevich, p196
20. *ibid*, p198
21. Lomax, p115
22. Seaton, p171

Chapter VII

'I never heard our men make such a yelling as they did this day!'
The Sandbag Battery

The opening round of the battle had been bad enough, but what now lay ahead of the British was to prove much more testing. The next hour's fighting revolved almost entirely around that most useless of fortifications, the Sandbag Battery, the seizure of which the Russians had come to view as a talisman of victory, and the loss of which the British saw as a sure symbol of defeat. It could easily have been ignored by the British as its capture made no difference to the security of Home Ridge so long as the cordon of defences was drawn tight against the slopes of the main position. In fact, had that been the case, control of the fighting would have been easier and firepower more concentrated. As it was, a substantial portion of the meagre forces available for the defence of the position as a whole were to be frittered away whilst the maverick general, Cathcart, jeopardised all that the British had achieved so far in the name of possession of the Sandbag Battery.

The next Russian onslaught was to be commanded by General Dannenberg who had arrived on the field with Pauloff's column and had there taken command of all of the Russian troops exactly as planned. To the north of Shell Hill lay sixteen battalions which had come out of Sevastopol with Soimonoff and had remained in reserve largely unharmed whilst the various, futile assaults were made against the British in the first hour and three-quarters. Dannenberg, however, chose not to use these men for his next attack selecting instead Pauloff's 11th Division, despite the fact that they had just arrived after a tiring march and knew nothing of the ground. Pauloff's force was nearly 10,000 strong and was made up of troops fresh to the Crimea but experienced in fighting the Turks. Indeed, it was these very troops whom Dannenberg had sought to protect from going into action on 4 November as it was the first anniversary of their defeat at Oltenitsa. Unlike that battle, however, at Inkermann these veteran troops would be supported by a vast number of artillery pieces. Marching with Pauloff were ninety-seven guns most of which were quickly brought up into support of those already on Shell Hill, so that by the time the assault started, Dannenberg had eighty-six guns in

97

action which stretched from the western extreme of Shell Hill right the way along East Jut.

Thirteen battalions were now to be used primarily against the centre and right of the British position. Approaching over the western slopes of Shell Hill, all the regiments advanced in the classic formation of skirmishers in the lead followed by two lines of company columns then one line of battalion columns. At the head of the host came the Okhotsk Regiment and a battalion of sappers who marched across Quarry Ravine, over the Tusk and emerged at the very top of St Clement's Ravine with the sappers leading, slashing their way through the thicker parts of the scrub. After them followed the four battalions of the Iakoutsk Regiment who took the same path until they reached the Quarry Ravine. Here they fanned out to the south with their right straddling the Post Road and their left brushing the right of the Okhotsk. Last came the four battalions of the Selenghinsk which passed to the rear and left of the Okhotsk thus both facing and over-lapping the Sandbag Battery and stretching right down into the gorge which marked the British right. The Selenghinsk had been in the eye of the Russian public during the fighting on the Danube after a celebrated incident at the battle of Oltenitsa where much had been made of the stoical defence of the regimental colours by a badly wounded non-commissioned officer. The storm of fire which they had met almost a year ago to the day must have been very much in the forefront of everyone's minds.

These, then, were the fresh columns which Brigadier-General Adams and his men saw emerging from the very glens down which the Taroutine and Borodino Regiments had just fled. As far as the British were concerned they could have been the same men who had simply re-grouped and come back into the attack after a brief respite. In fact, the lie of the land and the fog probably denied these fresh troops any sight of their broken, dispirited comrades despite the fact that they moved over almost the same piece of ground within minutes of each other.

To oppose this fresh attack Pennefather's forces were less than plentiful. Guarding the left rear at the head of the Wellway and the Mikriakoff Glen were about 1,000 troops or a third of his force. Muddled around the defences on Home Ridge and to the front of the 2nd Division's camp were several hundred soldiers of mixed regiments who had come in as picquets thrown together by the confused fighting in the early part of the battle. Many of their officers and non-commissioned officers had gone and all of them were short of ammunition, and whilst there was no absence of fighting spirit amongst them, they lacked any coherence. Colonel Percy Herbert recognised the need for these men, and tried to organise them, but met with little success. The remaining 1,400 or so consisted of the remains of Mauleverer's wing of the 30th holding the Barrier, 700 men made up of the 41st and three companies of the 49th under Adams at the Sandbag Battery and, on Home Ridge, three companies of the 47th, a handful of the 55th and most of the 95th. To support them there were eighteen guns.

These figures would be swollen somewhat by the reinforcements that were sent from various quarters throughout the next hour, but they never exceeded 4,700. The guns were supplemented by two further batteries, one from the Light Division and one from the First Division, whilst 1,200 guardsmen were to play a crucial role and 2,000 men under Cathcart eventually arrived and were spread across the front. Finally, two battalions of French infantry, about 1,600 strong, arrived.

The first Russian onslaught was on the British right against the 700 or so men of the 41st and 49th. The mist had cleared a little and Adams realised that he was about to be attacked by vastly superior numbers. Accordingly, he sent his Brigade-Major, Captain Armstrong, to the rear to seek reinforcements and he came upon the Duke of Cambridge with two Guards battalions on the bend of Home and Fore Ridge. Cambridge at once assured Armstrong that he would advance to support Adams's Brigade; so the Sandbag Battery began its career in earnest as a fatal magnet for British infantry.

Adams knew, however, that he could not wait for reinforcements and determined to attack the Okhotsk columns before they got a foothold on the lip of the Kitspur. His men had found the battery impossible to fire over as there was no fire-step and the embrasures were only wide enough for a couple of riflemen, so most of the defenders were lying down on both sides. With these men giving fire-support, Nos 3 and 4 Companies of the 41st were thrown out in front to deal with the cloud of Russian skirmishers who were leading the Okhotsk columns into the attack. The ground was steep and thick with undergrowth, but the 41st launched themselves into their enemies despite a withering fire from the Russians' leading troops.

Three officers fell in this rush. Captain Edwin Richards plunged into a group of Russians and was quickly surrounded; they signalled to him to surrender but instead he fired his Dean and Adams revolver about him, hitting four of them and slashed two with his sword before he fell to a bayonet thrust. The artistic Lieutenant Swaby who had had several sketches published in *Punch* magazine also perished. The circumstances of his death were summarised in a letter to his brother:

'His men, seeing themselves surrounded, begged of your brother to retire, but he answered "No, I shall not; I will fight to the last". He was seen to fire his revolver several times, and then to use his sword. His body was brought in three hours after the battle, pierced with nine wounds, the fatal one being a gun-shot through the abdomen. By his

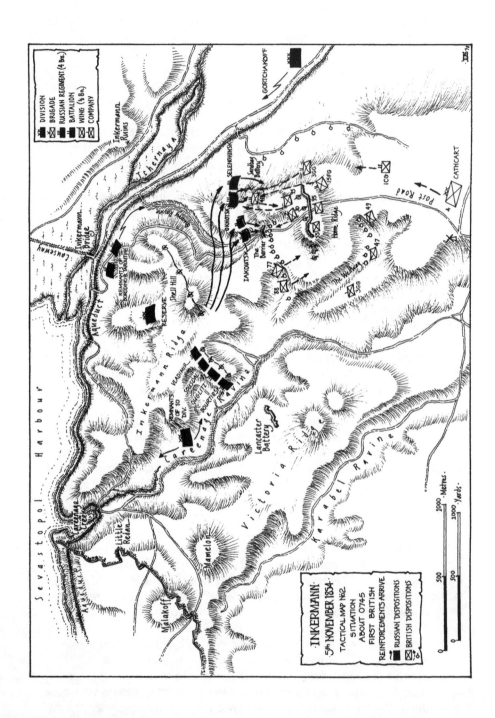

side was the dead body of a Russian officer with a deep sword cut through the head'.[1]

Simultaneously, Lieutenant Taylor died,

'Like a mediaeval hero. He was engaged in hand-to-hand combat with a Russian officer, when, seemingly by mutual consent, the Russian and British soldiers round about ceased fighting and formed round the contestants. Each officer ran the other through with his sword at the same moment, and as they fell the men took up the fight once more'.[2]

Steadily the superior Russian numbers began to tell and the two skirmishing companies were forced back upon the main body. The two leading battalions of the Okhotsk were thrown into confusion by the advanced companies of the 41st, but the two supporting battalions came on in good order with the Sapper battalion fighting particularly tenaciously. Whether these fresh troops were made of sterner stuff than those of the 10th and 17th Divisions, or whether the better visibility allowed the Russians to see the tiny numbers that opposed them, is not clear. In any event, as groups fell back under the steel or lead of Adams's men, more replaced them. There was none of the infectious panic such as that which had seized the Borodino, and the fighting ebbed back and forth across the Kitspur's ledge. Whether the supporting battalions of the Okhotsk began to outflank the defenders, or whether the Iakoutsk and Selenghinsk skirmishers were responsible will never be clear, but soon the little band was in severe danger of being cut off.

The tall Adams on his big, chestnut charger towered above the troops in the mist and musket smoke and appeared to bear a charmed life as the balls and splinters whined around him. He seemed unaware of the danger to his flanks, however, and roared to his men to hold their ground, while the 41st and 49th gradually lost any semblance of order and merged into a mass which was waging bitter little struggles all around itself.

The 41st's Regimental History recounts the story of the colour-party,

'. . . during this fighting the Colours were with the Regiment . . . it was a mystery why the Russians did not capture them. When the colour-party and escort were a little to the left of the Sandbag Battery, very close to the Russians in the midst of fog and smoke, Lieutenant Lowry was speaking to Lieutenant Sterling when the latter fell dead, shot through the left temple. As the Regimental Colour fell to the ground Sergeant Ford, one of the escort, picked it up. As the Sergeant did so a Russian seized the end of the pole and a tug-of-war took place until Ford drove him through with his bayonet when he let go. Another Russian came up who was driven off with a blow in the face from the butt-end of the Sergeant's rifle'.[3]

101

Neither was the commanding officer to be spared. Lieutenant-Colonel Carpenter, who had just managed to rejoin the Regiment from his duties as field officer, was knocked off his horse and fell into the hands of the advancing Russians who surrounded him and began to stab at him frenziedly, '. . . they bayoneted him in the stomach and clubbed him across the mouth',[4] but Private Thomas Beach dashed forward and beat them off with bayonet and butt, saving the Colonel and receiving a Victoria Cross for his bravery.

Seeing the danger as the British were forced backwards and into an ever narrower wedge as they sought to resist the Russians' outflanking moves, Major Eman told his buglers to sound the Regimental call and the 'halt'. The troops responded at once, found any cover that they could and tried to hold back the Russians with their fire. Slight though this fire was, the Russians checked and the situation might have stabilised had it not been for accurate and rapid artillery fire that was brought down on the British as the fog momentarily cleared. The situation became impossible and the defenders began to pull back towards Home Ridge carrying their casualties with them but pausing to fire as they went in order to keep the Russians at bay. In the nick of time Captain Hamley appeared with a half-battery of three guns which he sited just below Home Ridge in such a way that he was sheltered from the Russians' artillery but could bring his fire to bear on the battalions that were now occupying the Kitspur. Soon after liaising with Captain Hamley, Brigadier-General Adams was wounded in the ankle and carried from the field. He was to die from this wound and with his disappearance his Brigade, known as 'Adams's Forties' as it contained the 41st, 47th and 49th, lost a much loved leader.

With what remained of Adams's men relatively secure on Home Ridge, the flank protected by Hamley's guns and the Guards not yet committed, the British were in a good position to resist the next Russian move. However, the Sandbag Battery had fallen once again into the hands of the Russians and whilst there was no tactical sense in trying to recover it, honour demanded that the British should do just that. The bloodiest episode in the whole course of the battle was about to start.

The Guards were to be the first substantial reinforcements to arrive, but a strange piece of arrogance and xenophobia had already delayed the arrival of French assistance. General Bosquet had realised at once that the steady and determined firing from the British position on his left flank indicated an attack similar to that of 26 October and for which he knew his assistance would be required. Quickly assessing the manouevrings of Gortchakoff's forces on the Balaklava plain as a feint, he ordered two battalions to march northwards at best speed whilst he and his staff rode on ahead to link up with the British and find out where the reinforcements could best be deployed. Bosquet had seen much fighting in north Africa and was perfectly used to the confusion of battle; what he could not have anticipated was the frosty reception he was to receive from the two Napoleonic War veterans, Cathcart and Brown, whom he met on his way forward. Cathcart was on a similar mission; he had put as much of his Division as he could under arms and ordered them forward, and he was in advance of them trying to find out what was going on. Bosquet's offer of help was coolly rebuffed, however, both Britons suggesting that Bosquet would be better employed guarding the British rear and that the whole situation was in hand. Bosquet's instincts told him otherwise, but reasoning that the British must know what was happening better than he, he ordered both battalions to return to their original positions. Only sometime later did Bosquet set off again, lured by the din of battle and his instinctive feel for an emergency which had been underscored by an urgent plea for help from Raglan.

Two battalions of the Guards had arrived on Home Ridge and stood ready for use. In front stood 3rd Battalion Grenadier Guards with 1st Battalion Scots Fusilier Guards some little way to their rear. The third battalion of the Brigade, 1st Coldstream Guards, had come off picquet somewhat later than the other two and was still hurrying forward towards the sound of the guns when the Duke of Cambridge was trying to decide how best to use his troops. The Guards were to be plagued by being under dual command; Bentinck, their Brigadier, was with them but so was Cambridge, their Divisional commander who '. . . was not a man so constituted as to be proof against the contagion of surrounding opinion'.[5] To him and those who were with him the Sandbag Battery seemed to be the logical point to counter-attack, particularly in light of the fact that their support had already been sought by Adams's aide-de-camp. Before he launched his assault, however, Cambridge sent an officer to Bosquet to tell him that the attack was in earnest and that help was needed, whilst he sent two further officers to get a clear picture of what was happening on the slope below his battalions. The first officer, Colonel Hamilton, got only a short distance before his horse was felled. The second, Sir Charles Russell, met Captain Paynter who was trying to get his guns into position to reply to the increasing Russian fire and asked where the enemy were. Paynter replied, 'They are all around us, but thickest there',[6] pointing towards the battery. Russell's report decided Cambridge who moved both battalions east along the ridge into a position from which they could attack.

With the retirement of Adams's men, the Russians had continued to fan out and thirteen battalions now sprawled around the earthwork in a huge, dense crescent of men with the Iakoutsk edging forward to the west and the Selenghinsk moving sluggishly along the British flank in the east. The force which Cambridge was to attack most immediately with his 700 or so guardsmen were the nine battalions, about 7,000 men, of the Okhotsk, Selenghinsk and single Sapper battalion. The Grenadiers led the way. Under Colonel Reynardson the battalion aligned itself, fixed bayonets and set off at a steady tramp downhill towards their enemies. A volley was ordered, but the battalion, like so many others, had not had time to draw the charges from their rifles after coming off picquet and many misfired. This seems only to have infuriated the guardsmen more – they prided themselves on their skill-at-arms every bit as much as their steadiness on parade – and now the very weapons which had stood them in such good stead at the Alma were letting them down; there was nothing for it but to pitch into the Russians with the bayonet. In a fighting frenzy they cleared the battery in a single stroke and drove the Russians off the Kitspur lip and into the thick undergrowth which clung to the steep slopes below. Just like the 41st before them, by supreme efforts the officers managed to restrain the men from chasing the Russians into the valley and a little time was bought for the soldiers to clear their rifles by firing percussion cap after percussion cap into the damp powder in an effort to dry it enough for it to fire.

There was no sense in sacrificing the advantages of height which the new holders of the battery enjoyed on the Kitspur by chasing the Russians, but the lack of pursuit did allow them to re-group and return to the assault. This was precisely what happened and there followed a series of attacks in which the Russians came pouring over the Kitspur to be met by a steadily diminishing group of Grenadiers who hurled them back with a savagery that increased as their ranks reduced. Sergeant-Major Algar was killed as he climbed over the parapet of the battery in one of the rushes, whilst Alfred Tipping, one of the Grenadiers' officers records:

'After about three minutes to give the men breathing time we charged again but they were too many for us and would not move. Three of us got under the parapet and there they were with the muzzles of their guns close to our heads, but could not depress them sufficiently to shoot us and the moment their heads came over the top we had either a revolver or a sword to receive them with. They then hurled huge stones upon us'.[7]

Meanwhile, the Scots Fusilier Guards had been told to form on the left of the Grenadiers in order to oppose the columns coming out of St Clement's Ravine. A gap had appeared between the two battalions as the Scots lay down and held their ground and the Grenadiers eddied back and forth around the battery. Colonel Walker, the Scots Fusilier Guards' Commanding Officer, was cantering about the field on his charger trying to get a feel for the Russians' intentions and still keep in touch with the Grenadiers on his right when he saw two columns pushing up the ravine

104

to his front and emerging out of the fog. Getting his battalion to its feet he ordered it to move forward into a position from which it could make its fire tell to best effect when Cambridge's voice boomed out, 'Where the devil are you going to, sir? Form on the left of the Grenadiers!'[8] Despite the urgency of the situation, Walker chose to obey his commander to the letter and moved the battalion obliquely over the plateau, across the front of the advancing Russians, until they were hard up against the Grenadiers. Once here, Bentinck realised how ill-judged Cambridge's orders had been and, without finesse, told Walker to get his men back to their original position and deal with the threat emerging there. One can imagine the reaction of the soldiers being marched and counter-marched in the face of the enemy, but once back at the head of St Clement's Ravine, with the Russians only about fifty yards away, the Scots halted, faced their foes and delivered a crushing volley almost every round of which, at that range, must have found a billet. The Russians reeled back and Walker would have followed with the bayonet had an aide not arrived and told him not to pursue.

Further rushes put the Grenadiers under increasing pressure until the group within the battery became so frustrated at the Russian attempts to turn their flanks and their own inability to fire from within the sandbag wall that they rushed out and hurled themselves upon the Russians. So close had the fighting become, however, that no sooner had the Grenadiers left the position than a band of Russians dashed in and occupied it with loud hurrahs. Only able to see half a picture through the smoke-thickened fog, Colonel Walker (despite having his horse killed beneath him) immediately ordered one of his officers, Dawson Damer, to retake the battery whilst his Scots Fusilier Guards fired another volley into the flank of the next column that was ascending the hill and harassed them back down the slope farther than he had allowed the battalion to pursue before. So the attacks and counter-attacks continued with the numbers of guardsmen getting less by the minute and ammunition starting to run dangerously low. Reinforcements were beginning to be needed urgently and the Duke of Cambridge now rode in search of them.

The Duke's primary fear was that the Russians who were advancing in increasing numbers would get between the forces holding the barrier and his left, an expanse of ground which was very thinly held, and turn his flank. This piece of land which stretched for about 400 yards of undulating, boulder-strewn, brush-covered ground came to be referred to as 'The Gap' by Kinglake and was incredibly vulnerable. The little force holding the barrier had all its attention fixed on the considerable task that faced it; furthermore, it was hemmed about by the fog and the folds of the ground. Had not so many troops been focussed on the Sandbag Battery, then there should have been men enough to cover this area but, as it was, the men around the battery similarly had eyes for nothing but the Russians that kept scrambling up the Kitspur. So it was that the two groups fought in almost total isolation from each other and left open a hole in the line of defences which the Russians might find and exploit; there would then be little to stop them from being amongst the slender defences of Home Ridge itself.

It is not clear whether the Duke of Cambridge came across Cathcart or Pennefather first in his quest for troops, but his interview with the former met with no success. Sir George Cathcart was at a point on Home Ridge where he could see to the east, down into the gorge of the Tchernaya, when the fog cleared but not to the north and the area of the Gap. The Duke tried to persuade him of the danger that lay to the left of the Guards and that he should move his fresh troops up to plug the hole that existed there. Sir George at first seemed quite willing to assist, then, lifting the binoculars upon which his myopia made him depend heavily, his attention was held by the mass of the Selenghinsk Regiment that he could see through the gaps in the fog probing down the valley and threatening the British right. He dismissed the Duke's arguments, declaring that he would attack these Russians whom he believed posed a serious threat to the right flank. In fact, his judgement was faulty for he had decided to assault only the very tip of the Russian force rather than its core, but he began to make arrangements with his staff to execute his plans. We shall return to Cathcart and his attack in due course, but for the moment it is enough to know that Cambridge got no help from him.

Pennefather was more helpful, however. Reinforcements were beginning to arrive from those elements of the 4th Division which Cathcart was not keeping under his direct control and they were adding to the reserves which Pennefather now had at his disposal. The 400-strong 95th Regiment was still in reserve behind Home Ridge; Pennefather detached one wing under Champion to the Duke and one wing of 1st Rifle Brigade from the 4th Division under Colonel Horsford. Hurrying to the scene came Colonel Crofton's 20th Regiment, also from the 4th Division and unrested after a night in the trenches. One of their wings was also detached, thus '. . . three prime battalions'[9] were divided in half and used piecemeal rather than in a concentrated fashion. The Duke had intended all three wings to deploy well to the left of the Guards battalions and to plug some part of the Gap. Instead, the fight raging about the battery proved too attractive for the wings of the 95th and the 20th, both of which were instantly drawn towards the main contest. Only Horsford's Riflemen abided by the Duke's intentions, by spreading out in skirmishing order around the head of St Clement's Ravine and so going some way to achieving the main aim of the Duke's quest.

The fight around the battery was at one of its many heights, however, and only the most seasoned of commanders could have resisted the temptation to join in. The Okhotsk, Selenghinsk and Iakoutsk Regiments with the Sapper battalion in support had renewed their attack on the battery and captured it for a sixth time with the aid of a cross-fire of artillery support from Shell Hill. The fighting had been very bloody. Brigadier-General Bentinck had remained in command as the Duke sought help until he was wounded in the elbow. The commanding officer of the Scots Fusilier Guards, Walker, had already been wounded twice when he decided to move to his right and enter the battery in order to get a better feel for the importance of the earthwork. No sooner had he entered it than it was the object of a furious assault by the Selenghinsk whose soldiers, climbing up onto the parapet, began to shoot down into the guardsmen below. Walker was hit for a third time; a ball struck him in the jaw and left him unable to speak. Pouring blood, he indicated that Colonel Francis Seymour was to take over and made his way to the rear.

The death of one of the Grenadier officers killed during this mêlée marked a curious, double, family tragedy. Henry Neville had arrived with his Regiment in the Crimea some weeks before his brother, Grey Neville, had come ashore with the 5th Dragoon Guards. Thus Henry had been at the Alma and the establishment of the siege of Sevastopol whilst his brother chafed at sea and then at vedette duty: the lion's share of the fighting and glory appeared to be falling to the infantry. Both brothers wrote copious letters home in which they expressed their pleasures and frustrations and in which Henry showed a natural protectiveness towards his younger brother. At Balaklava, however, Grey was unhorsed, trampled, lanced and left gravely injured. Slowly he recovered and was well enough to write to his father that his brother's body had been found in the Sandbag Battery riddled with bayonet wounds. Whether the news of Henry's death affected him or not is unclear, but some days later Grey Neville went into a decline and succumbed to the wounds which he had received some four weeks earlier.

Meanwhile, the battery was to be captured again. Having been driven from the redoubt, what remained of the Scots Fusilier Guards and the Grenadiers stood at bay some way in the rear of the battery facing the hordes of Russians who were now crowding into their prize. In places the Guardsmen and the Russians were only six to eight yards from one another and both bodies blazed away at each other until ammunition ran short. So close were the assailants that stones and small rocks began to be hurled, but as these exchanges continued, so the bearskins of the Coldstream appeared to the rear of the battery. The Grenadiers, in particular, seemed to be inflamed by the idea that the Coldstream should not be allowed to see that their position had been lost to the Russians and, despite the fact that their retirement made perfect tactical

107

sense as it shortened the line and allowed firepower to be concentrated, the Grenadiers surged forward into the charge once more.

Captain Burnaby led the rush with the words, 'Charge again, Grenadiers!'[10] and the battalion went forward with the bayonet. So densely were the Russians packed that several were unable to get away from inside the battery as the Grenadiers fell upon them; there they died. The rest were pushed back over the lip of the Kitspur but the Guardsmen were held in check and not allowed to chase them down the slope. Some moments' respite were bought, but the Russians were soon surging back up the slopes and milling around the battery again. Soon Russian muskets were being thrust through the sandbagged embrasures and soldiers were clambering up onto its level top and shooting down into the defenders. Captain Percy found this intolerable and climbed on to the top of the sandbag wall himself only to be struck off by a hurled rock. Despite this bruising encounter, he climbed back again but this time the rock-thrower was more certain with his aim and caught him a blow on the forehead which sent Percy senseless into the mass of troops below!

In short order the Coldstream formed line on the right of the Grenadiers with part of Crofton's wing of the 20th on their right and the rest of them reinforcing the battery. Carmichael, one of the 95th's company commanders, recounts the advance of Champion's wing,

'. . . we could hear the cheering and hurrahing of the Russians over the din of the fight . . . an exclamation from one of my men drew my attention to my left, and turning round, I saw through the mist and smoke a line of the enemy's skirmishers close to my left flank. I wheeled my company at once to the left, and opened fire – at this moment the Duke of Cambridge rode up to me and not having, I suppose, noticed the enemy's skirmishers told me to take care, or that I should fire into the Guards. I pointed out who we had got in front of us, and he then rode on towards the left. Our fire drove the skirmishers, who were quite close to us back, and some of the men including Pte Timothy Abbot began to follow them with the bayonet, but I got them back, and we went on to the Battery, as having both colours with me, I felt anxious as to their safety . . . My men showed front chiefly to the left of the Battery, and the sergeant with the colours stood close to where those of the Guards were standing . . . our other two companies seemed to me to have formed towards the right but the men of different corps were very soon inter-mingled.'[11]

There followed a number of determined rushes by the Okhotsk against the left front of the battery which were generally kept at bay by fire and limited counter-attacks by the knotted groups of defenders who now held this part of the front. Captain Tower of the Coldstream was there,

'Several times I saw heads of Russian columns coming swarming through the bushes, the officers in front waving their swords and shouting to their men; but directly they saw us there was a hesitation, a huddling together, an indecision and a tendency not to come on. They fired quickly and nervously, and generally over our heads; they were so close to us before they saw us, and they were on lower ground than we were; if they had advanced in anything like a decided manner we must have been entirely swamped and annihilated . . . I kept taking ammunition out of dead men's pouches to feed the pouches of the living, screaming if I saw any fanatic Ruski that required shooting.'

Tower continues,

'It really was a critical moment in the battle, at least in our local part of the battle. Eliot fell from his horse shot through the head; Cowell staggered and fell by the same bush; young Greville was shot through the body. The enemy was frantic at this moment; the few men who charged with us were all shot, and I found myself entirely surrounded by flat caps . . . one fired at me, the powder almost singed my cap. I could see some bearskins on my right through the bushes, and accordingly made for them as hard as I could lay legs to ground, and I suppose Bob Lindsay and the men who were with us did the same . . . [now inside the Battery] we could see lines of bayonets outside the parapet, and could hear them howling and cheering one another on; it was now fearfully exciting . . . Our ammunition was beginning to fail, some of the men had not had a round of their own for a long time: the dead furnished the living; but now even that began to fail, and the men in their excitement threw stones, lumps of earth, anything they could see over the parapet amongst the Russians, and they came back again amongst us with interest. One of the most remarkable things about Russian troops is the noise they make in action, and I think it is catching as I never heard our men make such a yelling as they did all this day.'[12]

One notable assault rolled along the British line almost to the left hand embrasure of the battery but so spirited was the response that the Okhotsk fell back and a temporary lull descended on that limited sector of the Kitspur. To the east the Selenghinsk tried again and again to get over the lip of the plateau that faced them and then summon enough energy to press home their attack. Each assault would be preceded by a cheer, which served only to alert the defenders, then a ponderous, plodding advance that would grind to a halt in the face of sustained fire. Sometimes the Russians got close enough for bayonets and even butts to be used, but on most occasions, the Selenghinsk fell back wreathed in gun-smoke. Each time the Russians hesitated on the edge of the plateau they presented an almost irresistably tempting target for a bayonet charge and each time the men had to be restrained.

This lasted until Captain Wilson's company of the Coldstream could bear it no more. A Selenghinsk attack had got closer to the battery than all of the others and Wilson's men sprang forward to hurl them back. Control was lost; the fraught Coldstreamers unleashed all their frustrations and chased the Selenghinsk all the way to the bed of the Tchernaya gorge until they came under fire from some of Gortchakoff's men above them on the opposite slopes. With this display of indiscipline the whole nature of the fight in this quarter changed for watching events from the hillside above and poised to strike was Sir George Cathcart with six companies, the troops which he had earlier refused to give to the Duke of Cambridge to plug the Gap.

Whilst the fighting raged around the battery and more and more troops were drawn by its magnetism, the Gap remained open and more danger-ous than ever. In his search for reinforcements to secure his left, the Duke of Cambridge had, as we have seen, been refused by Cathcart and also by the commanders of the first French regiments to arrive on the field. After Bosquet had been snubbed by Brown and Cathcart in his initial attempt to proffer help to the embattled British, he had sent the two battalions that he was moving towards the 2nd Division's camp back to their own positions. Some instinct caused him to ignore the claims of the two British generals as the din of battle grew louder and he sent the 6th de Ligne and the 7th Leger back towards the scene of the action. Both battalions were strong: the 6th had over 700 men whilst the 7th Leger mustered over 900. Together they were larger than anything that the British had been able to put into the field and they were sorely needed to link the right of the force at the barrier with the left of the Guards around the head of St Clement's Ravine.

Both regiments had come up in good order with drums beating and bugles blowing jaunty calls, much to the delight of the mixed bag of British soldiery who milled around the rear slopes of Home Ridge. Cheers had rung out as the compact columns of the French approached the weary British; succour seemed to be at hand and plentiful succour at that. Delight turned to dismay, however, when both battalions advanced no further than the dead ground behind Home Ridge. The 6th came to a halt behind the bend of Home and Fore Ridge whilst the 7th Leger moved farther west, almost up to the Post Road, and formed square. In the British book, infantry only formed square when there was some danger of a cavalry attack, but there were no horsemen yet on the field of Inkermann nor was it ground that was at all suitable for the manoeuvring of massed horse. There was speculation that the square was adopted as

110

a useful expedient to control troops whose discipline was uncertain, for it was difficult for individuals or small groups to skulk away from so dense a formation. Whether this was true or not mattered little for the commanding officers of both battalions resisted the blandishments of both Pennefather and Cambridge to advance without orders from their superiors.

Pennefather's ire fell particularly heavily on the commander of the 6th de Ligne, Colonel de Camas. Without the direction of his brigade commander, Bourbaki, de Camas told Pennefather that he could not advance. Pennefather only relaxed his pressure when he noticed that the French officer 'had death on his face';[13] he believed that the Frenchman was not going to survive the battle; but the rest of the British troops were less understanding, and shouted insults were soon being heaped upon the French. Having realised that he would not prevail, the Duke of Cambridge asked the French officers to open the ranks of the Regiment in order to let him return to the Kitspur as quickly as possible. With punctilious manners, the French moved their ranks apart to allow the Duke to pass; he, with an expression of stony contempt on his face, rode through them and back to his guardsmen on the slopes below carrying with him only those few hundred reinforcements from the Rifles, 20th and 95th whom we have already met.

Meanwhile, on top of Fore Ridge, Cathcart's eye had been caught by the movements of the Selenghinsk in the fog-wreathed depths of the gorge below. By this stage of the battle, however, he had remarkably few of his 4th Division left with him. He had approached with five battalions of the Division but all of them he had given away in response to requests from others. A wing of the 21st was holding the mouth of the Mikriakoff Glen; both wings of the Rifles were accounted for; a wing of the 20th had been sent to the battery to support the Guards; the second wing of the 21st and the whole of the 63rd moved away to the left front whilst Brigadier Goldie with the second wing of the 20th and most of the 57th moved up to the line of the Post Road. So it was that at one stage Cathcart was totally deprived of troops, a strange state of affairs for one who must have been looking for every opportunity to prove himself.

Cathcart's salvation was at hand, however. Brigadier-General Torrens brought up some more men in the shape of six, depleted companies, two of the 46th and four of the 68th Light Infantry, a meagre force of fewer than 400. Both the commander and this handful of men had something to prove. We have already seen what pressures were at work on Cathcart's mind, but the composition of the soldiers bears closer examination. Neither the 46th nor the 68th had yet seen any serious fighting. Both had missed the Alma due to the indignity of poor navigation; both had been marched up to Balaklava and then remained inactive despite there

111

being opportunities to distinguish themselves; both had missed the glory of 26 October. Now both were arriving at what must have seemed a very late stage of another major engagement in which it was obvious that other regiments were already winning laurels. Added to all this, the 46th was the regiment that had been unable to embark as a whole battalion due to most of the officers being detained in England at the celebrated court martial occasioned by the treatment meeted out by the subalterns to one of their number, Lieutenant Perry. The 46th had been the subject of considerable public obloquy in the popular press, therefore both divisional commander and men had every incentive to perform whatever acts of gallantry they could that day.

Cathcart had already refused to assist Cambridge and his men were beginning to fire optimistically (for the 4th Division still had smooth-bore percussion muskets) into the brush in the depths of the valley below when direct orders came from Lord Raglan to take his men and plug the Gap. The orders were carried by General Airey, Raglan's principal staff officer, and there could have been no other individual except, perhaps, Sir George Brown, from whom Cathcart would have liked to hear them less. Cathcart regarded both Airey and Brown with contempt, for he believed that both officers used the name of Raglan to give weight to their own orders. Had it not been for the issue of the Dormant Commission, such friction might never have arisen, but Cathcart resented the fact that, despite his being the heir to Raglan's throne, he was seldom consulted and he had to take orders from officers whom he regarded as less able than himself. Cathcart was asked by Airey to cease fire and then to '. . . move to the left and support the Brigade of Guards, and not to descend or leave the plateau. Those are Lord Raglan's orders'.[14] An angry outburst might have been expected in response but Cathcart seemed in good humour, excited by the prospect of action merely remarking to Colonel Hardinge who was with Airey that he '. . . had so good a pack he did not want to be cautioned'.[15] There seems to have been no discussion over whether these orders would be obeyed or not, and there can be no question that Airey made Lord Raglan's wishes totally clear, having first gone to the trouble of getting Cathcart to break off the fire-fight in which he was starting to get involved. Cathcart seems simply to have ignored them, trusting his own judgement rather than that of his commander.

Cathcart ordered Torrens to attack. Most of his men had removed their greatcoats at some stage and were immediately noticeable to the Russians as almost the only British who fought that day in scarlet. They spread out into a wide, thin line and began their advance firing as they went. Contemporary accounts do not emphasise enough the difficulty of the ground over which they advanced for the slope to the south of the Kitspur is particularly steep, broken and boulder-strewn. Thickly covered in scrub and obscured by fog it would have made the control of an advancing line of excited, inexperienced soldiers almost impossible. The six companies broke into a tumbling, running charge that pelted into the flank of the leading troops of the Selenghinsk and drove them back. Control was not helped by many of the officers being struck down. Colonel Henry Smyth commanding the 68th was unhorsed, Major Wynne of the same regiment fell dead with a ball through the head whilst trying to keep his troops together, and Brigadier-General Torrens received a wound that disabled him then and there and from which he was to die several months later. As Torrens lay on the ground with his son, who was his aide, looking on, Cathcart, who had been following close behind the charging troops, said, 'Torrens, well and gallantly done!'.[16]

The actions of Cathcart and Torrens, however, started what Kinglake chose to call a 'great mischief', for once in the valley bottom they linked up with the Coldstreamers of Wilson's company who had already spilled over the lip of the Kitspur and started a stream of men that descended from the plateau above. Next to follow were Crofton's wing of the 20th. Crofton had led his men forward to the lip of the plateau when he was wounded. An approaching staff officer, Colonel Cunynghame, who had previously served in the 20th, was approached by Lieutenant Dowling who recognised him and said, 'Colonel, all our mounted officers are killed or wounded. Where shall we go?'[17] Accepting the command thrust upon him, Cunynghame advanced the men and volleyed into a column toiling up the side of the Kitspur. Here he left them, but as soon as he was gone the 20th surged forward driving the Russians before them tasting the same exhilaration as the others who had gone before them.

The fighting around the battery had not abated but the frustration of the constant charges and counter-charges to clear it of Russians was proving too much for the guardsmen and Line soldiers fighting there. On the left the cry went up, 'If an officer will lead, we will follow',[18] and Sir Charles Russell of the Grenadiers leapt forward through the left embrasure. Private Palmer was the only soldier to follow him, shooting a Russian who was in the act of bayoneting Russell as he did so, and the two shot and stabbed their way through a press of Russians as they made for a thicket of bearskins that they could see on the edge of the plateau. This towering headgear belonged to a group of soldiers from Captain Burnaby's company who had sallied out of another part of the battery. Burnaby had at first tried to get his men to follow him forward but had jumped over the parapet to find himself alone. Leaping back he killed a Russian with his sword who was closely pursuing him and yelled above the din, 'We must charge!'.[19] He was followed this time by Private Bancroft and a handful of others who immediately waded into the mass of Russians thronging about the battery. Bancroft tells how,

'I bayoneted the first Russian in the chest; he fell dead. I was then stabbed in the mouth with great force, which caused me to stagger back, where I shot this second Russian and ran a third through. A fourth and fifth came at me and ran me through the right side. I fell but managed to run one through and brought him down. I stunned him by kicking him, whilst I was engaging my bayonet with another. Sergeant-Major Algar called out to me not to kick the man that was down, but not being dead he was very troublesome to my legs; I was fighting the other over his body. I returned to the Battery and spat out my teeth; I found only two.'[20]

The move forward and down into the valley which had started on the right and been encouraged by Cathcart's charge was becoming infectious. The mass of troops in and around the battery suddenly started to move forward and soon the advance became general. The Duke of Cambridge could see how dangerous this was for all the advantages of a defence from the plateau were about to be sacrificed merely because the troops had become intolerably frustrated. He managed to keep the colour party of the Grenadiers and a small knot of about 100 men with him in the battery but all the shouting and imprecations that he could muster could not keep most of the defenders from surging forward and down the slope.

Carmichael's company of the 95th had been kept busy shoring up whichever part of the defences seemed to be in most trouble:

'. . . I went backwards and forwards between the flanks of the Battery several times, as at one moment one would be implored to bring assistance to the right, at another time it was the left that was pressed, and could not hold out any longer without help. The men behaved with great pluck and tenacity – I saw no flinching, although we were several times outflanked.'

Shortly afterwards a group of the 20th arrived to support Carmichael's men and

'. . . shortly after their arrival . . . the enemy's hold of the ground around the Battery was less firm, and their fire had most decidedly slackened, I proposed to an officer of the 20th . . . that we should try and drive them off the hill altogether by a charge – he agreed and we got together what we could, Guards, 20th and 95th and forming them up advanced with a cheer out of the left of the Battery. The enemy turned at once, several of those overtaken threw away their arms, and knelt down asking for mercy mentioning the name of Christ (Christos). These were taken prisoner and sent to the rear, but the pursuit was continued down the hill and into the ravine – I thought the battle was won, and the men were also exultant. A fine young soldier of the 95th,

Lance-Corporal Purcell came up to me saying, "We are driving them again, Sir", alluding to the repulse of the sortie of the 26th October, and at the same time was about to run his bayonet into a Russian's back . . . I cried out "Don't kill him!" and he then instead seized him by the belt behind and flung him to the ground, and took his weapon off him.'[21]

Carmichael, in the chaos of the battery, could be forgiven for thinking that he was the architect of the whole advance. In fact, the defenders advanced wholesale with his commander, Major Champion, leading the remnants of his wing of the 95th forward with a mass of men of other regiments attaching themselves to it. The 95th's adjutant spurred his horse through the left embrasure of the battery whilst Captain Sargent, slightly farther to the left of the battery with the 95th's Grenadier Company, at first hesitated as the shout of 'Charge!' became general. Sargent knew that it was unwise to forsake the high ground, but all around him those enemy that he could see were in retreat except for one, massed column that was struggling up St Clement's which threatened the flank of the troops who were pouring down the foggy slopes. The Grenadier Company launched into their opponents who broke and ran before they tasted the levelled steel behind them. Reaching the bottom of the gorge Sargent's men fanned out, some turning south-east chasing a group of Russians who had headed off down the valley and others pausing to draw breath and fire at the backs of their adversaries. The men were convinced that the battle was won.

Leading the charge, Champion had tried to ride down the steep, stony slope after the men accompanied by Macdonald, the mounted adjutant. It had proved too much for both of them, and as Champion was dismounting, he was struck by a ball. Macdonald had got a little farther than Champion but heard a call from the battery that a fresh, Russian column was advancing and would cut the pursuing party off. He returned to the battery but, realising that Champion was not following him, sent a party to go and try to find him before he rode off to bring in a small picquet that he had posted to the rear of the battery and which he was afraid would now be cut off. No sooner had Macdonald realised that more Russians were coming up unopposed than the troops in the valley came to the same conclusion. Carmichael records that,

'The men had got very scattered and were beginning to run very short of ammunition . . . I noticed just at this time, and the men near me also remarked it, that those following us but a good deal to the rear, were turning back, and soon after cries were raised "Come back, you are cut off!". I could see no cause to retreat and stopped those near me who began to retire thinking it was a false alarm, but the smoke and mist rolling away for a minute, a heavy Russian column became visible forming to our left on the high ground covered by a strong fringe of skirmishers . . . three or four of their companies were already formed and in order and the officers were busy marshalling the remainder . . . Not a moment was to be lost and it seemed to me more than doubtful if we could reach the Sandbag Battery before them.'[22]

These Russian columns were the two battalions of Okhotsk which had detached themselves from the fight earlier and four battalions of Iakoutsk who had been able to re-group, unmolested, in Quarry Ravine after their various sallies. They were now advancing through the very gap that Cambridge, Pennefather and Raglan had identified and tried to plug. Opposing these columns should have been the various wings that had been drawn in to the fight around the battery as well as the six companies that Cathcart had led into the valley. Had the high ground been held then they could have resisted these six battalions. As it was, impulsiveness had caused a very false victory to be won which was now in grave danger of being turned into a disaster.

The reaction of the troops cut off in the valley varied according to how far they had advanced down the gorge and the lie of the land. What remained of two companies of the 95th, the Grenadiers under Sargent and Number 2 Company under Captain Vialls, thought that their best chance was to melt into the brushwood and wait there for further developments. A party of guardsmen under Percy and Wilson and his Coldstreamers stole back under the lee of the lip of the Kitspur in parallel to a column of Iakoutsk who did not see them, whilst Captain Burnaby, less advanced than the others, was able to make it back to the battery in time to swell the Duke of Cambridge's force for their forthcoming battle. For the most part the men eventually managed to struggle back to the slopes of Home Ridge and join the crowd of disorganised troops who had gathered there after their various picquet actions earlier in the day.

Carmichael's experience was typical,

'With greatcoats on and pretty well blown, and impeded by the stiff oak brushwood, we made but slow progress back. My first idea was to climb up the side of the hill . . . to pass in front of the Battery, and to get in by its right; some appeared to be doing this, when recalled, and may have succeeded but the brushwood was so thick and the hill so steep, that I gave it up, and determined to follow those who were making for the left of the Battery by a narrow winding little footpath . . . up this we travelled in single file. I believe I was the last of this string the man just in front of me being a Guardsman, who I thought went very slow. In this manner we ran the gauntlet of their

116

skirmishers, and passed into the left of the Battery within six paces of their muzzles.'[23]

Meanwhile, Sir George Cathcart had become acutely aware of the danger of his position. Once in the bottom of the valley the Russians had retreated to a respectable distance and, whilst some sniping was going on, there was a lull in the serious fighting. It did not last for long, however, for no sooner had Cathcart spoken to the stricken Torrens than fire began to plunge into the scarlet coats in the valley from the high ground that they had just left. At first it was thought to be a mistaken volley from the Guards, but a quick inspection of the heights revealed a grey-clad, flat-capped column of considerable strength. They were, in fact, a battalion of the Iakoutsk who had advanced unopposed right through the Gap, along the edge of the Kitspur and now stood in the very spot that Cathcart's troops had just left, cutting off not just the troops of the 4th Division, but also the Duke of Cambridge's few men in the battery.

Cathcart's immediate response was to counter-attack, despite the fact that most of his command had disappeared into the brushwood and that he was faced by a very steep slope up which to assault. Having sent one of his staff, Colonel Windham, to recall the 46th and 68th, Cathcart turned to the troops around him and told them to prepare to attack. They were few in number, about fifty, and belonged to his Division but were not part of the force that he had led into such a predicament. They were part of Crofton's wing of the 20th who had been led down into the valley by Lieutenant Dowling and who were now milling about under fire from both sides of the ravine. Todleban recorded their attack:

'At this moment confusion began in their [Cathcart's] ranks but being quickly rallied, these brave troops made a supreme effort, and throwing themselves with desperation upon the Iakoutsk regiment, they succeeded in forcing its ranks, and cutting for themselves a way through the midst of our soldiers.'[24]

But there were only fifty against 800 and the Russian column was able to absorb the attack. Eventually those of the 20th who had not fought themselves to a standstill amidst the ranks of the Iakoutsk and fallen foul of a Russian bayonet or butt stroke, dropped back behind the cover of the slope and concealed themselves in the brushwood firing the odd round if they had any ammunition left.

A little way behind them was Cathcart and his staff whose retreat was now blocked and whose horses picked uncomfortably on the steep slope. He rode back and forth for a few moments before uttering one of the campaign's great understatements: 'I fear we are in a mess',[25] and then sent Major Maitland down the hill to try once again to rally the 46th and 68th. Maitland met with no success, however, for the remnants of the six companies complained bitterly that they were under fire from their own men, and when the reality of the situation was explained to them, they told him that they could not attack as they were out of ammunition. Maitland spurred his horse back up the slope to where Cathcart had taken cover in a rocky nook and, seeing him approach, Cathcart urged his mount forward a few paces to meet him. It was to be the last thing he did for he was shot through the chest by a Russian bullet and fell from his saddle mortally wounded.

To this day the Cathcart family have the leather wallet that Sir George had in his breast pocket when he was struck. It contains letters from his wife, is pierced by the bullet that killed him and the whole thing is crusted in dried blood. Those around him did not escape either; Colonel Charles Seymour was killed whilst Maitland was mortally wounded by the same fusillade. So it was that one of the most controversial characters of the campaign fell. Cathcart had every right to expect the expedition to add fresh laurels to his reputation. In fact, his last act was one of ill-judgement in a long series of mistakes and petty jealousies. Death in such romantic, even heroic, circumstances was the only thing that saved his reputation from being tarnished forever.

Meanwhile, the Duke of Cambridge was suddenly becoming aware that he was cut off. The Iakoutsk battalion to his rear had plainly identified the little band of bearskin-topped troops in and around the battery whose centre was clearly marked by the colours of the Grenadier Guards. They began to fire spasmodically at the party who at first thought that they were being fired at by their own people. Then the cry, 'Sir, you will be taken!'[26] ensured that the band were in no doubt that they were in the greatest danger and, tightly grouped together, they began to move off. To their left front the further two battalions of the Okhotsk had also started to move forward, heading directly for the battery and bringing a cross-fire to bear on the Duke's party. Joined by the group of men which Captain Burnaby had led up from the ravine, the party scraped along the front of the Iakoutsk which offered some resistance but, typically, when faced by British troops full of resolve, made no coherent effort to overwhelm them.

Whilst the Duke's group pushed through and past the Iakoutsk, the Russians were further distracted by another small knot of men who attacked hard into the flank of their column. These were a mixture of Line and Coldstream who also found themselves cut off but who had no officer at their head. Hardship inspires leaders, however, and Assistant-Surgeon Wolseley was there to provide just the leadership that was needed. Whilst medical men would not normally be expected to take a combatant role, Wolseley seized a rifle and bayonet and yelled to the group, 'Fix bayonets, charge, and keep up the hill!'[27] With a cheer the men followed him and buried themselves in the Russian column firing, stabbing and butting at the astonished Russians until they emerged on the other side. Whilst their casualties had been heavy, they had made their way to comparative safety and driven a wedge through the already confused Iakoutsk.

The two battalions of Okhotsk were behaving with considerably more vim than the Iakoutsk. Seeing the colours of the Grenadiers held aloft, their officers began to whip the Russian troops into a positive frenzy in an effort to close with the prize, but Burnaby had been able to grasp the situation perfectly as he toiled up the slope towards the Duke's group. He could see that, unless someone got between the Okhotsk and the rearmost men of the Duke's group, then the colours would be lost and the Duke overwhelmed and, shouting to his men to follow as best they could, he started a lung-bursting sprint up the Kitspur in an effort to get himself in a position to block the fast advancing Okhotsk. His party consisted of every regiment who had fought around the battery and was only about eighteen-strong; with these he intended to confound two battalions. Relying on the fact that attack was the best from of defence, Burnaby asked the men, 'Are you ready?'[28]; in reply they leapt forward into the Russians' skirmishers. A small space was cleared but the Russians came on, bayonets levelled. 'Get close together and charge them once more, my men!' Burnaby implored, and Private James Bancroft, still bleeding from his earlier bayonet wound in the mouth, thought it '. . . perfectly useless so few of us trying to resist such a tremendous lot; but for all that, I did so.'[29]

Corporal Isaac Archer of the Grenadier's No 3 Company was with Burnaby:

'Seeing the Colours surrounded we made to them. This was a struggle. I saw Sergeant Mann with the Colours. Likewise I saw Private Morris there. We closed about the Queen's Colour but two Russian columns coming upon either side of the Battery were closing upon us and would have seized it had not a few of us made a desperate resistance. We were not more than could have been covered by a sheet. We kept close together. Captain Burnaby was the officer with us but there were men of the Coldstream and the Line. He told us to keep close together and charge and as these two Russian columns were about fifteen yards from us we dashed through the few Russians who were between us and knocking them out of the way met the column. The blow was a desperate one. Some of us hardly were loaded. Step by step we prevented their advance until we nearly all fell and they eager upon the Colours pushed on. But it was too late to gain them.

The Colours had had time to regain the English lines and the French had come up.'[30]

This miniature charge had the effect of delaying the Okhotsk for vital minutes whilst the Grenadiers' colours put more ground between themselves and their pursuers, but eventually numbers told and the little rearguard was overrun. Burnaby slipped on the wet barrel of a musket and crashed to the ground as the Russian column began to fan out and change direction. Almost simultaneously the rest of the party were overcome, and they had the dubious pleasure of watching the Russians prodding the wounded and the dead with their bayonets. Lying next to Burnaby was a wounded Russian who seemed inclined to draw the attention of the other Russians to him; Burnaby knew that unless he did something he would be done for. Fortunately, he could speak a little Russian and pointing his pistol at the wounded man's head, he left him in no doubt about the consequences of giving him away. Surrounded by angry Russians, the impromptu rearguard had given themselves up for lost when, for no apparent reason, the Russian column, halted, uncertainty set in and then they began to melt away.

Help had arrived in the shape of the French 6th de Ligne who, at last, had been persuaded to advance. The fanning out of the Okhotsk which Burnaby had noticed had been the Russians' response to the new threat. De Camas, commanding the 6th de Ligne, had not dared to advance without higher authority, but on the appearance of his brigadier, Bourbaki, he had led his men forward, firing as they went. The French came on in good order driving the Okhotsk before them who fled back into St Clement's Ravine, but some Russians still stood around the Sandbag Battery, tightly grouped together and showing some resistance. This was too much for the 6th whose advance ground to a halt, much to the anger of a thin line of British who had emerged from the brush and formed a tenuous skirmish line in front of the French. Amongst these British was Captain James Armstrong, Adams's brigade major, who now wheeled his horse and tried to get the 6th to advance. Berating them in broken French, Armstrong managed to get the French officers to pull the Regiment's drums together and beat the 'pas de charge'; this, combined with shoves, pushes and even the flat of sword blades eventually got the French moving again. At this the Russians in the battery made off, and Colonel de Camas had the sense not to pause there but pushed on past the head of St Clement's Ravine where he linked up with Horsford's Riflemen who had stuck to their position whilst Russian columns flowed past them. Bourbaki already seems to have been here and he encouraged the 6th with the entirely inaccurate statement, 'Come on my lads, the English are in your front, forward!'[31], and led them up the western slope of the ravine on to the plateau that led down to the Inkermann Tusk.

*　　*　　*

Some little while before the French appeared there occurred an incident which is worthy of note on two counts. First, it showed a dedication between officer and soldier which modern theorists would have one believe did not exist in an army that many portray as being deeply riven by bigotry and class consciousness. Second, the British were acutely aware that the Russians at Inkermann were behaving in a barbarous fashion that they had not expected; wounded were seldom left unmolested and, as happened with Burnaby, went in fear of their lives.

We left Macdonald, the Adjutant of the 95th, riding uphill from the north-western slopes of the Kitspur having pulled away from the pell-mell pursuit of the Russians into the valley below. Alexander Macdonald, the last Chief of the Macdonalds of Glencoe, seems to have aroused great respect and admiration from the largely Irish soldiery of which 95th (The Derbyshire) Regiment consisted at that time. At the Alma, as a subaltern in the Regiment's Light Company, he had been in the thick of the fight and had been bowled over by a spent bullet which lodged in the whistle-chain ornament on his sword-belt. Worse was yet to come; at Inkermann:

'. . . I met the Duke of Cambridge who asked me who I was and whether our left was turned. I said that I had been on the extreme right all day and could not tell: I thought not but believed that we were pressed hard at all points . . . I rode after the Duke as requested and was shortly intercepted by a party of Russians coming towards me in skirmishing order, they must have got onto the plateau either between when I was in the camp or lower down than our camp. I think they must have been part of the column which cut off those of the two-gun Battery party who pursued the Russians with whom we had been fighting there . . . I am very near sighted and did not recognise the party till very close and I suddenly turned round and made off as fast as I could, intending to pass them on one of their flanks, but close upon this I met a very small party . . . returning and with Russians pursuing. I returned with them having the enemy both front and rear and very shortly afterwards on our right also coming from the direction of the two-gun Battery. I was standing in my stirrups looking round to see where we could charge through them with best chances when I received a ball through my right knee which gave under me and I fell from my horse.'[32]

Luckily for Macdonald, Sergeant Patrick Murphy stuck by him. In 1899 he recounted the incident from his point of view:

'I was placed in a position by Mr Macdonald, with all the other men on my left, and directed to keep up a fire to my front as quick as I could: the Regiment then retired: I kept up firing as directed. I could not tell how long I was in that position, but the ammunition was getting short. I neither looked to the right nor to the left, but kept on firing as directed. When I heard a horse galloping swiftly from the left, I looked in that direction and saw Mr Macdonald galloping towards me . . . 'Murphy, where are all your men?' I told him I did not know: he told me they were all dead but myself. 'Well now, Murphy, there are as many Russians in rear as there are in front; come along with me and we'll join this battalion of the Guards.' . . . I then started with him catching his left stirrup leather to help me along, I being very ill with dysentery at the time, and I came off the trenches that morning: my big coat was almost as heavy as myself, for it rained all that Saturday . . . We had not proceeded far when Mr Macdonald got wounded in the left thigh and was pitched about four yards to the left off his horse. I ran to him and lifted his head and asked him where he was wounded: he pointed to his thigh. I then saw for myself the blood oozing through his trousers . . . I made several attempts to get him up on my back . . . I told him I could not leave him in such an exposed position, for the enemy would surely kill him if they came across him, and they were looking and firing at us at the same time . . . leaving my rifle on the ground while stooping to get him on my back, he said 'For God's sake Murphy, let me down!' I let him down when I saw some Russians coming up at the charge. I made a grab for my musket and he told me not to fire: he fired with his revolver, and then I fired: when we could see, there were two or three on the ground and the others were retiring . . . I told him I might never show myself again in the Regiment if I left him. He told me to go, and if I lived to tell the Colonel what had happened: when I found there was no use in persuading him I left him . . .'[33]

Macdonald resisted the on-coming Russians with his sword and pistol as best he could, but eventually he was overwhelmed. His fingers were broken by the barrel of a musket; he was clubbed with butts; he received a sword thrust from a Russian whom he at first believed to be an officer who was trying to call his soldiers off; he was stabbed as many as twenty times with bayonets and left for dead. The next day his body was found under a thorn bush by some soldiers who recognised him but, noting that his shako was full of blood, they used the simple expedient of lifting him a few feet off the ground and then dropping him to see if he were still alive! His groaning was enough to persuade them that there was life in him and he lived to testify against the behaviour of the Russians, eventually dying peacefully in his bed in Teddington in 1876.

*   *   *

The past hour proved to be the bloodiest of the whole battle but, whilst attention was focussed on the extraordinary events at the Sandbag Battery, equally remarkable fighting was going on at the barrier. Though the barrier was only separated, as the crow flies, from the Sandbag battery by about 400 yards, the battery lay over the brow of the hill from the barrier making the two invisible to each other. Further to this, the scrub was dense between the two and the fog eddied thickly in the The Gap. So it was that the two fights went on in total isolation from one another, with neither force realising that if either gave way, or if the Russians managed to penetrate convincingly between the two, then the other position would be untenable. Also, all of the fighting in the British centre revolved around the defence being conducted at the barrier rather than on Home Ridge itself for Pennefather chose to continue his stance of fighting well forward and allowing the Russians to gain no ground. How much of this was by design and how much by chance is difficult to say and is very reminiscent of the fighting on 26 October when the picquets stuck too energetically to their task and prevented the artillery from being fully effective. The same phenomenon occurred again in the centre of the British position, for the top of Home Ridge had been fairly well prepared for defence whilst the barrier was only a crude, low breastwork and its protracted defence made it extremely difficult for the guns on the ridge to be used to full effect against advancing infantry. Whatever the logic, throughout the fight the barrier was held with every bit as much gusto as the Sandbag Battery.

We left Mauleverer's wing of about 200 men of the 30th having just thrown back the Borodino Regiment in fine style. Now they were catching their breath behind the barrier when two fresh battalions of the Iakoutsk Regiment came down the slopes of Shell Hill, wheeled into Quarry Ravine and attacked up the line of the Post Road. Most of the 30th's rifles were now back in commission, but ammunition was short and there raged a series of battles in which they fired and charged several times, inflicting casualties on the Iakoutsk and suffering many themselves, but each time losing a few yards in an effort not to allow themselves to be outflanked. Eventually they found themselves back at the gun positions on Home Ridge and linked up with remnants of the rest of the 30th under Major Patullo, leaving the barrier temporarily abandoned. Under the unobstructed fire of the guns the Russians hung back and many of the 30th fell down behind the breastwork, exhausted and, despite the din of battle, fell asleep.

To hand were a depleted wing of 140 or so men of the the Rifle Brigade under Major Horsford whom Pennefather now ordered to shake out behind the guns and charge the approaching Russians. The riflemen tore into the Iakoutsk who reeled back down the slope, past the barrier and into Quarry Ravine. The number of Russians who were left lying on the ground as the Rifles advanced was noticed by all on Home Ridge; but many sprang up soon after danger was past in best 'Resurrection Boy' tradition. Even more surrendered, throwing themselves to their knees and begging for mercy expecting, no doubt, to be treated in the same way that the Russians were serving the British wounded. Captain Bramston of the Rifles noted how '. . . extraordinary was the sudden change of every supplicant's countenance when he all at once learnt from kind gestures that there was no danger of his being despatched'.[34] The Rifles divided in two in their pursuit, but close behind came Major Hume's wing of the 95th, also about 200-strong, inadvertently plugging the gap that the Rifles had left. The Russians were now flooding back out of Quarry Ravine on a broad front and the 95th met them in line, fired, charged and checked their centre. Hume, who had been unhorsed, had his clothing riddled with shot whilst carrying the Queen's Colour at the Alma and had played his full part in the action of 26 October, was knocked from his horse and his wing lost its only mounted officer in a part of the field where the brush was particularly thick and control, therefore, especially difficult. Rifles and 95th now mingled together hitting the centre of the Russian column and preventing its left wing from getting any farther into the Gap. To the Russians' right, however, there was less resistance and a strong column swept past the troops around the barrier and were soon threatening the western part of the crest of Home Ridge. To counter this threat Turner's Battery, with no friendly infantry to its front, quickly came into action with canister, and the tattered remains of the column were soon staggering back down the slope up which they had so recently come.

For every body of Russians who were repulsed more seemed to come forward. The dozing 30th, who had played so exhausting a part in the earlier stages of the battle, had their rest disturbed by a column that was advancing steadily through the fog to the very crest of Home Ridge. With various bodies of British streaming forward towards the din that now marked the fight in the mist around the barrier, the 30th at first thought that the men plodding towards them in grey coats were British; then someone realised that danger was fast approaching and it was 'Up, 30th, up!'[35] and weary men were suddenly converted into charging devils as the Russians were once again forced back. Similarly, Colonel Upton with two companies of the Coldstream (who were the last of the battalion to march towards the fight) found themselves thrust forward to confront what was estimated to be about 1,500 men of what must have been the Iakoutsk Regiment who were moving towards the Gap. A rapid series of hard-hitting volleys made the Iakoutsk veer off to their right towards the barrier, saving the forces around the battery from being cut off.

Having sorted themselves out in the haven that Quarry Ravine provided, the Iakoutsk came on again, but this time they aimed more to the east of Home Ridge and were deployed amidst the brush with the two outer columns considerably in advance of the centre. Avoiding the defenders around the barrier they pushed up towards the crest which was, by this time, devoid of formed bodies of infantry being held by only the gunners and loose bodies of troops whom Herbert had continued to try to regiment. The second wing of the 20th was coming up, however, under the command of Colonel Horn who deployed them into line once they attracted artillery fire just to the south of the crest of Home Ridge, and then marched them on to the ridge itself as the Iakoutsk were getting closer to the breastwork than was comfortable. Without pausing on the ridge, the 20th fired, reloaded and pushed down the slope firing time after time into the Russians.

At first the brush broke up the ranks and prevented them from gaining the momentum that could have developed into a charge, but from the throats of the men there spontaneously arose a sound that was only known to this regiment. At Minden in 1759, the 20th had used a curious yell designed to terrify their enemies and regimental lore ensured that the custom was continued. Baying wildly the 20th drove the Iakoutsk down the hill and into the Quarry Ravine and they would have gone right down into its depths had a Russian light battery not been drawn near to the lip of Shell Hill to fire down upon them. The officer at the point of this advance was Lieutenant Vaughan; he had collected a number of men from other regiments as his troops swept past the barrier, many of whom, unlike the 20th, were armed with rifles. These he told to fire at the Russian gunners who quickly withdrew, but in the face of further columns in the bed of the ravine the little force pulled back to the area of the barrier and there it stood and held.

Hard on the heels of the 20th came another unit that also used its regimental history to spur itself on. The 20th's assault had cleared the centre and left columns of the Iakoutsk, but the right, forward column had been cut off from the rest in the mêlée and remained menacing the slopes of Home Ridge. Lying down in front of the parapet so that the guns could fire over them were the 57th, another regiment of the 4th Division which had yet to see any serious fighting. Known as the Die-Hards after Colonel Inglis had urged them to sell their lives dearly at Albuera in 1811, the 200 or so men were commanded by a youthful Captain Stanley, but amongst their ranks was the son of their hero, Captain Inglis. Brigadier-General Goldie, their brigade commander, approached the 57th and before unleashing them on the Russians who lay in front of them, he praised the 20th's spirited charge, the only evidence of which now remained was the cheering and firing in the fog and a litter of Russian bodies. Stanley got his men to their feet and with the cry, 'Men, remember Albuera!'[36] led the 57th forward. They fell upon the Iakoutsk and some stiff fighting occurred from which observers on Home Ridge at first thought the 57th would not emerge, but slowly the Russians gave and prodded by bayonets the column broke and ran down into Quarry Ravine on the tail of the rest of their shattered regiment. Soon Stanley was struck down and Inglis took up the command; he soon found himself as far into the ravine as Vaughan and his detachment of 20th. Like them, however, he was confronted there by fresh troops sheltering around the bend of the ravine and he fell back firing methodically until his little force was back behind the cover of the parapet on Home Ridge.

Rather less than two hours had now elapsed since the first shots were fired with the last hour's fighting around the battery and the barrier being particularly bloody. Dannenberg had taken no ground of significance and had been very severely mauled, whilst the British had defeated every body of troops that had been thrown at them with their own, slender forces and a few French reinforcements. Those troops which Dannenberg had used had taken over 1,000 casualties having fought their hardest over very difficult ground and faced artillery which Todleban believed '. . . sustained its infantry perfectly. It followed them everywhere, and opened fire at sufficiently close distance against the assailing columns of the Russians',[37] and rifles which decimated their ranks before they could even bring their muskets to bear. Whilst their ranks were thinned and each retreat into the ravines took more and more out of them, their morale, unlike that of the troops whom Soimonoff had led, held firm. In addition to these men, the next attack could call upon plenty more fresh troops for Dannenburg still had his sixteen battalions of over 9,000 waiting in reserve and, if he could just break through the defences of Home Ridge, he would be able to sweep down the slopes to the south and link up with Gortchakoff's men as they surged up from the Balaklava plain.

On the British side the picture was not so encouraging. Of the total of about 4,700 men who had defended the Inkermann position so far, at least half were now dead, wounded or incapacitated, whilst most of the remaining half had lost all battalion, wing or company cohesion and were lumped together in ammunition starved knots under self-appointed leaders. Furthermore, whilst the Russian infantry could be forced back into the ravines and some respite gained, over ninety Russian guns now played on the disorganised defenders without ceasing, to which the British artillery made increasingly ineffective reply. In support of these slender British resources there were two, relatively untouched, French battalions in the field, but their quality was uncertain and nowhere else were immediate reinforcements to hand. The next Russian onslaught would have to be faced by a group of men who had neither slept nor eaten, who were soaked by rain and sweat alternately, who were having to scavenge for ammunition amongst the pouches of the dead, who could detect the increasing volume of Russian artillery, and who had already fought themselves to a standstill. Those few who owned pocket watches and who had time to glance at them as the fog and smoke eddied around them in the brushwood would have seen that it was still only half-past eight.

Notes

1. Lomax, p225
2. *ibid*, p226
3. *ibid*, p226
4. *ibid*, p228
5. Kinglake, vol V, p197
6. *ibid*, p198
7. Kinglake, vol V, p199
8. *ibid*, p203
9. *ibid*, p211
10. *ibid*, p223
11. Carmichael Mss, p19
12. Tower Diary in *Guards* Magazine, p68
13. Kinglake, vol V, p213
14. *ibid*, p242
15. *ibid*, p243
16. *ibid*, p245
17. *ibid*, p246
18. *ibid*, p247
19. *ibid*, p249
20. *ibid*, p250
21. Carmichael Mss, p20
22. *ibid*, p23
23. *ibid*, p23
24. Russell, *Todleban's Defence of Sevastopol*, p198
25. Kinglake, vol V, p270
26. *ibid*, p273
27. *ibid*, p277
28. *ibid*, p281
29. *ibid*, p282
30. Ross, p213
31. Kinglake, vol V, p291
32. Macdonald Letters, undated, Author
33. 'I'm Ninety-Five', March 1899, p27
34. *Complete History of the Russian War*, p81
35. Kinglake, vol V, p300
36. *ibid*, p310
37. Russell, *Todleban's Defence of Sevastopol*, p203

Chapter VIII

'. . . should there be confusion in the enemy's batteries'
Diversions

Menshikov's overall plan, it will be remembered, was to launch Dannenberg's troops against the British holding the Inkermann position whilst distracting the rest of the Allied forces with both feint and real attacks. Gortchakoff was to hold the attention of Bosquet and the Brigade of Guards and prevent them from reinforcing the British flank until Dannenberg had overrun it. Once Dannenberg was visible on the plateau of the Sapoune, Gortchakoff was to surge up the slopes, link up with him and then push the Allies off the Chersonese thus raising the siege. Simultaneously, from Sevastopol, Timoviev was to attack the besieging forces and prevent their moving to the aid of the British. Gortchakoff's lack of activity has already been alluded to, but operations both within and without Sevastopol lasted throughout the fighting at Inkermann and need to be examined if their failure to prevent reinforcements coming forward, which caused the complete collapse of the Russian plan, is to be understood.

Starting with Timoviev, at nine-thirty the veteran artilleryman who had served against the Turks in 1828, sallied out of Sevastopol to the right of Number 6 Bastion (which lay at the far west of the defensive cordon) to attack the French. With him he had all four battalions of the Minsk Regiment and four light guns of 14 Artillery Brigade, veterans all, for the Minsk had faced the French attacks at the Alma and 14 Artillery Brigade had manned the Lesser Redoubt at the same battle. Issuing out of a cemetery, the force came under heavy musketry fire from the French trenches, but pushed on and one of the Minsk battalions under the command of Major Evspavlev '. . . broke into the defences of the batteries opposite Numbers 5 and 6 Bastions and spiked fifteen guns'.[1] French estimates have the number of spiked guns as eight, but whatever the actual number of guns put out of action, once the French had committed themselves to a substantial counter-attack, Timoviev had achieved his aim.

Forey, the commander of the French Siege Corps, had despatched three battalions under Monet to march towards the sound of the fighting at

Inkermann at eight o'clock that morning, but due to various delays, they had gone only about a mile or so of their six-mile journey when Timoviev's attack took place. Despite the fact that they had not gone far, the three battalions were allowed to continue, and De Lourmel's Brigade was sent to block the advance of Timoviev's force whilst D'Aurelle's Brigade was launched into its right flank. Levaillant's Division was moved forward in support, whilst Canrobert's orders for Prince Napoleon to be prepared to march the two battalions that remained at his personal disposal towards Inkermann were ignored and he moved both of them forward to help with the repulse of the sortie.

The experienced Timoviev meanwhile judged that he had done as much as he needed to and, with the French responding in much greater strength than he expected and starting to threaten his withdrawal route, he began to fall back on Sevastopol. Despite not having given any orders for his withdrawal to be covered, two battalions, one of the Brest Regiment which had not distinguished itself at the Alma and one of the Vilensk Regiment which was getting its first taste of field operations having been used exclusively within Sevastopol up until now, came out of the Russian lines to support him. De Lourmel led his Brigade on too fast trying to cut the Russians off and found himself sandwiched between their trenches and the Quarantine Fort. Caught in a murderous cross-fire, De Lourmel was fatally wounded and his Brigade was being very badly knocked about until D'Aurelle's Brigade and part of Levaillant's Division counter-attacked and extricated them. The whole affair was well handled by Timoviev (although it cost him a third of his force) and it took until half-past eleven for the French to have got themselves sufficiently well balanced to be able to send Prince Napoleon and his two battalions to help the British. By the time they arrived the fighting on the Inkermann position was all but over.

Lieutenant-General Moller, the commander of Sevastopol's garrison, had received very precise orders which told him that '. . . should there be confusion in the enemy's batteries [he was] . . . to storm those batteries'.[2] Menshikov had given Moller this crucial command despite his grave reservations about Moller's ability which had caused him to tell Prince M D Gortchakoff that 'I do not know what to do with him . . . I would be most grateful if you could write and ask me for him so that I can hide the fact that he is not wanted here'.[3] Menshikov's judgement of character was now proved to be entirely correct as Moller deployed not a single soldier against the besieging forces, despite the fact that troop movements away from the siege lines must have been evident to him. Presumably, Moller seeing no obvious confusion, failed to 'read the battle' and consequently missed an opportunity to tie down the troops that ultimately swung the battle in the Allies' favour.

General P D Gortchakoff's orders had also been precise telling him first to distract the enemy that faced him on the Sapoune and then to draw them on himself in an attempt '. . . to secure the approach to the Sapoune. Also, the dragoons must be ready to scale the heights at the first opportunity.'[4] Had these orders been obeyed with any degree of initiative, Bosquet and the Duke of Cambridge would have been pinned in their defensive positions by a convincing demonstration on the plain below them and Dannenberg's job would have been made immeasurably easier by a determined attack by 22,000 men deep in his enemy's right flank. There can be no doubt that Gortchakoff intended to link up with Dannenberg and that he would have been waiting, for some signal before he moved off, but his manoeuvrings were so feeble that it is difficult to credit them with any serious intent. Bogdanovich, the Russian historian, damns Gortchakoff's efforts: he

'. . . successfully denied himself any possibility of making a decisive contribution to the Sevastopol battle when he positioned half his force, seven battalions, 32 squadrons and 48 guns, behind the Tchernaya, and scattered the rest of his force, nine battalions, 20 squadrons and 40 guns between the Fedioukine hills and Redoubt Number 1'.[5]

Furthermore, those soldiers to the west of the Tchernaya only got to '. . . a distant cannon range of the Sapoune and opened artillery fire . . . this almost harmless activity lasted until 9 o'clock until the French became convinced that this was so and ordered their guns to stop firing'.

As already mentioned, Kinglake was convinced that the written orders to Gortchakoff were so very different from what he did throughout the day that they must have been bogus, designed to be intercepted by a spy with a view to spreading confusion within the Allied camp. How accurate this speculation is is impossible to say, but Gortchakoff, who had the tolerably competent Liprandi with him actually commanding the troops, does not seem to have put much effort into convincing his opponents that he was a real threat. Perhaps it is wrong to think that Gortchakoff had any idea what was happening on the plateau above him and that even if he had that he would have committed troops to an assault against the very steep scarp of the Sapoune which was topped with well prepared defences. As we shall see, Dannenberg waited in vain for his intervention; had it come, even in the shape of well and aggressively directed artillery fire, then the overall plan might have stood some chance of success.

Notes

1. Seaton, p170

131

2. Kinglake, vol V, p495
3. Seaton, p117
4. Kinglake, vol V, p496
5. Seaton, p177

Chapter IX
'We saw five columns of the beggars advancing on us!'
The Barrier

With the defences on Home Ridge looking increasingly sparse and no sign of substantial reinforcements on their way, Dannenberg now had the opportunity to brush the thin line of Allies that blocked his path out of his way and surge on to the plateau before him. However, few Russian records exist of this next phase of the battle due, no doubt, to the fearsome officer casualties that were incurred, so British accounts have had to be used with their understandable inaccuracies. Thus, from a British perspective, what came next was very different from anything that the Russians had tried before and was organised with extraordinary speed.

A single column of huge proportions was seen to be emerging from Quarry Ravine covered by the fire of the guns on Shell Hill. Quite how this column was made up is uncertain, for whilst the mist was somewhat thinner than it had been, gun and musket smoke from the artillery duelling between Shell Hill and Home Ridge and from the rifles and muskets in the hollow around the barrier hung thickly in the air. Certainly, before the column became obvious, Colonel Percy Herbert observing from Fore Ridge, had seen numbers of Russian infantry dashing down the forward slopes of Shell Hill at such a pace as to cause him to remark, 'Nicely blown those poor devils will be!'[1] and disappearing into the smoke and fog which obscured Quarry Ravine. The main trunk of the column consisted of what remained of four battalions of the Iakoutsk Regiment which, when one considers the mauling that the British believe they gave them and the number of skirmishes in which they were involved, is remarkable. If British claims are accurate then the Iakoutsk must have been made of very different metal than those regiments that Soimonoff had launched earlier for the latter needed no more than a couple of volleys and the threat of a bayonet charge to drive them off the field completely. The Iakoutsk, on the other hand, had already sampled lead, steel and canister; it must have been to their taste for they were now coming back for more!

Without detracting from any of the feats of arms of the British in the preceding sixty minutes or so, the fighting was at such close quarters and was so obscured by brush, mist and smoke that some of the accounts of

133

Russians falling in droves, abandoning their weapons and begging for mercy wholesale were perhaps exaggerated. Whatever the Iakoutsk's actual casualties had been, there was nothing wrong with their fighting spirit for they were now properly formed up and ready to advance with an enormous regimental flag waving above their two rear battalions. The central, regimental column was screened by battalion columns on either side and clouds of skirmishers in front and on both flanks. British observers believed the whole lot to be about twelve battalions strong; if so, from where did the other eight battalions come? It seems unlikely that the Selenghinsk were involved as they were still recovering from their assaults on the battery well below St Clement's Ravine. Some of the Okhotsk may have been there, but the 'Chasseurs of Soimonoff's 10th Division' were mentioned by Todleban as taking part. If this is accurate, these could only be the Tomsk and Kolivansk Regiments, the only two 'light' regiments in the 10th Division.

To oppose this mass of about 6,000, the British initially had about 2,000 men grouped in the vicinity of Home Ridge. About 600 were split up into little, independent parties fighting well forward of the Ridge amongst the brush; one wing of the 21st Fusiliers and the 63rd were advancing in line from the area of the Wellway to the left rear of the Ridge, also about 600-strong; and the remaining 800 were spread about Home Ridge itself, though mainly on the flanks rather than in the middle. To the left of the Post Road were about 100 men of the 55th with, after an interval, to their left 200 of the right wing of the 47th. Over on the extreme right was Colonel Upton's party of about 120 Guardsmen with 170 or so of the 57th behind the breastwork to their left. Coming up to the rear of the hill were the 7th Leger, 900-strong, whilst twelve French light guns under the command of Boussinière were also on their way. Their arrival was to be crucial for they swelled the number of artillery pieces on Home Ridge to forty-eight, a number which began to reply effectively to the Russian guns for the first time. Less easily accounted for was a small party of Zouaves whose battalion or regiment has never been discovered. It is thought that they had left their camp or perhaps even the trenches, against orders, when they heard the noise of battle, determined to play their part. Now they approached from the left rear of Home Ridge on the same path that Lieutenant-Colonel Egerton followed from the Mikriakoff Glen when he was relieved from his picquet duties there by the other wing of the 21st Fusiliers. So it was that with these other reinforcements on their way the Allied numbers rose to about 3,000 overall.

The outlying parties of British certainly annoyed and even delayed the protective columns of the main attack, but they simply did not have the strength or the artillery support to hinder the assault significantly. Added to this, the brush, smoke and mist were in parts so thick that it was perfectly possible for bodies of men to pass within feet of each other without knowing. So it was that one, advanced column of Russians sprang out of the mist against the extreme left of the Home Ridge position. Here lay three guns of Turner's Battery under the direct command of Lieutenant Boothby with the left-hand gun under Sergeant-Major Henry. They had already had one uncomfortably close encounter with Russian infantry and now, again, here they were at only a few yards' range directly to the front of the guns; a round of canister was fired with some effect but a smaller party had wheeled round to the left through thick brush and pounced upon Sergeant-Major Henry's gun. Unforgivably, the guns were not covered by infantry and the gunners had to fend for themselves. An order was given to limber-up, but the limbers and teams were some way to the rear so the men around the two right-hand guns fell back. Not so Henry and Gunner James Taylor who drew their swords and fell about their assailants. Taylor fell relatively quickly to a bayonet thrust but Henry, noting that the Russians were '. . . howling like mad dogs',[2] with his left hand grabbed the bayonet of one man who was trying to stab him whilst beating off others with his sword. Stabbed in the chest by a blow that lifted him off the ground, Henry fell to the ground being stabbed another fifteen or so times in the arms and back, but he lived to receive the Victoria Cross that his devotion to his gun had earned him.

Delighted with their prizes, the Russians stood around the three guns admiring them and trying to spike them with bits of wood. A spark of initiative would have told them to drive a bayonet point into the touch holes with the butt of a musket, snap the bayonet off quickly and then turn their attention to more important things. Had they moved sharply to their left they could have swept up the unsuspecting British left flank, clean on to Home Ridge itself right into the gun positions that were so weakly held. In fact they did nothing beyond mill about and this was precisely the pause that the wandering band of sixty or so Zouaves needed. There is some suggestion that the Zouaves were guided on to this point by Sir George Brown; in a private despatch he tells of the English position being denuded of troops and

> '. . . it was that circumstance which enabled a few of the enemy to break through to take temporary possession of three or four of our guns, which rendered the arrival of the French infantry so opportune. It was in leading on them [sic] that I received a musket-ball in the left arm, which compelled me to quit the field'.[3]

The Zouaves made short work of the Russians; a brutal fracas occurred around the guns with bayonets and butts being freely used and the Russians fell back with the French colonial troops in close pursuit.

To the right rear of the Zouaves came the right wing of the 21st Fusiliers

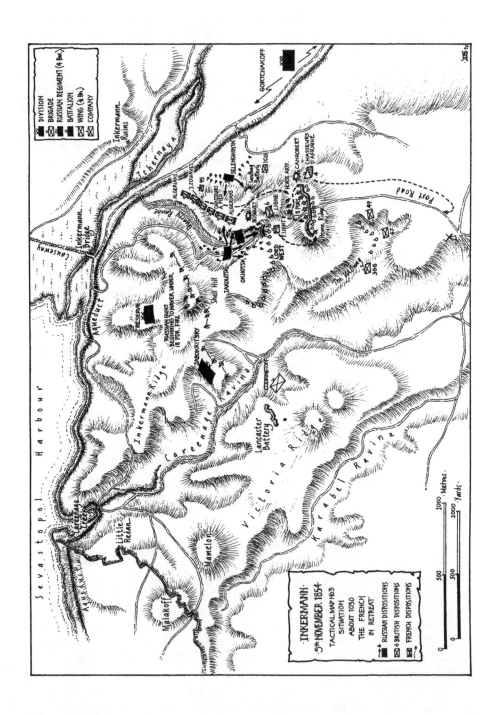

under Colonel Ainslie and 450 men of the 63rd under Colonel Swyney. The 21st Fusiliers were a comparatively mature regiment which had had time and opportunity to be well trained, but the 63rd had only recently received a vast batch of recruits drawn mainly from Dublin and who had had little opportunity to train. Furthermore, neither regiment had been actively involved in this sort of fighting before. Indeed, Ensign Vaughan Lee, an eighteen-year-old Etonian carrying the Regimental Colour of the 21st Fusiliers, mentions in a letter to his father of 27 October that he '. . . had a delightful fight at one of the picquets three days ago . . . my men were delighted as they were the first Russians they had shot'.[4] Now he found himself

'. . . passing through a storm of round shot, grape and shell which luckily did not hurt us. When we came up to the top of the hill, we found the Russian troops almost into the camps of the 2nd and 1st Divisions, and our skirmishers retiring behind the lines of the 21st and 63rd who were comrades. We formed line and laid down to allow our Artillery to play over our heads.'[5]

The 21st Fusiliers and 63rd pushed the Russian column that the Zouaves had started to shift before them and wheeled round to the east before lying down. Thus they found themselves in an irregular line with its right almost on the part of the crestwork from which Boothby's three guns protruded and its left about 120 yards away to its north-west. Under fire from Shell Hill they would not have to pause here long for events to their immediate right were about to plunge them into further action.

To their right lay about 100 men of the 55th under their acting commanding officer, Lieutenant-Colonel Daubeney, whilst Colonel Warren (their actual commanding officer though at Inkermann he was commanding the Brigade whilst Pennefather commanded the Division) was also close by. Daubeney was busying himself around two guns which had become fouled and refused to fire and had called up their limbers to extricate them when he suddenly became aware that a group of grey-clad men quietly approaching his front through the fog were Russians and not British. A bugler not of the 55th but, with a few other stragglers mixed up with them, sounded the retire; the 55th faltered and in no time the Russians overwhelmed them, taking some prisoner and causing the others to withdraw whilst farther to the right the rest of the same column threatened to overrun the other three guns of Turner's Battery. One round of canister was fired before the guns got away, but suddenly there were Russians in strength along the left part of the gun position on Home Ridge. As the fog lay thinner to the rear of the ridge, those Russians had a clear view all the way down as far as the Windmill, about a mile away, and, with the exception of one battalion, nothing seemed to stand in the way of their objective. If they could surge forward down the slopes the way would be clear for Gortchakoff to come up from the plain, the link-up would be complete and victory would be theirs. The battle was at its most critical point and all that lay between the Russians and their goal were the 900-strong French 7th Leger.

The 7th Leger deployed into line, shook out and advanced in such a resolute manner that the Russians halted and took stock. The 7th came on and then, for no apparent reason, also halted. A British staff officer rode up to them and called on them to advance; he recalled the glories of their forebears in the Peninsula and generally tried to embarrass them in his best French. It worked; the line advanced but only until the British officer was struck by a ball and was forced to retire. His withdrawal was all that was needed for the 7th's fragile resolve to buckle and they broke and ran down the slope up which they had come, shaving past the 200-strong wing of the 77th under Egerton who were moving forward from the Mikriakoff Glen, the scene of their earlier triumph. Disgusted, one of Egerton's officers grabbed hold of a retreating French officer but released him when he saw the terror in his eyes and heard him say, 'Mais, Monsieur, voilà les Russes!'.[6]

A few moments' grace were bought by the Russian artillery pounding their own men on Home Ridge with a barrage that would have done great damage to any British who had been there. In fact, some of these rounds skipped through the ranks of Raglan's headquarters which had just witnessed the rout of the 7th Leger and which was grouped together discussing what should be done. General Strangeways, the artillery commander who had survived Leipzig and Waterloo, had a leg torn off and was borne away asking to be allowed to die amongst his gunners. Two staff colonels had horses shot from under them and several other mounts were brought down by these falling horses, and for a moment the whole of the headquarters was in disarray. In short order Raglan, mightily displeased with the French, sent an aide away to give orders which might retrieve the situation. Ignoring the 7th Leger, the aide was told to head for the remnant of the 55th now rapidly reforming just to the rear of the point from which they had been driven.

The 55th were only a handful but they had been horribly embarrassed. Added to which, still standing on the spot where they had been overrun was Colonel Warren, untouched by the Russians who flowed around him and in a towering temper! There could be no better incentive for the 55th for they were under the eyes of Raglan and their furious brigade commander was waiting impatiently amongst the Russians to be rejoined by his men. Only a matter of minutes after they had been forced out, the 55th counter-attacked the parapet and, after a number of grisly combats where the bayonet was freely plied and officers used both swords and pistols, the Russians retreated. Indeed, it was in this fight that

Lieutenant-Colonel Daubeney was crossing swords with a Russian officer when a soldier of the Rifle Brigade dashed up and ran the Russian through with his bayonet saying, 'There you are, Sir!'[7] as he did so. The Russians did not go far, however, for they had tasted victory and they knew that there was plenty of support to hand with which to attack again.

In the centre of the Ridge, however, the rest of the Russian column still stood gazing down towards the remnants of the 2nd Division's camp. They were probably dazed by the effects of their own artillery and they must have been aware of the fate of their right when it was attacked by the 55th, for they were sufficiently supine to watch Egerton move his 200 or so men of the 77th directly across their front from west to east, halt, turn to their left, take their dressing and start a steady advance up the hill towards them. Having got themselves under control and seeing the example of the 77th to their left front, the 7th Leger joined in the advance although this time they moved in their more usual columns rather than the British-style line that they had previously tried to ape. They moved quickly and took ground to the right of the 77th, which meant that upwards of 1,100 Allied troops were now attempting to recapture the vital crestline. The Russians saw that they stood little chance of being able to resist such an attack and fell back from the parapet, allowing the 77th and 7th Leger to establish themselves just behind the crest of Home Ridge.

These troops, though, were only the vanguard of the powerful Iakoutsk column which was even now at the point of the Post road where the barrier lay. The outlying Russian columns, either by chance or design, had skirted around the barrier, the defenders of which now found themselves cut off to their rear, low on ammunition and facing a powerful and compact column. These men were, perhaps, 200-strong and made up of Captain Bellairs's remnants of three companies of the 49th, Vaughan's party of the 20th and elements of the Rifles, 95th and assorted guardsmen, and they were preparing to make a stand when a staff officer rode up and gave the command, 'Retire!' On seeing this '. . . as was natural, the men connected the words of the officer with the example he seemed to be giving them, and at once began to run.'[8] Bellairs took hold of the men, however, calmed them down, and ordered a measured withdrawal through the brush with those men who had ammunition stopping and firing. The little group could do little against such strength, however, and by moving so stubbornly they inadvertently helped the Russians whilst hindering them little for all the while that the British lay between the head of the column and the Ridge the guns could not fire.

As well as the guns, Bellairs and Vaughan were hampering the force that Pennefather had moved from the crest to a point some way down the forward slope of Home Ridge. When the 170 or so men of the 57th under Captain Inglis had withdrawn from their successful tussle with the Iakoutsk in the Quarry Ravine some time before, they had re-grouped behind the cover of the parapet on Home Ridge and then moved forward about 150 yards, halted and faced north-east. Pennefather's Headquarters was nearby and this style of meeting the enemy suited him admirably. So too did the approach of a captain of Zouaves, probably the commander of the party of sixty who had recaptured the three guns, who, with eyes alight with the fire of battle, asked Pennefather where he would like him to take post and what he would like the rest of the French forces who were present to do. Why the Zouave thought that he had the authority to deploy other French troops was entirely unclear to Pennefather, but he knew better than to question such enthusiasm and asked the Zouave to get the 7th Leger to come forward from behind the Ridge and form on the right of the Zouaves who, in turn, were to form on the right of the 57th. Much to everyone's amazement the 7th came forward in column and halted just as Pennefather had asked!

So, around 1,200 stood waiting for a column of about 2,000 some way forward of Home Ridge, but over three-quarters of that force were the 7th Leger, a young battalion which had already proved unsteady. In column, in normal circumstances, they would probably have opened fire at about 100 yards and continued file-firing and reloading so that a continuous ripple of fire would have struck the enemy. As it was, the mist prevented them from seeing 100 yards, and the first troops that appeared to their front were the defenders of the barrier who were moving very slowly and only a few yards in front of the approaching Russians.

Vaughan realised that his men were hampering the 7th and broke clean from the Iakoutsk and doubled his men round the right flank of the French. Bellairs, however, had to be told by an irritated French officer that his men were in the way – 'Mais retirez vous! Nous allons ouvrir!'[9] – before he moved them around to the left flank; but by causing this delay he provoked an emergency. The Russians were so close to the 7th when the first round was fired that the French found themselves deploying into file-fire formation as their enemies were near enough to charge with the bayonet. Despite the French rifle fire tearing into the Russians and causing heaps of bodies to build up as each round passed through more than one rank, the Iakoutsk came on whilst the French desperately tried to load their second volley. The firing stopped and Colonel Vaissier's inexperienced 7th Leger found themselves handling their ramrods within spitting distance of their foes. A seasoned battalion would have seized the moment and charged the dazed Iakoutsk before they had time to recover themselves, but the 7th were raw and they had already tasted panic.

The flanking companies began to give, crumbling away by ones and twos and filtering back to the shelter of the rear of the French centre. To their rear had formed up Bellairs's men on the left and Vaughan's men on the right, and for a while these men, growling their contempt, served to keep the French in place. The sight of the Russians was too much, however, and whilst the left of the French line responded to Pennefather and his staff riding up and down amongst them and appealing to their patriotism to stand and fight, the right began to give way. A knot of French and British officers sprang forward, caps raised on swords and tried to rally the 7th, but the Iakoutsk, no longer beset by fire, launched themselves at the French with a shriek of triumph.

Just as suddenly as the Russians started to advance, they stopped; something in their rear was amiss; the cheering ceased, soldiers began to look uncertainly over their shoulders and the charge halted in its tracks. This was precisely what the 7th needed, for the same officers who had leapt to the front still stood their ground and around them their troops began to rally. A voice from the rear yelled, 'Avancez, les tambours!'[10] and the pas de charge began to thunder out, stinging the 7th with its warlike tempo. The Iakoutsk's unease was caused by one of those anomalies with which the course of the battle was studded, for their rear was being attacked by only a handful of British troops, but a handful whose attack was so frenzied that it shook the whole regiment.

As Pennefather faced the Russian column and tried to get the 7th Leger to stand, he sent an aide back to the parapet on the crest behind which the remains of the 55th crouched to ask Lieutenant-Colonel Daubeney, 'Why don't you charge?'[11] Daubeney, still smarting from the indignity of the 55th's recent withdrawal needed no further prompting and, taking no more than thirty men with him, he set off over the breastwork obliquely down the hill. He chose as his target the second battalion of the Iakoutsk which was just in the process of wheeling to its right with a view, presumably, to putting itself in a position to enfilade the flank of Pennefather's little force. With no great finesse, the 55th lanced into the side of the column firing a little but mainly stabbing and hacking at the Russians, as Sergeant Walker, '. . . a fine, powerful man . . . distinguished himself greatly in the charge . . . using the butt end of his rifle with great effect'.[12] Some were wounded and some killed but the press of bodies was too great for weapons to be wielded to full effect, and eventually what remained of the thirty men of the 55th burst through on the eastern side of the Russian battalion.

The leading battalion, now close pressed by the French, had their confidence swept away by the din to their rear and, under renewed attacks from the 7th Leger, they began to give way. The British noticed how eager the French were to prove their prowess; all of them were shouting encouragement to one another and asking that their deeds should be noticed. The Zouaves were particularly keen to be praised; one British soldier, whilst busily reloading his rifle, was asked, 'Ah well, come, we French, you see now, we are good for something after all. Are we not?'[13] With the two, front, Russian battalions giving way the rear two followed suit, and soon the whole mass were being herded down into Quarry Ravine on the points of French and British bayonets.

The outer columns were still advancing, however, oblivious to the fate of their comrades in the centre. To the east, part of Pennecuick's Battery had been firing into the left-hand column with only limited results until Captain Yelverton, who was on horseback, approached and, having a better field of view from the saddle, told the gunners that they were firing too high. Jumping from his horse, he depressed one barrel himself, had the satisfaction of watching a round of canister tear into the Russians and then ordered the other guns to adjust their lay. Firing methodically, the guns cleared the Russian column most effectively, being helped considerably by the arrival of Boussinière with his horse artillery who deployed his men forward of the crest and harried the Russians all the way down into Quarry Ravine.

The column to the west was met by the 600 or so men of the 21st Fusiliers and the 63rd. The first volley that they delivered was bedevilled by the same damp powder that had affected almost everyone else, but slowly their muskets were made to fire and the whole column advanced obliquely across the field pushing through the brush that was particularly dense in that part. The Russians fought hard; their musketry was good and they were, from time to time, well supported by the guns on Shell Hill. The 63rd lost heavily amongst its officers: the commanding officer, Swyney, was knocked off his horse by a ball that killed him; his successor, Dalzell, was unhorsed; the adjutant and three captains were struck; and both ensigns were hit. Ensign Clutterbuck was remembered in a letter from Private George Evans:

'In the thick of it fell poor Mr Clutterbuck who was carrying the Queen's colour and cheering the men on. I think that the last words he said were "Come on 63rd!" then he received a shot right through the neck and died instantly. I never saw a braver man in the field that day'.[14]

Pushing the Russians down the hill, the 21st and 63rd realigned themselves on the Post Road having a particular tussle with their enemies at the barrier. The Russians held the earthwork from the north for a while but they were ejected with the bayonet and slowly edged right down to the point in the road where the British had cut a trench across it. Protected from the Russian guns by the steepness of East Jut, the men used the ditch for cover and fired hard at the Russians massing in the bottom of the ravine. Vaughan Lee again:

'Our Colonel got on his horse and said "Fusiliers, prepare to charge!"

Up we all got and gave a cheer and rushed through the brushwood (for it was all bush fighting) and down we went with fixed bayonets. Stephens was then struck in the arm by a grape shot. A sergeant took his colour from him; I still went on with my sword drawn in one hand and my pistol loosened in my holster . . . they pelted us with stones then ran off. We went on, men were falling on all sides of me and we saw the Russains retreating down the hill. We then saw five columns of the beggars advancing upon us, so we retired behind a breast-work.'[15]

The 'beggars' to whom Lee refers were the next columns of Russians to issue out of Quarry Ravine. The easterly column brushed against Colonel de Camas's 6th de Ligne which had been waiting stoically at the start of the Inkermann Tusk for some time. Colonel de Camas was mortally wounded (fulfilling Pennefather's hunch), the regimental standard bearer was struck and the eagle fell to the ground. The guns which Boussinière had brought forward would have been able to support the 6th, but many of their team-horses had been killed and they had had to be drawn back into cover, so the 6th fell back with little covering fire. Seeing this, their brigadier, Bourbaki, ordered the 7th Leger to move down from the slopes of Home Ridge and form alongside the 6th whilst he brought up a battery of guns in support, but it soon became clear that the French did not believe that they could hold their position without substantial reinforcements.

So it was that the party holding the forward trench on the Post Road were out-flanked to their right. Lieutenant-Colonel Haines of the 21st Fusiliers, now commanding this group, had realised that he could hold his forward position so long as his left flank was secure, and his men happily poured fire into the advancing Russians. Another column was soon forcing its way up on his left, however, and seeing that his position would soon be untenable, this little group of British who had got themselves into an impossibly forward position, began to fall back upon the barrier.

In overall command of this sector of the battle was Brigadier-General Goldie, commander of the 1st Brigade of the 4th Division. He busied himself someway to the rear of the barrier by banding together whatever wandering soldiers he could, organising ammunition supplies and trying to find reinforcements. He even sent back Major Ramsey Stuart of the 21st Fusiliers, the only remaining mounted officer who was not directly commanding troops, to '. . . send up the camp-guard or any other available men'[16] but few were found. The commander at the barrier, however, remained Haines. His little force was now beset time and again by Russian columns, the repulse of which must rate as one of the finest feats of arms of the whole battle. Haines tells the tale:

'At the Barrier, finding I was the senior officer, I at once busied myself in making the post secure . . . on the left I posted a small party of the 68th with an officer, under cover of a broken wall. Some of these men had Minie rifles, they were directed to fire deliberately on the Artillery on Shell Hill, and to observe any movement in that direction. We were subject to a very heavy cannonade, and were attacked frequently both by the road and the ravine, but no attempt was made on our left. After we had repulsed the first of these attacks, I asked Major Roper [sic] of the 1st Bn Rifle Brigade to report our position to General Pennefather, and to request support, as our ammunition was nearly expended. He begged me to send someone else as as he did not know the ground. I told him I would go myself and handed over the post to him as next senior officer . . . I had no difficulty in finding the General. I explained to him the state of the case, the importance of the post, our want of ammunition and our weakness in numbers.'[17]

Ammunition was provided but only one augmented company of the 77th could be spared. Under Lieutenant Acton the 77th marched off down the Post Road but were surprised to be told by Pennefather '. . . to go fast down the Post Road and shout as loud as they could'.[18] Unnecessary cheering and shouting was strongly discouraged in normal circumstances, but Pennefather wanted to give the impression of greater numbers so, somewhat bemused, the little column headed off into the fog yelling as hard as they could and, having been given the scantiest of orders, with very little idea of precisely where they headed. The din of shot and shell passing overhead was terrific, and when a column of Russians loomed up out of the ravine to the right and below Acton, he found himself having to bellow in the ear of the nearest soldier to get the Company to move as rapidly as possible into the comparative safety of the barrier. Their arrival, and soon after a company of the 49th under Lieutenant Astley, immensely cheered the defenders who had begun to fancy themselves forgotten and cut off.

Haines continues:

'This small reinforcement had the best effect, for it showed we were in communication with our own people and not cut off as the men were beginning to imagine . . . Brigadier-General Goldie . . . joined us here – I explained to him how we were posted, that I should like to visit the party on the left and that I would report to him in ten minutes. I found the party all snug, but no firing from it, it appeared that they had been so plied with grape in reply, that the officer in charge had ordered the firing to cease – in this he was right for the position was exposed and valuable merely as a lookout. On my return to the Barrier I found Brigadier-General Goldie mortally wounded'.[19]

Goldie had already had one horse shot from under him and this wound was to prove fatal; so Haines continued to defy the enemy as the fighting became desperate.

Vaughan Lee was in the thick of the fray;

'. . . from behind the breastwork we poured into the enemy showers of musket and Minie balls, for besides our own men we had some of the Rifles and other corps, and even some of the Guards . . . the Russians advanced to our work . . . we then rushed out with a cheer and charged the Russe, who then turned tail and fled double quick. We had again to retire, and this time poor Hurt was struck, and I was so done up I could not retire and fell struck down by a splinter of a stone. A sergeant took my arm and I was brought up and only escaped being made a prisoner by a few yards. I laid down under the breastwork, and when the Russians came up to within twenty yards of the place where I was lying, I gave the five barrels of my revolver with great gusto'.[20]

Haines saw Hurt struck down and an act of great bravery:

'When we retired from our advanced position on the road Mr Hurt was left for dead. Subsequently from the Barrier, Sergeant Higdon observed that he moved and asked my permission to bring him in. I gave it and Rutherford volunteered to accompany him. These two sergeants advanced under very heavy fire and brought in the young officer. I thought so highly of this act that I recommended Sergeant Higdon for the Victoria Cross'.[21]

Again and again the Russians came and each time they were met by fire and sometimes a charge as they tried to leave the narrow neck of Quarry Ravine. The defence of the barrier was an epic every bit as bloody and hard contested as that of the Sandbag Battery; the difference was that the actions of Haines and his men made perfect, tactical sense and every drop of blood that was shed here was shed for good reason.

At about half-past nine the only original order that Raglan had given in the battle so far came to fruition. Seeing the Russians' superiority in artillery he had ordered two 18-pound guns to be brought up from the Siege Train. How the first order had been misdirected and valuable time lost has already been explained, but as soon as word arrived at the gun-park, the two guns were in motion for such a directive had been anticipated. These long, iron guns each weighed 42 hundredweight and 150 men were harnessed up to drag them and their ammunition into place. The men toiled over the broken ground, eager to get to the fight and Colonel Gambier, who led them, pressed into service every horse that he came across as they advanced, thus speeding up the excruciatingly slow progress of the guns over the difficult terrain. As the guns approached Home Ridge they immediately attracted fire and Colonel Gambier was struck from his horse. Colonel Collingwood Dickson took command, and he and another officer cantered forward to try to select fire positions on Home Ridge.

They carefully selected a point right on the bend between Home and Fore Ridge which faced Shell Hill and where a small, thick bank, about two foot high, had been constructed with gabions and sandbags, the beginnings of a gun position. Three field guns were rapidly withdrawn from this point and the two 18-pounders were quickly in position and as quickly drawing fire. Their first round fell short but the second ripped into a Russian battery and the range was found. All of the Russian guns that could be spared now fired on the two guns and the shot fell thickly around them furrowing the ground and showering all with earth, pelting the men with branches and twigs cut by the projectiles as they tore through the undergrowth and hitting horses, ammunition boxes and men without discrimination. In the first quarter of an hour seventeen men were hit, but as one fell so he was immediately replaced.

The effect of these guns was remarkable, for the Russians had mostly 12-pounders but also several 32-pound howitzers amongst the ninety or so guns which were still in action on Shell Hill. Yet the British weapons were striking gun after gun on the heights opposite them whilst both of them remained untouched. The Russian fire was certainly accurate, but many rounds struck the little bank behind which the guns and their detachments sheltered, and whilst a 32-pound shell would '. . . tear itself into fragments and send them crying for blood with their harsh, grating, truculent "scrisht" – the most hated of all battle sounds',[22] the British guns continued to fire. Shell Hill was marginally higher than Home Ridge so many of the Russian guns were skylined to the British, but the fact remained that the 18-pounder was a longer range gun, able to hit harder than anything that the Russians had. The Russian artillery was firing almost at the limit of its capability and furthermore, the British gunners were fresh whilst the Russians were not. Not only had the Russians been hard at it since the beginning of the engagement, they had all seen action before, either on the Danube, at the Alma or in subsequent battles. Having had a gruelling approach march, having seen their infantry constantly repulsed, having been under perpetual fire and then being the target of accurate fire from heavier guns being handled by fresh gunners, their resolve began to give.

In the second fifteen minutes of the action, British casualties became fewer and the 18-pounders began to get the upper hand. The Russian fire started to slacken and Boussinière brought forward twelve heavy guns on to the crest to thicken up the fire of the British. Until now the Russians had been able to dominate the artillery battle with guns that they seldom had to move; some had been struck, but on the whole, they had fired with relative impunity from positions from which they had been able to gauge the range and stick to their lay. Now they had to move or be hit; with movement came a lessening of fire; and with a lessening of fire came a crisis of confidence.

By failing to break the stranglehold that the tired and rapidly diminishing British exercised on the exits from the ravines, Dannenberg lost an opportunity to reach his goal. Perhaps if he had thrown his plentiful reserves into the fray he could have broken through, though the ground was choked with the numbers already involved. Perhaps if he had used the sixteen fresh battalions rather than those which had already been in action then he might have succeeded. That said, it is impossible to criticise the bravery of the Russian troops used over the last hour and a half, particularly the gallant Iakoutsk who attacked time and again. Perhaps if he had massed his artillery against a specific point instead of using it piecemeal or tried to get it farther forward, making use of the lighter pieces' mobility he might have enjoyed more success. He had now lost his chance, however, for the French were on the move in strength and their arrival, so long delayed by the feints and sallies from Sevastopol and on the flanks, was now imminent. But it is easy to identify such a point in a battle in retrospect; it is simple now to say that Dannenberg would have done better to cut his losses and get back to Sevastopol whilst he could, or perhaps he should have dug in where he was, held the ground that he had gained and waited for orders.

None of this accounts for the ghastly confusion of this particular battlefield, however – the difficult, unknown ground, the noise, the lack of communication as more and more officers and gallopers became casualties and, above all, the caprices of the smoke-thickened fog which allowed a commander to see everything one minute and almost nothing the next. Fifty or so years before, the great military theorist, Clausewitz, had described such unpredictable battlefield factors as 'friction'. Here Clausewitz's 'friction' was writ large and the circumstances of this battle made both sides, as we have seen, more than usually vulnerable to it. Whilst it would be wrong to credit the Allied command, and the British in particular, with any great tactical acumen, they at least had commitment. The circumstances under which Dannenberg had been sent into battle were far from ideal and now, having missed one opportunity, he simply did what he understood best – he battered away at the same obstacles as the Allies brought more and more men and guns to resist him. It was now ten o'clock.

*　　*　　*

Notes

1. Kinglake, vol V, p316
2. *ibid*, p324
3. *ibid*, p325
4. Lee, Letters, p18
5. *ibid*, p23
6. Kinglake, vol V, p331
7. Hume, p72
8. Kinglake, vol V, p342
9. *ibid*, p344
10. *ibid*, p350
11. Hume, p72
12. *ibid*, p73
13. Kinglake, vol V, p353
14. Slack, p72
15. Lee, Letters, p23
16. Haines Mss, p3
17. *ibid*, p4
18. Kinglake, vol V, p368
19. Haines Mss, p5
20. Lee, Letters, p25
21. Haines Mss, p6
22. Kinglake, vol V, p375

Chapter X

'. . . save your guns, all is lost!'
Lost Opportunities

The extra French who were rapidly approaching the field of battle were led by Bosquet himself. With him were further troops of Bourbaki's Brigade, namely 450 men of three companies of Chasseurs à Pied, whilst 2nd Algerian Battalion and 2nd Battalion of the 3rd Zouaves, both regiments of D'Autemarre's Brigade, a further 1,500 men, were hot on their heels. Some little way behind this group were several squadrons of British and French cavalry, whilst to their rear but marching hard towards the sound of the guns came D'Autemarre himself with the 2,300 infantry (1st Battalion 3rd Zouaves and two battalions of the 50th de Ligne) that remained of his Division and an additional artillery battery. So, Bosquet would be able to face the Russians immediately with, if the 6th de Ligne and the 7th Leger were included, over 3,000 infantry and, if he waited for D'Autemarre to arrive, a powerful, all-arms force of over 5,000. Had Dannenberg known that these fresh troops were about to arrive, his withdrawal might have been understandable. As it was, his continued attacks can only have been based on one of two things, a cool assessment of Allied fighting power and high expectations of a French mistake, or tactical ineptitude that would not readily admit defeat.

With the Russian artillery tamed by the two 18-pounders the field had fallen relatively quiet with the only noise of sustained battle now coming from the fog-wrapped barrier. Bosquet therefore should have had time to dispose his troops carefully around the field based on the advice of those who had been fighting there for the last four hours or so. Full account, though, has not yet been taken of the doings of Bourbaki and his two regiments, the 6th de Ligne and the 7th Leger. We left them falling back together from the plateau of land that leads on to the narrow top of the Inkermann Spur with less fire support than they might have wished. Neither regiment had proved particularly resilient in the face of the enemy and, despite the fact that they were not yet under serious attack, the lack of artillery support was such an article of faith to the French that panicky messages began to filter back to Bosquet. Kinglake recounts that:

'An officer of the French staff – bare-headed and extending his naked sword in the air – came galloping back . . . vehemently asking for Bosquet, said his people were turned by the movement made on their flank and declared that unless they could be supported – nay, supported by two or three regiments – they must be again falling back'.[1]

Such a message would have lent wings to Bosquet's feet and caused him to press forward urgently without seeking British guidance. When he came within sight of Home Ridge, however, he must have expected to see the battle raging with his own troops alongside ranks of hard-pressed British. Instead, the arena was almost subdued with small knots of British lying behind the breastwork on the Ridge – some even asleep, stretcher-bearers and others helping the wounded to the rear and some wandering back to their camps in the search for more cartridges. The history of the French 2nd Division points out that Bosquet '. . . vit tout le terrain en avant de la droite des Anglais évacué par nos Allies; il n'y avait plus d'occupé que la crête qui précède de vingt pas le premier rang des tentes.'[2] With such a sight before him and Bourbaki's worrying message in his mind, Bosquet committed the same mistake that the British had done before him, for he chose to secure what he believed to be the wide-open right flank by counter-attacking the Sandbag Battery!

The Russian column which had forced the two French battalions to fall back had, in its turn, ceased to push forward as support from their guns on Shell Hill lessened once the 18-pounders came into play. Two further columns were now just beginning to emerge from Quarry Ravine, and their skirmishers were forcing what remained of Colonel Horn's men of the 20th back up the slope when the 450 Chasseurs came rushing down the slope and formed up to block the advancing Russians. On reaching Home Ridge, Bosquet had ordered Bourbaki to return to the offensive immediately and sent the Chasseurs down to clear the Sandbag Battery. The Chasseurs, however, had seen a better target in the shape of these new Russian phalanxes and had sheered off to the left of the Kitspur to meet this threat; here they now stood with the 20th on their left preventing the Russians from coming any farther. The two bodies exchanged fire for some little while with the British doing what they could with those few rounds that were available to them. Colonel Horn soon fell wounded, however, and shortly afterwards the Chasseurs broke off the fight and moved away to their right apparently following orders to return to their original course farther to the right of the Kitspur. This move was executed as the Russians had temporarily fallen back to re-group, leaving only a few files of the 20th to face another onslaught. None materialised, however, and the 20th clung to their lonely post waiting for the next move.

*   *   *

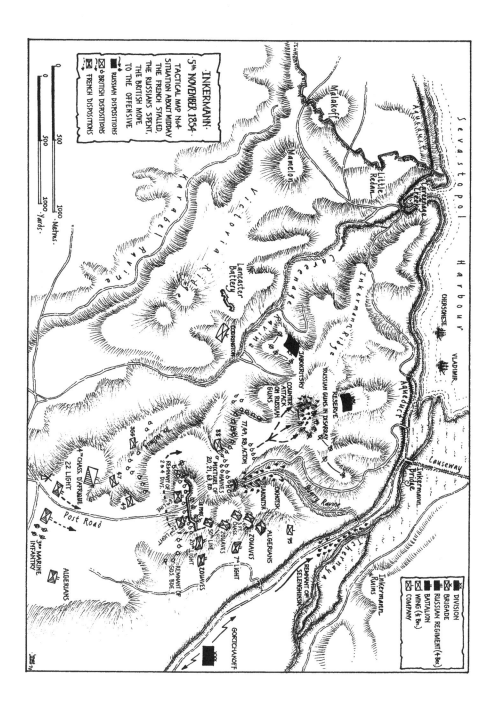

151

The 20th did not have long to wait, however, for Bosquet had meanwhile lined up over 3,000 infantry supported by twenty guns and several squadrons of cavalry on the right of the Post Road. With the artillery battle now being won, Bosquet could have chosen to launch these fresh troops wholesale against an enemy that was proving less and less willing to stand. Instead, he sent forward less than two battalions and deployed them in a way that betrayed his complete lack of understanding of what had happened in the battle so far. So, leaving some companies behind in reserve, 2nd Battalion 3rd Zouaves under Dubos and the Algerians under Colonel Wimpfen headed off down the slopes of Fore Ridge picking up the Chasseurs on the way. They advanced with much excited drumming and bugling with the Zouaves' '. . . vivandière gaily moving in her pretty costume fit alike for a dance or a battle, and . . . not . . . minded to loiter whilst taking her lads into battle',[3] sweeping past the 20th on to the slopes of the Inkermann Tusk.

Today the Tusk is a remarkable piece of ground, a great chalk finger sticking out jaggedly with steep ravines on either side that give way to sheer cliffs and culminate in a drop from the edge of which one can look straight across the Tchernaya valley. In 1854 it would have been little different except that it would have been surrounded by swirling mist that might have hidden the fact from someone who did not know the ground well that the only way off the Tusk was to retrace one's steps back the way that you had come. Once on the flat top of the Tusk the French began to attract fire from East Jut which, as the crow flies, is less than 500 yards from where the French stood and within easy shot. Bosquet and his small escort rode off to the left, perhaps to link up with the British whom they imagined to be there, but instead they met a column of that most persistent regiment, the Iakoutsk. At first the French thought that the grey-coated columns were British, but quickly recovering and summoning six of Boussinière's guns, Bosquet covered his own withdrawal, but not before the Iakoutsk had fallen upon one of the guns, driven off the other five and found themselves partially blocking the end of the Tusk which the French would have to use to escape.

As the French saw Russian troops to their left so they began to be fired at from their rear by elements of the Selenghinsk, who had been probing up from the Tchernaya valley towards the Sandbag Battery for some time. The Selenghinsk had realised that if they ignored the Battery and placed themselves farther forward on the Kitspur, then the French could easily be brought under fire. So, things were beginning to get uncomfortable for Bosquet's men with musket balls coming from their rear and their exit route blocked, but they were saved by the inertia that so beset the Russians at critical moments. First, the Iakoutsk had failed to close with Bosquet when he and his group were surprised and only a few yards from the nearest Russians. Indeed, Bosquet was under the impression that the Iakoutsk were more inclined to salute him than to attack, so over-awed were they by an officer of high rank, albeit an enemy one! Now they had the opportunity, with their guns firing in support from East Jut, to hem the French in on the Tusk, push them towards a sheer drop and destroy them piecemeal or simply accept their surrender. So narrow a front could the French have presented on the top of the Tusk, which is only about 150 yards across at its widest point, that little fire could be brought to bear with the French herded into a target so dense that the Russian guns would have found it impossible to miss.

The Iakoutsk dithered, however, and, Zouaves leading, Bosquet's troops extricated themselves from a very ugly situation by skirting along the eastern edge of the Tusk which the Russians had not yet blocked. The whole lot doubled up towards the crest of Home Ridge as quickly as they could in an attempt to get under the cover of Boussinière's guns, but their withdrawal proved infectious. The 6th de Ligne and the 7th Leger had seen what had befallen Bosquet's men and had taken themselves back to the shelter of the south side of Home Ridge, out of direct artillery fire and some way to the left of the Post Road, so negating any support that they might have given to their forward regiments.

So the French found themselves everywhere in retreat; to add to their misfortunes the Zouaves' sutler, or vivandière, had been killed and, much more importantly, Boussinière's guns had started to take heavy casualties. In no small measure this was due to the fact that the initial panic amongst the Russian artillery, caused by the British 18-pounders, had begun to subside as the gunners found positions that were less vulnerable to their fire. Also, the 18-pounders' rate of fire had slackened somewhat as ammunition began to dwindle. To add to Boussinière's difficulties, his guns had occupied a very cramped position on the forward slope of Fore Ridge and they now began to pay the price as men, horses, limbers and tumbrils started to be hit. Boussinière, with incredible sang froid, remarked to Collingwood Dickson, 'We are getting massacred; well, after all, this is war'![4] Under increasingly heavy fire, though, he had to withdraw or lose his guns and, moving one battery to the right to deal with any eventualities there, he took the other battery off to the left of the Ridge to an apparently less vulnerable position.

Canrobert, the French commander-in-chief had now arrived on Home Ridge in person and, to restore a situation that must, on the surface, have appeared dire he took the unusual step of committing the cavalry which had come up with the other reinforcements. These troops were the 4th Regiment of Chasseurs D'Afrique, the regiment which had so distinguished itself at Balaklava, and following behind them were the remnants of the British Light Cavalry Brigade, about 200 in number. Despite the fact that the Chasseurs D'Afrique were more used than most to riding across rough and broken ground, to use them on the sort of terrain that the field of Inkermann presented was almost an act of desperation; it was most unlikely to be successful and demonstrates how serious Canrobert must have thought the situation to be.

As they picked their way across the slopes, however, a Russian shell burst near one of the squadrons and the whole regiment retired at speed from the field only re-forming once they had reached a point just north of the Windmill. Some way to the rear of the Chasseurs D'Afrique rode the shadow of what had once been the Light Cavalry Brigade commanded this day by Lord George Paget in the absence of Lord Cardigan who had yet to emerge from his yacht in Balaklava harbour. As the French cavalry moved off, Paget had received a most precise message from Canrobert that great importance would be attached to the support of the British light horse. Somewhat nonplussed by the fact that a 200-strong cadre of what had once been five, magnificent regiments could be needed with such urgency, Paget nonetheless set out to support those who had supported him so gallantly on 25 October. The advance of the Chasseurs caused Paget to take his men forward, and they soon began to feel the effect of the Russian artillery, losing five killed and as many wounded in a very short space of time. Seeing that the ground was utterly unsuitable for his troops but determined, nevertheless, to advance behind the French, Paget was mightily relieved when the French quit the field. Thus the Light Cavalry Brigade were able to leave this scrimmage with no further, useless sacrifice and with their honour intact.

So French infantry, guns and now cavalry had suffered reversals and, despite the fact that they had taken no serious numbers of casualties, they seem to have convinced themselves in a very short space of time that they and their Allies were now on the point of defeat. Indeed, one French officer rode up to Colonel Dickson, who was overseeing the firing of his 18-pounders, and told him, 'My officer, save your guns, all is lost!'[5] Dickson had other ideas and continued banging away, much to the bemusement of the Frenchman who, after several more attempts to make Dickson see sense, rode away bemoaning the loss of the British guns which he now believed to be inevitable!

The French distress must have been based on the fact that they believed their enemies would react to their disarray in the same way that they would. Canrobert could see no formed bodies of British troops that would protect his men from the Russian advance that must now be on the point of looming out of the fog, his guns had had to withdraw and his last trump card, the cavalry, had proved useless. All of this fear, however, was based upon the logical reactions of a fresh, numerous and vigorous enemy that was trained to use its initiative and to seize opportunities. There can be no doubt that with only the British artillery and those men who fought around the barrier to oppose him, and with French morale on the point of breaking, Dannenberg now had the opportunity to deal one decisive blow that would shatter the French and drive them from the field which, perforce, must lead to the collapse of the British.

The fact that Dannenberg did little to follow up the withdrawal of the French is easy to criticise, for he certainly missed a great opportunity to confirm the fears of the French and finish the battle. But those columns which had moved up on to the Tusk ran out of drive and melted back into Quarry Ravine under the fire of the French guns and there was no further attempt to exploit the situation. Nevertheless, the question has to be asked, did Dannenberg even know that there was an opportunity to be taken? To his front the barrier was resisting manfully and, even if there had been a slackening of fire, the 18-pound guns continued to punish his artillery. With the possible exception of the duel between his guns and those of Boussinière, there had been no marked combat with his troops from which messages would have returned telling Dannenberg that he was gaining ground. Furthermore, the significance of the capture of one gun and the incident with the Iakoutsk on the Tusk would probably have been missed.

History is littered with examples of one side feeling that they have been spared from the pursuit of their enemies by virtue either of skill or good fortune whilst their foes have, in reality, read the situation very differently and attached little importance to it. So it was with the French at Inkermann; Dannenberg's men had already fought long and hard against determined foes and the incidents that made the French flee were, to them, unremarkable. French reinforcements had responded to messages of near panic and reached the battlefield expecting to find disaster at hand; a bad mistake had been made and, despite their deliverance with few casualties, defeat had become a self-fulfilling prophesy. In the circumstances, Dannenberg would have to have been a remarkable and highly intuitive commander to know what an opportunity had presented itself.

As the British continued at their business apparently unconcerned, and as Dannenberg failed to pursue his unwitting success, French morale began to recover. It was helped by the arrival of over 2,300 men of D'Autemarre's Brigade namely, 1st Battalion 3rd Zouaves and both battalions of 50th de Ligne with whom Bosquet determined to retrieve the situation by making '. . . a supreme effort'.[6] Keeping the fresh troops in reserve on the Ridge, the Zouaves under Dubos and Wimpfen's Algerians were launched at the Selenghinsk in the Sandbag Battery, both regiments, despite their recent experiences, returning to the offensive with great dash. A number of British troops who had been waiting for such a moment amongst the brushwood now emerged from their lairs and joined the advance. Wilson and what remained of his

Coldstreamers appeared like wraiths from the brush on the slopes of the Kitspur and attached themselves to the Zouaves; similarly, Carmichael of the 95th, now with no more than a few British of mixed regiments around him joined in. He recollects that

> '. . . the French bugles rang out the charge and a battalion of the Algerian Indigènes in column advanced at the double close to where I was standing. A big black or negro with his musket held in the middle, and high over his head led the column by some paces waving his weapon in the air. The French officers and N. C. officers were all shouting 'En avant, en avant'. I advanced with the Indigènes who charged into the Battery, and drove out the enemy. A French officer jumping on the parapet, and waving a tricolour flag for a few minutes. The Indigènes swept down into the ravine, where I did not at first go, thinking it possible that the same incident might happen to them as had befallen us'.[7]

Both regiments pushed the Russians before them just as the British had done earlier, but this time there was no sign of their being cut off, despite Carmichael's understandable fears. In the bottom of the gorge waited another body of British who had quietly remained well in advance of the rest of their own troops where they had been marooned after their own downhill pursuit. Captains Vialls and Sargent with about 100 men of the 95th had disappeared into the brush and stayed undiscovered there whilst column after column of Russians had trudged around them up the slopes towards the Kitspur. It seemed that they were now discovered and they were just preparing to sell their lives dearly when the Russians were distracted and then began to fall back around them as fast as they could go. The Zouaves were approaching fast; they had their blood up and were eagerly pursuing their adversaries down the glens when they came upon this group of British. One of the Zouaves patted a 95th soldier on the back and in excellent English told him, 'There! it's our turn now: you go to the rear: you have had your share!' Sargent noted that '. . . the accent and address of the Zouave were such as to show that he must have been an educated Englishman'.[8] Without stopping to consider this oddity further, he led the little group back to Home Ridge.

The attack by the Zouaves and Algerians had the effect of finally ridding the battlefield of the tenacious Selenghinsk. Against much smaller numbers of now thoroughly battle-weary troops, the French enjoyed rather more success than the British had done when they pursued the Russians off the Kitspur and down into the valleys. The Selenghinsk were allowed no respite and their pursuers only called off the chase once the Russians had split into many fleeing groups once they had reached the other side of the aqueduct which ran across the bottom of St Clement's Ravine. Utterly routed, the Selenghinsk were to fight no more on 5 November.

The launching of these two regiments was meant to be accompanied by the advance of the 6th de Ligne and 7th Leger whom Bosquet had ordered to advance with the rest of Bourbaki's brigade as part of the 'Supreme Effort'. In fact, neither regiment did anything more than move a couple of hundred yards down the Post Road and halt some way in the rear of the barrier where Haines's men continued to protect the Allied centre against repeated assaults where Russian bodies were now '. . . lying 4 and 5 deep as every shot told on their enormous columns.' The strain on these few men must have been considerable as Vaughan Lee continues:

> 'Haines and I were the only two officers at that work, the rest being either killed or wounded, and we only escaped by the providence of God, for indeed it was a fearful sight to see so many brave men falling around one. I was covered with blood from a man about three quarters of a yard from me whose brains were dashed out by a round shot.'[9]

In fact, the forward movement of the 6th de Ligne and the 7th Leger marked a distinct change in the tempo of the battle for once Bosquet's troops were drawn in, Canrobert took stock of the situation alongside Lord Raglan. As he was deliberating, further French reinforcements were arriving in the shape of three new battalions under de Monet. This brought the total French strength up to over 7,000 infantry of whom rather fewer than 5,000 were completely fresh and ready to be launched into the fight. Canrobert's position was enviable, for with the fire of the Russian artillery waning fast and no sign of Dannenberg's reserves being brought forward, with the British holding firm and newly supplied with rifle cartridges and gun ammunition, and with those Russians who were at the forefront of the fighting having been under fire for over six hours, the conditions were perfect for victory to be clinched. It was eleven o'clock and Canrobert's hour had arrived.

Canrobert had been lightly wounded by shrapnel in the arm, and whilst his wound was being dressed, Raglan sent one of his aides-de-camp away to Pennefather to see how things stood with him. The aide, Captain Somerset Calthorpe, found Pennefather in bouyant mood for he had detected a lessening of Russian fire whilst their infantry's probing attacks were losing their sting; his experience told him that the moment had now come for an opportunity to be seized. Calthorpe returned to the little knot of commanders and reported that Pennefather had said that if he were reinforced he could win the fight with the Russians and 'Lick them to the devil!'. This boast obviously appealed to Canrobert who exclaimed, 'What a brave fellow! What a brave man! What a good general!',[10] but Raglan unwittingly spoilt things by asking Pennefather to come forward in person and present himself to Canrobert, presumably with a view to impressing his ally even more with his aggressive intentions and the need for French reinforcements to carry them out.

Pennefather arrived beaming confidence and Raglan asked him what forces he had left at his disposal. Raglan cannot have wanted the precise answer that he got for Pennefather had just been told by Colonel Daubeney of the 55th, now commanding the 1st Brigade of Pennefather's Division, that the Brigade alone could muster over 750 men. It would have suited Raglan better to get a vague but confident and encouraging answer that could make it seem that the British held the position comfortably rather than with a handful of weary troops. Canrobert, however, had already been bested despite his thousands of fresh troops and that all important arm, his artillery, had been mauled. Furthermore, with the exception of Pennefather, nothing that he had seen of his Allies so far had convinced him that they were in a position to support him. He must have thought the British horribly over-confident and his enthusiasm rapidly waned from that moment on with the French infantry and cavalry taking no further aggressive part in the battle.

They held Home Ridge, the Sandbag Battery and the upper slopes of the Kitspur securely, trying long shots with their rifles whilst their gunners battled on manfully against their opponents on Shell Hill, but advance to clinch victory they would not. Indeed, French official sources claim that the battle all but ended once the French arrived: 'Depuis l'arrivée des francais le Lt.-général Dannenberg s'est décidé de battre en retraîte. A partir de onze heures, ses troupes n'ont 'fait aucun mouvement offensif. Le combat a continué de loin à coups de fusil et à coups de canon'.[11]

The truth was rather different, for on Shell Hill Dannenberg had no intention of retreating. Certainly, the Russians had gone from offence to defence for everything that they had tried had been thwarted; but the fact remained that they were still in possession of a very considerable chunk of ground that dominated the Allies' north-eastern flank. If he could not break through the British defences and sweep down onto the plateau to join up with Gortchakoff, then he could at least hold his ground and wait for Gortchakoff to draw off the Allies. If he husbanded his resources then he might still be in a position to attack the British and French in the flank as they responded to Gortchakoff's sally from the Balaklava plain. Further to this, Menshikov's despatch after the battle on 6 November makes interesting reading for he states:

'The siege artillery of the latter [the British] was placed in position on the field of battle, and it was not possible for our field-artillery to contend against them with advantage. The superiority of the enemy's long-range rifles occasioned heavy losses amongst the horses and men of the artillery. This circumstance did not admit of our completing, without a great sacrifice of life, the redoubts which we had commenced during the fight upon the points which commanded the enemy's position, with the intention of connecting them with the works of the town of Sevastopol.'[12]

Just like Federoff's sortie of 26 October, most of the Russian infantry had arrived on the field carrying sappers' long-handled digging tools rather than the shorter ones that they had for immediate use. Also, a number of regiments had carried gabions up to Shell Hill, although these were soon abandoned when the mobile nature of the fight became obvious. However, nowhere in Menshikov's orders is there mention of any intention to fortify Shell Hill, nor, after the battle, was there very much evidence found that the Russians had tried to dig in. Despite this, the holding of Shell Hill and its incorporation into Sevastopol's defences as a post both to harass the Allies and to protect the Sapper Road makes perfect sense and fits with the plan on 26 October. Whether it really was at the core of what Menshikov intended or whether it was simply wishful thinking in the wake of the defeat of the day before will never be known, but inactivity on the part of the Allies was now precisely what Dannenberg needed if he were to consolidate his position.

Something of a lull now spread across the field as the French took stock, the Russians changed tack and the British came to realise that further efforts would be needed from troops that had already been fought to a standstill if the Russians were not to be left unmolested in possession of Shell Hill. The lull was accentuated by a lessening of fire from the mighty 18-pounders which had at last come to the dregs of the first batch of ammunition with which they arrived. It was to demand superhuman efforts of Captain Chermside to bring up another hundred rounds for both of the guns over appallingly difficult ground, and in the meantime both fell silent. In fact, other than for the sporadic fire of the lighter guns, the field was calm except for the one spot where the battle ground on relentlessly. The barrier was the area with which the Russians still had difficulty, for at first it had merely blocked their way to the approaches to Home Ridge and had to be cleared. Having failed to achieve this, however, it now threatened the security of Shell Hill as a defensive position for it was at the toe of the ground that the Russians had seized and, whilst it remained in the hands of their enemies, the position could never be properly secure. To eradicate it the Russians continued to throw column after column at it, and as often as they came Haines and his men repulsed them bloodily.

* * *

Throughout the day parties of troops, sometimes formed, sometimes not, had been trickling forward to the barrier in response to the continuing roar of battle there. On the left of the position, amidst the scrub, those armed with Minie rifles had orders to snipe specifically at the Russian gunners and they had been enjoying considerable success. Now, as the 18-pounders thundered into action again with their fresh ammunition, the Russian artillerymen began to suffer anew. But with enormous fortitude and total dedication to their task, the Russians limbered up, moved to new positions, unlimbered and came into action to be greeted immediately by 18-pound rounds or the bullets of the riflemen in the valley below. After the battle it was remarked how many of the dead gunners' mouths were full of earth and grass having literally 'bitten the dust' as they died. It was a phenomenon that was explained by Kinglake thus

'. . . this muscular action is apt to occur when a man has been arrested by death in the act of strenuous bodily exertion; and no doubt an artilleryman whilst hotly engaged, and vehemently serving his gun, must in general be much harder at work than an infantry soldier busied with his firelock'.[13]

As the guns thundered on, the French held back and the British commanders tried to decide what to do. In a way that was typical of this mighty battle, the key to victory was already being turned by the regimental officers and the little party of infantry that held the barrier. Some days before the battle Haines and his fellow major from the 21st Fusiliers, Lord West, had chosen to roam all over the Inkermann position expecting that it would sometime be the scene of an onslaught such as the one in which they were both now engaged. As the 21st Fusiliers had come forward, Lord West's wing had been detailed off to guard the top of the Mikriakoff Glen against any further attacks such as that tried by Soimonoff earlier in the battle and things had been fairly quiet for them despite the fact that they were only about 400 yards away from where the other wing of the 21st battled under Haines at the barrier. Almost at the same time that Haines realised that his riflemen's fire was beginning to tell against the Russian batteries, and that the time might now be right to try to exploit the situation, so West came to the same conclusion. Leaving the Mikriakoff Glen, West moved over to Lieutenant Acton and his fifty or so men of the 77th and told him to gather the remnants of two other companies of different regiments that were nearby and attack the westernmost battery on Shell Hill which was currently firing in his general direction.

The orders given to Acton were specific enough: he was to capture the battery or drive it off. Accordingly, he moved his men into the gap in the scrub between the other two companies and called for their officers telling them, 'If you will attack the battery on either flank, I'll do so in front'. The plan appealed to neither, however, and they refused to entertain the idea, saying that the little force was not strong enough. Acton was quite clear in his resolve, however, and said, 'If you won't join me, I'll obey my orders and attack with the 77th!' Sadly, the 77th, who had already seen more than their share of fighting that day, also declined to join him. Saying, 'Then I'll go by myself!', Acton set off alone up the slope. The effect was precisely what Acton wanted, however, for first Private James Tyrrell sprang forward exclaiming, 'Sir, I'll stand by you!'[14], then another soldier from one of the other companies followed his example, and for a few moments the lonely trio trudged up the hill together. The spectacle was too much for the 77th, and soon all of them were fast in pursuit of their leader who rapidly organised them into three parties under sergeants and sent them at the run against the Russian guns. As the 77th led the way the other two companies took their courage in both hands and followed on both flanks some little distance behind.

Simultaneously, Haines at the barrier had discerned the same signs.

'Feeling strong and that the enemy was becoming decidedly weak, an aggressive movement seemed feasible. The men armed with the Minie were collected and placed under the command of Lieutenant Astley of the 49th who had orders to advance in skirmishing order through the brushwood towards the artillery posted on Shell Hill, and harass the gunners as much as possible. I have always ascribed the retreat of these batteries and the abandonment of eight ammunition waggons to the very efficient and enterprising manner in which the duty was carried out. I had wished to attack the artillery on Shell Hill in such force as to ensure the capture of the Batteries, but my proposal was disapproved of, and I contented myself with sending out Major Horsford with part of the 1st Bn Rifle Brigade to support and reinforce Lieutenant Astley – this he did, taking up the ground as the enemy retired and securing the trophies abandoned by them.'[15]

Haines's account tells only part of the story, for as his men advanced with those despatched by Lord West, so the fire of the 18-pounders switched to the batteries that this mixed and disjointed force of perhaps 300 was now attacking. Certainly, the rifle fire of the approaching infantry would have galled the Russian gunners, but the telling factor would have been the round shot of the 18-pounders which howled over the heads of Acton, Astley, Horsford and their men and tore into their enemies. By the time that the infantry reached the crest there was little to be seen beyond dead and dying horses and men, one dismounted gun, smashed limbers and the ammunition waggons already mentioned. So British infantry found themselves in the heart of the Russians' gun-line on the crest of Shell Hill – the very ground which all the blood of the last few hours had bought. For Dannenberg there could now be only two courses of action open to him: run or counter-attack.

Coming as this blow did hard on the heels of all the disasters of the morning and as something of a surprise as the fresh, French troops – from whom an assault might have been expected – remained inactive on the slopes opposite, Dannenberg's resolve suddenly crumbled. Without even consulting Menshikov (who was a little over 500 yards away to his right rear in company with the two young Grand Dukes), Dannenberg gave the order to break off and retreat. He still had plentiful reserves that were untouched by battle and a counter-attack against the paltry British force now on Shell Hill would certainly have succeeded in retrieving the situation, but Dannenberg was hardly likely to be in the calmest frame of mind as he found his precious guns in danger of being overrun. Throughout the day he had met nothing but defeat, whilst all around him his staff and regimental officers had become casualties. Indeed, the majority of Russian officers in the field that day were now either dead or wounded, and Dannenberg himself had had two horses shot from under him. Furthermore, he had waited in vain for help from Gortchakoff as his infantry suffered most horribly, and now that most prized of Russian arms, the artillery, was threatened by a handful of men who simply would not give up. The whole affair must have seemed grossly unfair to Dannenberg as he stared the imminent loss of guns in the face and listened to the shriek of the 18-pounders that had pulverised his own much larger artillery force. Human nature could stand only so much, and the moment had come to save his loyal and brave men from further sacrifice; he directed that the batteries that had taken the worst punishment should be withdrawn first.

To cover the withdrawal of the forward troops the Sousdal and Vladimir Regiments were ordered up, whilst a further eight of the battalions that had been kept in reserve were told to support the lighter batteries that were not to move until the heavier guns had got away. Once the Sousdal and Vladimir battalions were far enough forward on Shell Hill so the remains of the eight battalions of the stalwart Iakoutsk and Okhotsk Regiments were to move out of Quarry Ravine and away from the field upon which they had handled themselves so well. So it was that at about one o'clock the Russians began to withdraw and the battle was effectively won.

Baron Del'vig, the Russian brigade commander who was ordered to cover the withdrawal from Shell Hill, interpreted his task in a rather more aggressive fashion than might have been expected, for the Vladimir Regiment were thrown forward into a spirited counter-attack. From the

British gun-position on Home Ridge most of the Russian artillery had been seen to start withdrawing and their fire slackened accordingly. Horses, men and limbers were busy about the guns and a general movement away from the fight had become evident when, suddenly through the fog, a mass of over 2,000 infantry were seen to be moving down the forward slopes of Shell Hill at a smart pace. Quite what impelled the Vladimir is unclear, but their advance against hopeless odds may have had a lot to do with the reputation that had been built around them after the Alma.

After that battle their ponderous bayonet charge from the Great Redoubt had become something of a legend. In fact, on the fiftieth anniversary of the battle, so famous had their modest achievement become that a massive bronze statue was unveiled on the site depicting a Vladimir soldier in the 'on-guard' position. Today only the base remains, the statue having been removed during Khruschev's time, but the seeds of the renown that led to the statue being erected now propelled the Vladimir forward. Moving from company column into battalion column of attack the Vladimir seemed to be making straight for the bend on Home Ridge where both the 18-pounders lay. They could not have chosen a worse target, however, for these two guns now depressed their barrels and fired round after round into the dense target. Solid shot and common shell were used to great effect causing the Vladimir first to check, then to stall and then to recoil up the slopes down which they had come. To their credit, however, the Vladimir did not break and, despite terrible casualties, they moved back over the crestline and into safety in good order.

Now Canrobert had another opportunity to unleash his forces. Most particularly, his Chasseurs D'Afrique, had he been able to persuade them to return to a point on the field from which they could be launched, would have been invaluable over the less rough ground of Shell Hill so redolent of their native Africa. Now was their chance to catch the Russians at their weakest and turn the near-panic of a retreat into the horror of an all-out rout. In a private letter to the Duke of Newcastle dated 31 December, Lord Raglan sums up events:

'Towards the close of the battle Major-General Pennefather proposed that the French troops on the right, aided by the English in front, should make a forward movement, and hurry the departure of the Russians. General Canrobert was unwilling to act upon the suggestion, and has often since, as I understand, expressed his regret that he did not attend to it.'[16]

Sometime after one o'clock Menshikov became aware of the retreat that had started without his sanction and cantered forward to Dannenberg's position in an attempt to influence the battle for the first time. He demanded, 'Is it you that have ordered the retreat? It is impossible for us to fall back!'. Dannenberg replied that his men had fought like lions, that they were exhausted and that his artillery and infantry were utterly spent; then pointing to Gortchakoff's position, he asked why he had received no help from that quarter. Menshikov's reply was terse, 'Stop the troops here', pointing to the ground upon which they stood and which Menshikov, according to Urosoff, his aide-de-camp, considered to be covered by the fire of the distant Malakhov redoubt. Dannenberg's answer was uncompromising, 'Highness, to stop the troops here would be to let them be destroyed to the last man. If your Highness thinks otherwise, have the goodness to give the orders yourself, and take from me the command.'[17] Menshikov made no reply; wheeling his horse he made off in the direction of Sevastopol.

Meanwhile a classic fighting withdrawal was being conducted by Dannenberg's men. Under merciless Allied artillery fire, four guns at a time were pulled back from the Russian gun-line which then followed one of two routes down from the heights either along the Sapper Road or down through St George's Ravine and along the shore of the roadstead. The infantry used both the Post Road and the bed of the Quarry Ravine until all that was left were two batteries occupying folds in the crest of Shell Hill that the 18-pounders could not reach. Raglan, seeing that the French would not advance until the last Russian gun had ceased to fire and anxious that there should be some attempt made to harass the main Russian body, took the unusually perceptive step of ordering Colonel Collingwood Dickson to cease fire. Shrewdly, he had realised that the Russian gunners needed some valid reason to stop firing and to limber up and that a halt in British fire might give them this excuse and so prevent them from buying more time for the main body to put distance between themselves and the Allies. It worked perfectly; the 18-pounders stopped firing, the Russian guns withdrew, and at about three o'clock the two steamers, the *Chersonese* and the *Vladimir*, opened covering fire from the bay sweeping the crest of Shell Hill with their broadsides.

Here was another opportunity for Canrobert who could now have pushed his horse artillery and cavalry forward to fire into the crowd of guns and infantry who were jostling along the routes into Sevastopol. The fire of the ships, however, caused the French to delay further, and another half-hour's reprieve was bought before two battalions of Zouaves and the Lainsecq Battery picked their way up on to East Jut. The French light guns came into action and were starting to cause havoc amongst Pauloff's rearguard when they were answered more accurately than they might have wished from the ships in the bay. Scrambling back under cover, the French pursued their advantage no longer.

Only the French were in any condition to pursue, and their apparent lack of enterprise was heavily criticised by the British. Several years later, however, Sir William Russell asked Todleban what effect a pursuit would have had on the fleeing Russians. Generally, Todleban's views are less than objective but on this occasion they are more than usually worthy of note:

> 'I would have desired nothing better. I honestly think you would have incurred disaster. The batteries – our works – the forts – the ships and an army of 40,000 men would have inflicted tremendous losses on you. A retreat in front of us then might have lost you your trenches. Though Gortchakoff was incompetent, he must have come up from the Tchernaya on your flank with 20,000 excellent troops. No, you did very well – too well. I only wish you had come on.'[18]

Perhaps the judgement of the French commanders was right; with more recent battle experience than the British, perhaps they assessed the risks of chasing the enemy to a point where he was under the protection of his guns and with fresh reserves to hand as being too high.

It was not quite all over, however. Throughout the day supporting fire had been directed against the Russians by mainly Light Division units on Victoria Ridge. The job was frustrating but crucial, for the troops who lay there throughout the battle were under constant fire and yet, due to the tactical importance of Victoria Ridge, they could not be allowed the satisfaction of abandoning it and going into the attack. To add to the Light Division's anguish, along Victoria Ridge, across the Careenage Ravine and up the slopes to the north-west of West Jut came Colonel Waddy with fifty-six men of No 7 Company of the unblooded 50th Regiment, a 3rd Division unit which had just managed to get away from trench duty to join the battle. Daringly, they pushed over the ridge-line and found themselves looking down onto a press of guns, limbers and their horses which had become horribly jammed on the Sapper Road as they fled from the bloody slopes of Shell Hill. Using the brush for cover, the 50th opened fire into the totally unguarded flank of the demoralised, battle-weary gunners. A satisfying chaos ensued which looked set fair to spread amongst the rest of the Russian host had it not been for the presence of Colonel Todleban. He had been entrusted with the task of overseeing the construction of field defences on ground seized from the British and, self-evidently, he had not been over employed! Fortunately for the Russians, he was now at hand to grip a situation that could have caused the whole retreat to disintegrate. A company of the Ouglitz were sent skirmishing forward; they were followed by two battalions – nearly 3,000 men – of the Bourtirsk and four guns to add weight of fire. In the face of such odds the 50th could do little except harass the Russians with rifle fire, and as their rounds thumped into the infantry who had been sent to clear them, Todleban despatched the young naval lieutenant, Skariatine, to Admiral Istomine in Sevastopol for assistance. It was not long in coming, for two battalions of sappers and a large body of sailors were quickly on the scene helping to manhandle the guns and carriages back along the road and into the haven of Sevastopol's walls.

The last round was fired about four o'clock and by eight o'clock the rearmost guns were back in Sevastopol and the fight was over. Recriminations and excuses immediately began to fly with one non-commissioned officer of the Taroutine's 2nd Battalion hearing a group of officers bemoaning their lack of mountain experience; others thought that battalion column should have been used rather than company column, whilst everyone agreed that their training had left them totally unprepared for modern war. That same soldier's thoughts evoke the reaction that all the Russians who were present on the field of Inkermann must have been experiencing:

'A weak sun lit up the hill, where the bodies were strewn about, some still stirring in their dying torment. There was little firing and every-thing became quiet as we crossed the bridge on the way to our previous day's billets, taking our wounded with us on carts and limbers; the men marched listlessly and unhappily, looking around and asking the fate of their missing fellows. We took possession of the same huts, but whereas last night there had been six or seven of us in each now there were but two or three. Where yesterday there had been chatter, noise and mirth, today there was melancholy and emptiness.'[19]

Notes

1. Kinglake, vol V, p381
2. '. . . saw that all the ground in front of the English right had been evacuated by our allies; nothing was occupied beyond the crest which lay twenty paces in front of the first row of tents.' *ibid*, p383
3. *ibid*, p390
4. *ibid*, p396
5. *ibid*, p397
6. *ibid*, p405
7. Carmichael Mss, p22
8. Kinglake, vol V, p409
9. Lee, Letters, p27
10. Kinglake, vol V, p409
11. 'Before the arrival of the French, Dannenberg had decided to beat a retreat. From 11 o'clock his troops had not made any offensive movement. The battle was continuing in the distance with musket and cannon fire.' *ibid*, p504

12. *ibid*, p411
13. *ibid*, p505
14. *ibid*, p425
15. Haines Mss, p7
16. Kinglake, vol V, p410
17. Seaton, p175
18. Russell, *Todleban's Defence of Sevastopol*, p188
19. Seaton, p172

Chapter XI
'They lay as they fell, in heaps'
Aftermath

When visiting the field of Inkermann today, it is hard to believe that so many men fought so intensely over so restricted an area. Even by the standards of nineteenth-century battlefields it is small, whilst the number of men engaged and the weapons that they were wielding made heavy casualties inevitable. Added to this, the valleys and glens would have tended to pack the protagonists together tightly making engagement ranges shorter than usual due to the broken nature of the ground and the poor visibility. These factors and the very high number of artillery pieces involved meant that casualties would be unusually high so long as both sides fought in earnest; and fight in earnest they did, for Inkermann was one of the few battles of the gunpowder era in which the combatants closed with one another over a sustained period and the injuries inflicted on both the dead and wounded bore testament to the ferocity of the fighting. Whilst small-arms had been deadly enough, artillery had done most of the damage and its effects were frightful:

'One poor fellow of the 95th had been struck by two 24-pounders in the head and body. A shell afterwards burst on him and tore him to pieces, and it was only by the fragments of cloth, with the regimental buttons adhering, that you could tell the rough bloody mass which lay in the road had ever been a human being.'[1]

The sheer numbers of dead and dying were overpowering:

'Yet I shall never recall the memory of Inkermann Valley with any but feelings of loathing and horror; for from around the spot from which I surveyed the scene lay upwards of 5,000 bodies. Many badly wounded also lay there; and their low, dull moans of mortal agony struck with horrible distinctness upon the ear; or, worse still, the hoarse, gurgling cry and vehement struggles of those who were convulsed before they passed away . . . Outside the battery the Russians lay two and three deep. Inside the place was literally full with bodies of Russians, Guardsmen, 55th and 20th. The fine, tall forms of our poor fellows could be distinguished at a glance, though the grey great-coats, stained with blood, rendered them alike externally. They lay as they fell, in heaps; sometimes our men over three or four Russians, and sometimes a Russian over three or four of ours. Some had passed away with a smile on their faces, and seemed as if asleep; others were horribly contorted, and with distended eyes and swollen features, appeared to have died in agony but defying to the last. Some lay as if prepared for burial, as though the hands of relatives had arranged their mangled limbs, while others, again, were in almost startling positions, half-standing, or kneeling, clutching their weapons, or drawing a cartridge. Many lay with both their hands extended towards the sky, as if to avert a blow, or utter a prayer, while others had a malignant scowl of mingled fear and hatred, as if, indeed, they died despairing.'[2]

So broken was the ground and so confused was the fight that many wounded had crawled away into crannies or scrub-covered folds to die. There their bodies lay undiscovered for weeks until covered by the winter snows; even after the fighting had finished almost a year later, corpses were still being dragged from the undergrowth and taken to one of more than a dozen cemeteries that held the dead of Inkermann. As Sir John McNeil wrote, having ridden across the field more than six months after the battle, 'It has been said that there are sermons in stones, but I have heard few sermons that filled me with thoughts so solemn and so little connected with the amenities of life as that ride over the field of Inkermann.'[3]

History is full of bloodcurdling accounts of bayonet charges and hand-to-hand fighting, but rarely do the facts support the stories. Usually it is the case that when one side shows the firmness of resolve to close with their enemies, that same firmness has been prompted by the other side's obvious desire to quit the field; in most cases those who are charged break and run long before the fight gets to close-quarters. Not so at Inkermann for both sides went at each other with a vengeance; bayonets were freely used as were swords, fists, boots and even stones. The casualties that Wilson of the Coldstream noted after the battle demonstrated its nature very clearly; those that had been bayoneted had died agonising deaths '. . . their features convulsed, leaden orbs bulge from their sockets; their mouths wide open, their blackened tongues protrude; mud and grass are held in their clenched fists.' There were others that had been bludgeoned to death to which '. . . the shocking aspect of faces, every feature beaten down into purple jelly'[4] bore witness.

But what had caused both sides to fight with such savagery? The question is rather more easily answered in the case of the British for, as already suggested, they were well disciplined, volunteer troops who were relatively new to warfare and whose only experience of battle so

170

far had been of victory. The unfit had been carefully combed from the regiments before they had left home and their places filled by volunteers from other units. Furthermore, the Army had been feted by the British public and every man was spurred on, to a greater or lesser extent, by regimental rivalry. So, there must have been a certain sense of privilege to be in the Crimea at all, and whilst that would have been blunted by the tedium of the journey to the seat of war and then by the rigours of the campaign, the name that the British soldier had earned for himself at the Alma, Balaklava and on 26 October must have re-awakened that pride on the morning of Inkermann.

Added to this, whilst there was little evidence of inspired leadership amongst the British senior officers (with some notable exceptions), there was real affection and trust between the troops and their regimental officers as so many incidents that day demonstrated. That strength of feeling is exemplified in a letter from Captain Strange Jocelyn of the Scots Fusilier Guards to his sister-in-law. In it he asks her to look after the widow of one of his sergeants who was '. . . one of the noblest and finest fellows that ever breathed . . . his loss to me was as great almost as a brother's. I had great affection for that man and would do anything for his widow and children.'[5] It was that sort of mutual respect that allowed small numbers of British troops to pit themselves against overwhelming columns of Russians time and again, following their youthful officers often to certain death.

There was always another factor which guaranteed that the British soldier would fight well. Simply put, he had no alternative. The Allies were fighting in a corner of a hostile peninsula from which there was no escape other than by giving oneself up to the Russians. Unlike the Spanish Peninsula, say, where a battle-shy individual might roam across a large and relatively friendly countryside and simply melt away from his regiment, such a man could not hide in the Crimea. He might also expect a savage reception from the Russians; the expectation that they would be less than civilised to their opponents was certainly borne out at Inkermann.

The British were quick to note and admire the pluck of their opponents, however, whose determination is rather less easy to understand for there was no question of their being volunteers. Indeed, British public opinion about the Russians was much inspired by the account of the Pole Hodasevich who deserted from the Taroutine Regiment shortly after Inkermann. In it he ascribes every sort of military vice to the Russians, constantly damning their abilities and ridiculing their leadership. Furthermore, popular papers like *Punch* mocked the Russians incessantly. In an issue shortly after the battle there appeared two illustrations, one entitled 'How the Holy Men of Russia Inspire their Soldiers' which shows Orthodox clerics pouring grog down their soldiers' throats and another which shows a winged spur hanging from a ribbon and entitled 'New Jewel for the Fourth Order of Russian Bravery, in Honour of the Princes Michael and Nicholas who won their Spurs at the Flight From Inkermann!' Whilst such mawkish sentiments could be expected from the British papers and the deserter Hodasevich might be expected to criticise the leadership and attitude of the Russian Army from which he had fled, no contemporary accounts by British troops nor Hodasevich himself, an officer who had been in the thick of the fighting both at the Alma and Inkermann, ever questioned its courage.

Indeed, Hodasevich is quick to point out the gallantry of his own Regiment:

'The next day (7th November) we were told that the Grand Dukes would inspect us, and about one o'clock they came up to us, thanking us in the name of their father for the gallant manner in which we had fought; they added that they thanked us too in their own names, as our regiment was the first in the two-gun battery, and that for our gallantry they had each received the cross of St George, which they pointed to on the breasts of their grey great-coats.'[6]

Added to this, whilst some British accounts speak of the Russian propensity to fake death and then spring up once the tide of battle had passed, and Russian columns were often seen to break and reel back under British fire, none seems to have observed outright cowardice.

In fact, most who were there spoke openly of their courage: 'The Russian soldiery being men endowed with great bravery, and a more than common share of physical strength',[7] wrote Kinglake, whilst an eyewitness account reproduced in the *Illustrated London News* was typical of the British soldiers' admiration for the stoical courage of the Russians:

'Until I saw it I never in my life could have believed that any troops in the world could have retired under such a murderous fire in such perfect order. The French and English, with a whole mass of artillery followed close upon the retreating battalions, pouring in volley after volley . . . it was a perfect carnage. Yet, in spite of this, the enemy kept their order, retreating almost at slow time, and every five or ten minutes halting and charging desperately up the hill.'[8]

Interestingly, it was the regiments that were involved in Soimonoff's initial attacks which distinguished themselves least. The Tenth Division, already mauled at the Alma, attacked well enough but then failed to press home their advantage and fought with little of the tenacity of Pauloff's men despite the fact that they had only just completed an ardous march from Silistria and had had no opportunity to rest. Who can doubt the

172

courage, though, of regiments like the Selenghinsk and the Iakoutsk, who came back into the attack time after time despite bloody repulses? These were men who were willing to cross bayonets and hurl rocks at troops who had already gained the reputation of being 'red devils' and yet it was they whose commander had begged for them to be given a day's grace rather than attack on the anniversary of their defeat at Oltenitsa. Certainly they showed an allegiance approaching worship to the Tsar and the presence of his sons might have helped to inspire them. Indeed, the *Illustrated London News* even reported that on the eve of the battle the Russian troops had been told that

'. . . these English heretics have in their camp an enormous sum, which God will give into your hands . . . every one of you soldiers will receive 580 roubles. To the wounded the Emperor promises a month's pay and rations. As to those of you chosen by God for a glorious death, your Emperor will permit you to dispose of your share in the booty by will.'[9]

Furthermore, there can be no doubt that at regimental level the Russians, like the British, were well led. In every assault the Russian junior officers were to be seen waving their swords and leading their men from the front; as a result casualties amongst the officers were disproportionately heavy. Whilst they might have lacked initiative and flair there was no shortage of gallantry, and the only person to criticise them and their soldiers' courage was their own commander. Menshikov continually told the Princes that '. . . the troops would not fight', but Prince Nicholas, suspecting the truth, visited the battalions and saw that they had taken heavy casualties and were in disorder but 'disordered because they had been badly directed'. Nicholas went on to visit the Katherinberg Regiment, a unit that had reputedly been reluctant to close with their enemies. He found that '. . . many of the men carried bloodied bayonets and the officers had British rifles.'[10] The Russian soldiers had fought well and hard and with a ferociousness that had shocked the British; they deserved better than commanders like Menshikov.

This mixture of poor leadership and stoical courage carried its own reward for the Russians had suffered terribly. Of the 35,000 Russian troops who had assaulted the Inkermann position 3,286 now lay dead, whilst 7,673 had been wounded or taken prisoner, a very high proportion of which were officers. Similarly, of the fewer than 8,000 British who had fought throughout the day, 635 had been killed and 1,938 wounded of which a great many were officers. The French, who by the end of the day had fielded rather more than 8,000 men, had emerged with surprisingly heavy casualties with 175 being killed and 1,530 being wounded, though there were suggestions that these figures included their sick-list. A useful measure of the ferocity of the fighting can be found by comparing the number of casualties with the number who took part. By doing so it can be seen that both the British and the Russians, the main protagonists, lost about one third of their number, an unusually high proportion, especially for the British who had been defending a position which the Russians regarded as very strong. Both sides' most recent experience of fighting of this intensity had been at the Alma where the Russians, who had been on the defensive, had lost one sixth of their force, whilst the attacking British had lost about one tenth and the French about one twentieth. Little wonder, then, that many contemporary accounts speak of Inkermann as a much sterner contest than the Alma and, as Clifford put it, 'Our loss has been a sad one and we are but ill able to stand such "Victories".'[11]

Some Russian accounts after the battle tried to claim that the disparity in numbers between themselves and the Allies was not great, and that they were opposed from a strong defensive position by a force of similar size. Undoubtedly they are wrong, for the Russians put almost twice the number of troops into the field compared with the Allies' total at the close of the fight, and for most of the time no more than 8,000 British opposed more than four times their number. Why then were the Russians who had carried out an armed reconnaissance of the ground and pre-sited their artillery, who had opposed weary troops with many who were veteran troops but fresh to the Crimea, who had almost total surprise on their side and who attacked with overwhelming numbers of troops and guns so soundly beaten? The answers fall into two categories: physical and moral.

The physical reasons can easily be understood. First, the Russians could not compete against the long-range, accurate rifle fire of both the French and British infantry. The Minie rifle bestowed an enormous advantage on the Allies, for not only did it allow the dense Russian columns to be mown down wholesale, to which they were powerless to respond with their smooth-bores, but it also allowed the Russian artillerymen to be constantly plagued by bullets fired by far distant infantry. Every Russian account speaks of the superiority of the Allied rifle fire and the galling effect that it had on the one arm in which they enjoyed a superiority – their artillery. Furthermore, that artillery, whilst very much more numerous than its opponents on Home Ridge, was soon outclassed by the two British 18-pound guns which were such a feature of the latter half of the fight. What is not clear, however, is why neither of those two guns was dismounted by the Russian artillery which were generally well handled. Luck could have had much to do with it, but when the effects of Minie fire which was specifically directed at the gunners laying the guns is remembered, then the Russians' lack of accuracy is more easily understood.

Secondly, the ground favoured the British despite their many accounts which make it seem to be a desolate, open, coverless plateau. Certainly, the position in front of Home and Fore Ridge was an unpleasant place to be, being dominated as it was by the Russian-occupied Shell Hill and having a dearth of pre-prepared defences on it, but there was dense scrub everywhere which favoured the defender, especially one who had been trained to skirmish and in whose interest it was to conceal from his enemy his lack of numbers. Furthermore, one of Pauloff's men who had just arrived in the Crimea, who knew not one foot of the ground, and who had to face the prospect of climbing a slope like the Kitspur which he could see was topped by the Sandbag Battery, could be forgiven for feeling at a disadvantage. Also, the steepness of those slopes should not be underestimated, for a fit man unencumbered by equipment and weapons would find a climb up St Clement's Ravine today an exhausting prospect. When the weight of a soldier's kit is added, plus the debilitating effects of fear, then there is small wonder that the Russian infantry arrived at the top of such hills thoroughly blown and with little energy to deal with the ferocious defenders whom they found waiting for them.

Allied to the ground was the visibility. The fog interfered with the artillery of both sides, but gave a real advantage to the British for, like the scrub, it allowed them to conceal their paucity of numbers. Even a Russian who had seen the British method of fighting in line before might have been justifiably confused by the long ranks of British who sprang from the fog at close quarters and been excused for thinking that their formations had much greater depth than they in fact did. For someone who had never before seen the British fight, it would be perfectly logical to assume that the wide rank that could be seen through the mist was backed up by many others in much the same way that a Russian column was. At the Alma Hodasevich had noted the apparently weak line formation of the British and had observed: 'This was the most extraordinary thing to us, as we had never before seen troops fight in lines of two deep, nor did we think it possible for men to be found with sufficient firmness of morale to be able to attack . . . our massive columns.'[12] By the same token, the shrouding mist may have given some reassurance to isolated groups of British who, had they been able to see how few supports they really had, might have thought better of continuing the unequal fight.

Leading on from the way that the British fought, another crucial factor was the dense column which the Russians chose to adopt. Hodasevich has already alluded to the feeling of security it bestowed, but in reality it could not have been less suitable for the fluid, bush fighting that Inkermann required. With a frontage of but a few men, only a small proportion of the column's muskets could be brought to bear at any one time, and the whole, dense edifice was remarkably vulnerable to both rifle fire and all types of artillery rounds. Coupled to this, the Russian infantry were not only taught to fill the spaces of any who fell, but the column encouraged the herd instinct where men tend to club together more closely when under fire. Against this, the British line triumphed every time, for it permitted well-drilled fire to be delivered from almost every weapon that was available and also allowed a bayonet charge to outflank and flow around a cumbrous column permitting it to be attacked from several sides at once which the majority could do nothing to resist.

The moral reasons for Russia's losing the battle are less tangible. First, the commanders had no confidence in what they were about. The pressure that the Tsar was putting on Menshikov to attack before Sevastopol was assaulted, and his lack of enthusiasm for such a venture, has already been examined. With no staff to support him properly, and no reconnaissance having been conducted, his plans were imprecise, disjointed and lacked cohesion. Had his orders encouraged the field commanders to use their initiative, to 'read the battle', then Gortchakoff might have attacked to support Dannenberg; reserves might have been deployed at an opportune moment, and the Russian advantage in men and guns properly exploited. As one Briton who had survived the day told his son,

> 'We only succeeded in beating the Russians because of their failure to co-ordinate their attacks. Huge columns came up the three ravines in succession and we just managed to drive each attack back before the other developed . . . if they had arrived together we would have been swamped.'[13]

Similar accusations, though, can be laid at the feet of the commanders in the field, for talented and determined men would have pushed ahead despite the shortcomings of the overall commander. Competent commanders would not have issued contradictory orders within hours of the start of the battle; Soimonoff would not have disobeyed the orders he had received and embarked on an assault on the British right before Pauloff had arrived to support him. Most telling of all, however, was Dannenberg's plea to be allowed to attack the day after the anniversary of Oltenitsa. True, his men were tired from their long march from the interior and the ground was unknown, but a confident commander would have grasped the opportunity to attack on the anniversary of a defeat in order to prove to his men how all their fortunes had changed.

At regimental level it has already been seen that there was neither lack of courage nor aggression, but a determination to seize advantages and press home victories was entirely lacking. There were countless incidents of complete inertia by Russian troops who had prevailed in a skirmish and then had the opportunity to exploit their advantage but who, in Hodasevich's words '. . . stood like sheep . . . having gained possession of the Battery, no-one ever thought of pushing on, nor did we know what direction to take.'[14] The habit of obedience was too deeply ingrained, so captured guns were left un-spiked and opportunities such as the Iakoutsk had to pin a superior force of Frenchmen on Inkermann Tusk and destroy them piecemeal were thrown away.

In a similar vein, the ground was new to the Russians and the mighty slopes and ravines must have been intimidating, the more so when the Russians knew that having toiled to the top of such hills they would have to face men whose fighting reputation preceded them. The Alma and Balaklava had soon disabused the Russians of the popular notion that the British Army were simply misguided and half-trained sailors turned soldier. Those regiments that had faced the British before knew what was waiting for them, and it is interesting to note how badly Soimonoff's regiments, who had mostly been in action against the British before, fought compared with those of Dannenberg who were newly arrived.

The last point has been alluded to already; most of the Russians had seen action before and knew all about defeat whether at the hands of the British in the Crimea or at the hands of the Turks on the Danube. Numbers of Russian dead were noted to have the marks of old wounds upon their bodies and few men would be keen to repeat such an experience. Perhaps the Russians had seen their share of the horrors of the battlefield already; in the jargon of the twentieth century, perhaps they were 'battle-weary' before they even set foot upon the field of Inkermann. What is certain is that they were facing men who had enough experience to make them useful in battle and not so much that they would take risks no more. Furthermore, the Russians' opponents were fighting for their very existence; the British knew that the job had to be done by them and them alone and that to fail meant total defeat. The Russians did not have the same spur of desperation; if they had, the result might have been very different.

Inkermann was to be the last great battle of manoeuvre in which the British were involved. The combined casualties of the Alma, Balaklava and Inkermann meant that the British simply did not have the strength to push on with their plans to assault Sevastopol before the onset of winter, and without the British the French could not continue alone. So, whilst Inkermann was a tactical defeat for the Russians, it at least guaranteed that the Allies sat on the Chersonese uplands throughout the winter and let those most effective Russian generals, January and February, waste them away as supplies proved difficult to bring up from the ports to the siege lines and reinforcements only trickled in over the stormy Black Sea. The besiegers soon became the besieged, and throughout the long winter suggestions arose again and again that operations should be abandoned and that the Allies should re-embark.

Of the Allies the British suffered the more from the winter conditions due to an almost complete breakdown in their administration, but with spring came reinforcements; with more manpower trench work became less arduous and less risky as duties became less frequent. The noble regiments which had fought so valiantly in the previous summer and autumn, but which had shrunk to mere skeletal cadres over the winter months, began to fill up again; turn-out was looked to once more and esprit-de-corps began to return to troops who were justly proud of their achievements of the year before. But as the Allies took heart, so the Russians began to prepare themselves for the onslaught that they knew to be inevitable. Over the winter they had not been idle and, whilst their defences grew stronger by the day and the garrison swelled as reinforcements were received down the umbilical cord of the Sapper Road, Sevastopol became an ever more daunting target to attack.

In January 1855 Sardinia entered the war on the Allied side, and in early June a bombardment followed by an assault by the French enjoyed partial success. To capitalise upon this, the anniversary of Waterloo was picked as an auspicious date for a full Allied assault on Sevastopol and so, on 18 June both British and French attacked the south-eastern earthworks of the city. For months the Allies' trenches and saps had been approaching the Redan and the Malakhov, and the Russians had had more than enough time to prepare themselves. The attack failed with heavy casualties, and a little while later Lord Raglan died officially from diarrhoea but in reality from a combination of physical exhaustion and depression.

On 16th August the Russians mounted another attack against the Allies in circumstances that were not so very different from those of Inkermann. In February the Russians had attacked Eupatoria and had been repulsed by its Turkish garrison. Tiring at last of Menshikov's incompetence, the Tsar removed him and put Prince M D Gortchakoff in his place who now took over the Army of the Crimea whilst continuing as commander of the South Army in Bessarabia. Once again pressure from the Tsar caused the commanders in the field to go unwillingly onto the offensive, and with many of the same misgivings that had prevailed before Inkermann, Gortchakoff attacked the Fedioukine and Gasfort heights to the north of Balaklava which were now held by French and Sardinian troops. The aim, once again, was to unhinge the Allies from the north-west and distract them from the prosecution of the siege, but the battle of the Tchernaya, as it came to be known, failed in as spectacular a fashion as Inkermann had, and the Russians were bloodily defeated without gain.

On 8 September the Allies attacked a Sevastopol which was no longer tenable; the French took the Malakhov, but the British failed to capture the Redan and took very heavy casualties in the process. With their main redoubt in the hands of the enemy, the Russians abandoned the southern half of the city moving across the harbour by an ingeniously constructed pontoon bridge to the Severnaia, and with their withdrawal the siege came to an end. A series of minor operations followed, but for the most part both sides contented themselves with long-range, desultory artillery fire, whilst the British and French started the business of a systematic destruction of Sevastopol and its facilities. Winter saw a change in fortunes for the British who were now well dressed, equipped and housed, whilst the French suffered a remarkable breakdown in their administration and became victims of the same sort of diseases and privations that had swept the British the year before.

The spring of 1856 found the British 90,000 strong, well equipped and raring for a fight, whilst the French had lost interest. The King of Sweden had been wooed during the previous winter with a view to bringing him into the Alliance and transferring operations from the Crimea to the Baltic, but little had come of it beyond a defensive treaty. Thus, with the attention of the French distracted by political developments at home, Austria mediated and an armistice was declared on 30 March 1856. By the so-called Peace of Paris, the integrity of Turkey's empire was guaranteed by France, Austria and Britain, whilst the Black Sea and the Dardanelles were denied to warships, and naval ports and installations on its shores were banned. Sevastopol had been razed and so the Allies determined it would remain.

For fifteen years the Russians abided by the conditions of the treaty, but in 1871 the rebuilding of Sevastopol and the Black Sea Fleet began, and in 1877 Turkey was once more the subject of a Russian attack. So it was that all that the Allies had struggled for, and all the sacrifices that they had made, came to nought. Sevastopol rose again from its ashes, but this time it was watched over by the bones of thousands of Britons some of whom lay in formal cemeteries each grave marked by a headstone; some below the cairns so carefully erected once the tide of war had swept on; and some in shallow, unmarked scrapes.

Today a visit to the scene of the fighting is not a simple matter for someone from the West. The Crimea is now part of the independent Ukraine, and whilst the Iron Curtain no longer precludes visitors entirely, a powerful suspicion of sightseers and a bureaucracy of Byzantine proportions remain as a legacy of the Communist era. As most of the occupants of the Crimea are Russian by descent and seem to hold that country in far greater esteem than the Ukraine, the whole area is a flashpoint, the sensitivities of which are exacerbated by the issue of which country owns the Black Sea Fleet. Officially, Russia has now given up claims of ownership of the powerful fleet which lies at anchor, rusting in Sevastopol harbour, but everywhere graffiti proclaims the loyalty of the Crimea to Russia and the fact that the ships belong, if only emotionally, not to the Ukraine. Furthermore, whilst Sevastopol is no longer a closed city, a visitor is meant to have a military pass which can only be procured in Kiev and which can take anything up to three days of frustrating waiting to get whilst one is referred to bureau after bureau and hard currency sweeteners are demanded.

Once armed with a pass, the visitor can see Sevastopol in all its glory for the old port has been extensively rebuilt after the fighting of the Second World War which razed it. It is now once more a very attractive city with wide streets and classical architecture, reminiscent of Paris. The outskirts are less lovely, however, with high-rise blocks of faceless, concrete flats now standing in the old Korabelnaya suburb where the earthworks of the Redan and the Malakhov have almost entirely disappeared. The ground remains the same, however, and it is possible to drive out of Sevastopol along the old routes to the north and visit the totally unspoilt battlefield of the Alma which remains much as it was in 1854, save for some memorials. Similarly, the field of Balaklava can be easily visited and, other than for a ribbon of buildings and a light railway that have appeared in North Valley, little has changed. On the Causeway Heights stands the stone memorial which was erected in 1855 pockmarked now by the fragments of German shells fired at it, one presumes, as a test of marksmanship during Mannstein's advance on Sevastopol, whilst close by an increasingly tourist-conscious Sevastopol City Authority has recently had a further memorial erected in the shape of a stone of massive proportions with a metal plaque fixed to it which bears a suitably obscure statement about the events of October 1854.

Looking north-west from the valleys of the Balaklava plain the Sapoune looms above in precisely the same way that it did over the carrying parties toiling up from the harbour. Similarly, if the valley of the Tchernaya is followed to the north, the edge of the Chersonese plateau dominates the little, wine-growing town of Inkermann. From the town can be seen the top of the Kitspur from which, so clearly, guns in the Sandbag Battery could have brought the whole valley under fire. The old Post Road still winds up out of the valley with massive shoulders of hill either side which quickly become recognisable as East Jut and Inkermann Tusk until the site of the barrier is reached. Today it is nothing more than the minor road junction that it always was, and gone are any signs of breastworks or trenches. At this point it becomes obvious, however, why the Ukrainian authorities are so reluctant to give permission for the visitor to go to Inkermann. First, it must be very difficult for the Ukrainians to understand why anyone should want to visit a piece of scrubby wasteland on the outskirts of the suburbs of Sevastopol where there is nothing to be seen; second, right in the centre of the old British positions on Home Ridge there now stands a coastal defence rocket battery complete with sentry towers around its perimeter and lazily revolving radar antennae. There is also a suggestion that dug deep into the limestone in the side of Quarry Ravine there are magazines for nuclear warheads. Whatever the truth, visitors are precluded from the battlefield, and any officially sanctioned trip is limited to staring at its skyline from across the Tchernaya valley.

Once the fighting had subsided after the fall of Sevastopol, the British dedicated much of their plentiful time to the clearance of the battlefields and the erection of memorials. Inkermann, as already mentioned, took months to clear of all the dead, but immediately after the battle large, mass graves were dug into which the dead of all sides were lain. Weapons and equipment were removed, as were any useful items of clothing such as boots; other than that, corpses were buried fully clothed, and the tops of the graves were covered over by rocky cairns. There were several main graves and numerous smaller ones which were created as more dead were found amidst the rock and scrub over the months, and on the saddle between Home Ridge and Shell Hill an elegant, white obelisk was erected to mark the mid point of the opposing sides. Additionally, many of the dead officers were taken to a spot adjacent to the headquarters of the 4th Division which became known as Cathcart's Hill in recognition of this rash but gallant officer who lay there surrounded by so many of his staff and regimental officers.

Despite all the difficulties, the determined visitor can get on to the field of Inkermann, but he will find that all signs of the battle on that Sunday in November are gone. The memorial has disappeared, the top of the Kitspur has been ploughed into terraces for young fir, and no clue remains of the precise position of the rampart of the Sandbag Battery. Yet the ground is covered with jagged, metal fragments, and if the scrub which still dominates the whole position is investigated, trenches and dugouts can be found. These are the remains, however, of a far more recent and no less bitter fight, and Mauser and Mosin-Nagent cases still litter the parapets of rapidly eroding weapon-pits. On the edge of St Clement's Ravine, however, there remains a cairn, one that was not levelled when Khruschev ordered the removal of all memorials. Around it has been built a crude metalwork fence, and from its top protrudes an iron, Orthodox cross. It is all that remains to mark the resting place of thousands, and scattered amongst the scrub are human bones scooped from below the stones by grave-robbers in search of trinkets to feed the military antique markets of America and Europe.

Over on Cathcart's Hill all traces of headstones are gone, but in their place there stands a modern memorial of stunning ugliness funded by British appeal monies and built in the plain style of the Communist era monuments which dot the surrounding countryside so liberally. The inner walls of the memorial are faced with metal plaques recording the number of casualties suffered by each of the regiments who were present in the Crimea. There can be no better indication of how quickly the memories of this war have faded than when these plaques are scrutinised, for the regimental authorities who advised those who designed the memorial have, in several cases, got the old designations of their regiments wrong and there even exists one plaque for a regiment that never served in the Crimea!

Whether headstones, graves and monuments have vanished or not, no one can remove the atmosphere of this curiously small battlefield. Standing on Shell Hill, where Dannenberg's gun-line stood, Home Ridge seems only a stone's throw away. Just below is the site of the barrier where Haines and his men held out against the columns that would have poured up Quarry Ravine, whilst the slopes at one's feet are still clothed in the scrub that gave Acton and his little band such vital cover. A few moments' walk away it is possible to stand on the junction that now marks the position of the barrier and realise just how close were the breastworks on Home Ridge; the advance of so many regiments down that gentle slope must have been the work of moments even when the fog made it terribly difficult to see the way. Standing on the junction of Home and Fore Ridge, all that Pennefather would have had before him can be seen at a glance. At first his task seems relatively simple, but when the sheer press of numbers, the noise of the guns and capricious fog are added, it is easier to understand why most commanders failed to distinguish themselves that day. Set against this backdrop, Pennefather's singular achievements seem all the more remarkable.

Seen from Home Ridge, the Gap is merely a scrubby ridgeline the tactical importance of which it is difficult to grasp at first sight. It is only a couple of hundred yards from the barrier to the Sandbag Battery, yet so much revolved around mastery of this stretch of ground that morning. Farther to the south-west lies the slope down which Cathcart and his six companies charged, and peeping from the undergrowth is the rocky shelf where he fell. Nothing marks the spot, and his body lies a league from the scene, yet it takes little imagination to grasp how events must have unfolded there. Some have found buttons and other scraps on the field, and someone claims to have dug a Minie ball from the limestone face of Inkermann Tusk, but such artefacts are not necessary to know that the gullies and bushes teem with ghosts. If the field is visited on a frosty, misty morning and one's eyes are half-closed, it is not difficult to see grey greatcoat-clad wraiths crouching in the oak scrub, cursing their damp rifles and damning the artillery that thumps around them so incessantly.

The last word belongs to an anonymous eyewitness writing in the *Illustrated London News*: 'From the nature of the ground no generalship could prevail. It is alone to the undying pluck of the officers and men that we are indebted for preservation. To the survivors generally, not the slightest credit for the display of any military talent is due. It was essentially a struggle between pluck and confidence, against obstinacy backed by numbers.'[15]

*   *   *

Notes

1. *Complete History of the Russian War*, p89
2. *ibid*, p91
3. *Illustrated London News*, p487
4. Wilson, p316
5. Airlie, p176
6. Hodasevich, p210
7. Kinglake, vol V, p244
8. *Illustrated London News*, p491
9. *ibid*, p571
10. Seaton, p176
11. Clifford, p93
12. Hodasevich, p70
13. Hamley, p221
14. Hodasevich, p196
15. *Illustrated London News*, p497

Bibliography

Published Books

Airlie, Mabel Countess of, *With the Guards We Shall Go*, Hodder & Stoughton, London, 1933
– (ed.) *Little Hodge: Letters and Diaries of Col. Edward Cooper Hodge, 1854–56*, Leo Cooper, London, 1971
Anon., *Complete History of the Russian War*, New York, 1896
Barthorp, Michael, *Heroes of the Crimea*, Blandford, 1991
– *The British Army on Campaign, 1816–1902*, Osprey, London, 1989
– *The Crimea*, Osprey, London, 1987
Bell, Sir George, *Rough Notes of an old Soldier* (1867); reprinted as *Soldier's Glory*, Bell, London, 1956
Blackmore, Howard L, *British Military Firearms, 1650–1850*, Herbert Jenkins, London, 1961
Buchan, John, *History of the Royal Scots Fusiliers, 1678–1918*, Nelson, London and Edinburgh, 1925
Butler, Sir William, *An Autobiography*, Constable, London, 1911
Cavendish-Taylor, G, *Journal of Adventures with the British Army in the Crimea*, Hurst & Blackett, London, 1856
Clifford, Henry, *Letters and Sketches from the Crimea* (ed. C Fitzherbert), Michael Joseph, London, 1956
Curtiss, John Shelton, *Russia's Crimean War*, Duke University Press, Durham NC, 1979
Fortescue, The Hon. J W, *History of the British Army Vol. XIII*, Macmillan, London, 1930
Gowing, T, *A Soldier's Experience: A Voice from the Ranks*, Thos Forman, Nottingham, 1895
Hamley, Gen. Sir Edward, *The War in the Crimea*, Seeley, London, 1896
Hibbert, Christopher, *The Destruction of Lord Raglan*, Longman, London, 1961
Higginson, Gen. Sir George, *Seventy-One Years of a Guardsman's Life*, John Murray, London, 1916
Hodasevich, A, *A Voice from Within the Walls of Sevastopol*, John Murray, London, 1856
Jocelyn, Col. J R J, *The History of the Royal Artillery, Crimean Period*, John Murray, London, 1911
Kinglake, A W, *The Invasion of the Crimea*, Vol III (1866), Vol. IV (1868),

Vol. V (1875), Vol. VI (1880), Vol VII (1882), Blackwood, Edinburgh and London

Lysons, Gen. Sir Daniel, *The Crimean War from First to Last*, John Murray, London, 1895

Parry, D J, *Britain's Roll of Glory*, Cassell, London, 1895

Pemberton, W Baring, *Battles of the Crimean War*, Batsford, London, 1962

Rait, Robert S, *The Life of Field-Marshal Sir Frederick Haines*, Constable, London, 1911

Ray, Cyril, *Regiment of the Line: XX Lancashire Fusiliers*, Batsford, London, 1963

Regimental Officer, A (Col. C T Wilson), *Our Veterans of 1854*, Skeet, London, 1859

Ross of Bladensburg, Lt-Col., *The Coldstream Guards in the Crimea*, Innes, London, 1897

Russell, W H, *Despatches from the Crimea* (ed. Nicholas Bentley), Panther, London, 1970

– *Todleban's Defence of Sevastopol*, Tinsley Bros, London, 1865

Russian Account of the Battle of Inkermann (trans. from the German), John Murray, London, 1856

Seaton, Albert, *The Crimean War: A Russian Chronicle*, Batsford, London, 1977

Small, E (ed.), *Told from the Ranks*, Melrose, London, 1898

Spiers, Edward M, *The Army and Society, 1815–1914*, Longman, London, 1980

Steevens, Lt-Col. N, *The Crimean Campaign with the Connaught Rangers*, Griffith & Farran, London, 1878

Strachan, Hew, *Wellington's Legacy: Reform of the British Army, 1830–54*, Manchester University Press, Manchester, 1984

– *From Waterloo to Balaklava: Tactics, Technology and the British Army, 1815–54*, Cambridge University Press, Cambridge, 1985

Ward, S G P, *Faithful: History of the Durham Light Infantry*, Nelson, Edinburgh and London, 1963

Whinyates, Col. F A, *From Corunna to Sevastopol: History of C Battery RHA*, W H Allen, London, 1884

Windham, Lt-Gen. Sir Charles Ash, *Crimean Diary and Letters* (ed. Maj. Hugh Pearse), Kegan Paul, London, 1897

Wood, Sir Evelyn F M, *The Crimea in 1854 and 1894*, Chapman & Hall, London, 1896

Privately Printed

Bannatyne, Lt-Col. N, *History of the 30th Regiment*, Liverpool, 1923

Champion, Maj. J G, (95th), *Sketch of the Life and Letters* (ed. Anon.), 1856

Hume, Maj.-Gen. J R, *Reminiscences of the Crimean Campaign with the 55th Regiment*, 1894

Lomax, D A N, *History of the Services of the 41st Regiment*, Devonport, 1899

Moore, Geoffrey, *Vincent of the 41st*, 1979

Neville, The Hon. Henry and The Hon. Grey, *Letters from Turkey and the Crimea*, 1870

Petre, F Loraine, *History of the Royal Berkshire Regiment, Vol. I*, Reading, 1925

Slack, J, *History of the 63rd Regiment*, London, 1884

Whitehorne, Maj. C A, *The Welch Regiment, 1719–1914*, Cardiff, 1932

Woollright, H, *History of the 57th Regiment*, 1893

– *Records of the 77th Regiment*, 1909

Wylly, Maj. H C, *95th (The Derbyshire) Regiment in the Crimea*, London, 1899

– *Regimental Annual, The Sherwood Foresters 1934*

Manuscripts

Armstrong, Lt-Col. J W, Testimonial re. Capt. Astley, 49th

Carmichael, Lt-Col. G L (95th), Notes on the Battle of Inkermann (National Army Museum, 6807–264–1)

Fisher, John (Rifle Brigade), Scraps from a Corporal's Notebook (National Army Museum, 7606–38,39)

Haines, Maj.-Gen. F P (late 21st), Recollections of Inkermann (National Army Museum, 6807–146–2)

Image, Lt J G (21st), Journal (Manitoba Museum)

Lee, 2nd Lt Vaughan Hanning (21st), Letters, 22 August 1854–13 June 1856 (Maj. F Myatt MC)

Macdonald, Lt A (95th), Letters, September 1854 and undated (Author)

95th Regiment, Record of Service (Sherwood Foresters Museum)

Shervinton, Capt Richard (46th), Journal (Duke of Cornwall's Light Infantry Museum)

Periodicals

Guards Magazine (1987), Diary, 4 Mar-8 Nov 1854, 3483 Sgt William McMillan, Coldstream Guards

Durham Light Infantry Journal, Vol. I, p150

Illustrated London News (July-December 1854)

'I'm Ninety-Five', Regimental Magazine of the Derbyshire Regiment (1896–7)

Jackman, S W (ed.), 'Crimean Experiences of Gnr. William Love RA', Vol. LX, 103

Journal of the Society for Army Historical Research, Vol. LX, p103, Jackman, S W (ed.) 'Crimean Experiences of Gen. William Love RA; Vol. LVIII, pp96–8, Lagden, A A (ed.), 'Letters, Lt-Col. F G Ainslie, 21st RNB Fusiliers'; Vol. XLIX, p44, Selby, J M (ed.), 'Lt Anthony Morgan, 95th, 20 Sep-26 Oct 1854'
Punch, Vols XXV-XXVII, 1853–4
Torrens, Capt H D (23rd), Letter, 3 April 1856, *Guards Magazine* Vol. I, p150 (1987)

Tradition

Anon. Surgeon, Letter, 8 November 1854 (no. 31)
Connor, Sgt J (77th), Letter, 6 November 1854 (no. 28)
Corporal-Drummer (Scots Fusilier Guards), Letter, undated (no. 28)
Evans, Pte George (63rd), Letter, 6 November 1854 (no. 28)

Index

189